AMY VANDERBILT

answers the most frequently asked questions about etiquette in this unique guide to good manners. Here is down-to-earth advice on what to do for hundreds of personal, social and business occasions.

MANNERS

for teen-agers, divorcées and widows, children, doctors, tourists, business associates, acquaintances, close friends and relatives.

ETIQUETTE

for funerals, christenings and other special occasions.

ENTERTAINING

hosts, guests, parties, celebrations, gifts, food and drink.

ENGAGEMENTS AND WEDDINGS

showers, the reception, manners and dress for bride, groom, parents and guests, second weddings, invitations, gifts, anniversaries.

AMY VANDERBILT'S
EVERYDAY ETIQUETTE
COMPREHENSIVE, EASY TO USE,
UP TO DATE.

2ND REVISED EDITION

Amy Vanderbilt's everyday etiquette

Answers to Today's Etiquette Questions
Drawing by MARY SUZUKI
and ANDREW WARHOL

AMY VANDERBILT'S EVERYDAY ETIQUETTE
Answers to Today's Etiquette Questions
*A Bantam Book / published by arrangement with
Doubleday Company, Inc. (Hanover House Division)*

PRINTING HISTORY

*Doubleday edition published March 1956
2nd printing ...... March 1956
New revised Doubleday edition published 1967*

Dollar Book Club edition published July 1957

*Bantam edition / June 1957
22 printings through April 1970
New Revised Bantam edition / November 1970*

2nd printing . November 1971	6th printing .... October 1974
3rd printing .... August 1972	7th printing .... July 1975
4th printing .. February 1973	8th printing .... June 1976
5th printing .... May 1974	9th printing .... May 1977

Cover photo courtesy of Otto Stupakoff

ISBN 0-553-11025-X

Published simultaneously in the United States and Canada

*Bantam Books are published by Bantam Books, Inc. Its trade-
mark, consisting of the words "Bantam Books" and the por-
trayal of a bantam, is registered in the United States Patent
Office and in other countries. Marca Registrada. Bantam
Books, Inc., 666 Fifth Avenue, New York, New York 10019.*

This is a question and answer book based on questions the author has received through her column in the *Ladies' Home Journal,* her daily newspaper column syndicated by the *Los Angeles Times* Syndicate, as well as from television programs on which she has appeared. For a fuller and more complete treatment of the complex subject of etiquette, please see *Amy Vanderbilt's Etiquette* published by Doubleday & Co. Inc. of which over 2½ million copies have been sold.

TO MY STEPCHILDREN—
CURTIS BRADBURY KELLAR, Jr.,
LUCIA, WILLIAM, BETSY
and
MARTHA

CONTENTS

INTRODUCTION

This is a practical, basic etiquette book for today's busy people. It avoids involved discussion of elaborate ritual in favor of answers to specific questions I have received from my readers over the past years. It covers much of what the well-mannered person needs to know about the conduct of his ordinary daily life. There is much here for the managers of small households, for business people, and for the teens.

We are in the midst of a social revolution. Manners are changing but the essential need for manners of some kind remains the same. Good manners are the traffic rules for society in general—not in the purely "social" sense. Without good manners, living would be chaotic, human beings unbearable to each other.

A knowledge of what constitutes good manners makes us comfortable within ourselves and with other people. *Automatic* good manners under difficult circumstances increase our security and our ability to help others achieve social poise, too. Reduced to a phrase, good manners is consideration of other people in respect to their feelings, their safety, their privacy and their full social rights and privileges.

AMY VANDERBILT

New York City

Dear Miss Vanderbilt:

THE SOCIAL GRACES

TABLE MANNERS

Who is served first at table and when is the proper time to begin eating? F.G.P., GARDEN CITY, NEW YORK

The hostess is not served first unless she is the only lady at the table or is alone with her husband and children. If Grandmother or even a young girl guest is present, the dishes are first presented to her after inspection by the hostess. When the hostess is serving from in front of her place, with or without the aid of a servant, she is served next to last and her husband last. For her to serve herself earlier will mean her food will be cold and her filled plate in the way.

After several people have been served, urged by the hostess, guests begin eating so their food will not be cold. And, except at breakfast, the polite husband waits until his wife has been served before beginning to eat.

• •

Is it considered bad manners to take anything to drink to your lips while there is still food in your mouth? B.C.J., DENVER, COLORADO

Yes, because this may leave particles of food in the beverage or leave an unattractive smear on the glass. Your mouth should be empty before you take anything to drink. Certainly you should avoid the effect of "washing down" food that is already in your mouth. It is amazing how many people are guilty of this breach of etiquette.

1

• •

Which is correct—the American way of holding the fork in the right hand, or the Continental custom of holding it in the left? M.F.P., ST. LOUIS, MISSOURI

Either is correct, but a combination of the two systems is now often seen and is quite acceptable. Even when one uses the American zigzag method it is sensible to convey cut food to the mouth with the fork in the left hand, with the tines of the fork down. Also, in eating a bit of bread and gravy—by impaling the bread on the fork (in either hand), tines down, and sopping up the gravy—it is now usual to convey the bit to the mouth with the fork tines down rather than up.

• •

How do you get stray bits of food on a plate onto your fork? O.L., ATLANTA, GEORGIA

A combination of European and American style eating is very usual among sophisticated people and makes it easy for a diner to retrieve skiddy bits of food—like peas—on his plate by using his knife in his left hand as a pusher. But the completely American system is to use a bit of bread as a pusher. One never uses the fingers for this purpose.

• •

Please tell me if it is permissible to "dunk" doughnuts, cookies, etc., either at home or elsewhere. O.E.C., WICHITA FALLS, TEXAS

Dunking doughnuts or cookies, eating chicken, pie, and other things with your fingers depends very much on the circumstances. If you are having coffee with a friend in the kitchen, dunk if you wish. If doughnuts or cookies are served at a tea, you would be uncomfortable doing so, I am sure. So many of these things depend on good sense and appropriateness. As a general rule I would say don't dunk publicly except under very informal circumstances, and if you dunk, break the doughnut or cookie in half, just as you would break your bread, rather than bite into the whole slice.

• •

Is it proper to tip soup or dessert dishes? And when is soup eaten with a spoon? I sometimes see people drinking bouillon, etc., directly from the cup. Is this correct? E.H., NORWALK, CONNECTICUT

The tipping of soup or dessert dishes is acceptable if the plate is tipped away from the spoon, not toward the eater. Soup or bouillon served in a handled cup or (Oriental fashion) small, cup-sized bowl may be drunk. If there are vegetables or other garnish floating on top, these may be lifted off with the spoon before the soup is drunk. Noodles or other things which may be in the bottom of the cup are spooned up after the liquid has been drunk.

• •

If bouillon is served in a cup, do you drink it? Should you take part of it with the spoon? What if the cup has two handles. Do you use both hands? P.O., STATEN ISLAND, NEW YORK

Spoon up part of the bouillon before taking it up to drink. If the cup has one handle, hold it in one hand. If it has two handles, hold it by both handles. If the bouillon has solids in it, take them up with the spoon before drinking the bouillon.

• •

Does one open one's napkin in the lap as soon as sitting down at table, or is it proper to wait until the food is served? D.O., MACON, GEORGIA

Guests wait until the hostess has taken up hers before placing their own, entirely open if they are lunch-size, or in half if they are dinner napkins. Napkins are tucked in only for children. Guests' napkins at the end are gathered and laid casually to the left of the place setting. Overnight—or longer—guests return napkins to rings and leave them on the right.

• •

My husband insists on pouring gravy all over everything on his plate. I feel this is bad table manners. What do you think? MRS. D.T.A., BUTTE, MONTANA

Gravy—unless it is a gravy in which meat, fish, or other protein is incorporated (rarebits, curries, blanquettes, chilis, etc.)—is never poured or ladled onto rice, noodles, or other than meat on the plate. It is an insult to the cuisine to inundate everything with gravy —or that American favorite, catsup. If you want to eat your potatoes with gravy, dip a forkful into the gravy that has escaped from the meat.

• •

When conserves and jellies are served, are they placed on the butter plate or on the dinner plate? U.T.R., RED HOOK, NEW YORK

These may be served at dinner or lunch with meat and are placed on the side of the plate, as are horse-radish, cranberry sauce, relish, etc. They are incorporated onto the fork as the food is taken into the mouth. Only liquid sauces (mint, Worcestershire, etc.) meant for the meat are poured on it.

• •

What do you do when you discover you have taken some "spoiled" food into your mouth—bravely risk ptomaine and swallow it? Or is it acceptable to spit it

calmly into your napkin as though nothing had happened? H.F.B., NASHVILLE, TENNESSEE

Nothing, not even a bad clam, is ever spit, however surreptitiously, into a napkin. But it is sheer masochism to down, for the sake of manners, something really spoiled. Certainly, a partly chewed mouthful of food looks unappetizing if it has been necessary for you to deposit it from your fork on the side of the plate. It should be screened, if possible, with some celery leaves or a bit of bread. And, in taking it out of your mouth, try not to look as if anything were the matter. After all, if you were eating stewed or canned cherries, you would place the pits in the spoon with which you were eating and place them on the side of your plate without anyone thinking your procedure disgusting.

• •

When you find that you have taken some "foreign matter" into your mouth—gravel, stones, fish bones and such—are they removed with the fork with which you have been eating? V.F., PERU, ILLINOIS

No, do not use your fork. Foreign bodies accidentally taken into the mouth are removed with thumb and forefinger, as are fish bones and other tiny bones.

• •

When you have to use your handkerchief at the dinner table, should you excuse yourself and leave the table, or should you excuse yourself and turn your head to use the handkerchief without leaving the table? MRS. N.J.MCC., CONCORD, MASSACHUSETTS

You turn your head slightly, use your handkerchief as quietly as possible, and do not excuse yourself.

• •

My husband and I like to make experimental visits to restaurants where foreign foods are served. Is is bad manners for us to order different dishes so that we may taste each other's food? C.M., CHICAGO, ILLINOIS

This is informal but permissible, though only if a fresh fork or spoon is used, with the possessor of the dish then handing the "taste" implement, handle first, to the other person. The other must not reach across the table and eat from a companion's plate, no matter how many years they have been married! If one of the two has had included some item in his order and doesn't wish it, he asks the waiter to serve it to the other, if desired—he doesn't take it on his plate, then re-serve it.

• •

I was taught never to reach for anything at the table that wasn't directly in front of me, but this rule seems very much relaxed nowadays. What is your opinion? MRS. S.C.H., HARRISBURG, PENNSYLVANIA

Reaching at table is now preferred to asking neighbors to pass things one can well take up himself, but one should not have to rise out of his seat or reach in front of others.

• •

Who is in charge of the conversation at dinner, the father or the mother? Is the rule for conversation the same when guests are present as when the family is dining alone? MRS. B.B., NEW HOPE, PENNSYLVANIA

The mother is always the head of the table and is responsible for the leading of the conversation, whether or not guests are present. At a very long table, when there are guests, the father would lead the conversation at his end. When husband and wife are alone with the family at the table, the husband and wife share the responsibility for the dinner table conversation.

• •

When, if ever, is it permissible to smoke at table? R.N.,
HOBOKEN, NEW JERSEY

Smoking at table is tolerated by some hostesses *at the
end* of the meal. Ash trays at the table indicate only
that smoking after the dessert course is permissible. It
is downright bad manners to go to any dinner table
with a lighted cigarette or to smoke during or between
courses.

• •

**Is it ever proper for a guest to ask for a second help-
ing?** D.G.S., BOISE, IDAHO

At an informal meal, when he sees that there is plenty
of the dish he'd like to have, it is very flattering to the
hostess for him to ask for a second helping. However,
the hostess should anticipate his request for more.
The only reason he might not ask, himself, for another helping would be if there were only one or two
more portions on the plate and he knew that there were
servants still to partake of the meal. Where food is
served from the kitchen, plate style, obviously the guest
must wait for the hostess to suggest a second helping,
because there may not be more in the kitchen.

At a formal dinner, a guest never asks for a second
helping. This is because formal meals have many
courses and it is assumed that no guest would want a
second helping for this reason.

• •

**When you are a guest, or eating in a restaurant, is it
bad manners to eat everything on your plate, or should
you leave a little "for manners."** D.S., NEW ORLEANS,
LOUISIANA

You eat what you wish. It was a Victorian notion that something should be left. Today you please yourself in the matter.

I see a lot of people doing it, but is it really correct to drink bottled drinks right from the bottle? If so, under what circumstances? MISS T.S.L., LOUISVILLE, KENTUCKY

This is something like eating a wedge of pie right from the hand. It tastes better and under certain circumstances is quite acceptable. Drinking bottled drinks from the bottle is certainly informal and may be done when people are standing around in a playroom or outdoors at a picnic, at the beach, etc. When they are seated at a properly set table such drinks are poured into glasses or mugs, just as the pie would then be eaten from a dessert plate with a fork.

• •

Can you tell me the proper way to eat bacon—do you always eat it with a fork or can you eat it with your fingers? What about broiled or fried chicken? B.L., HOLLYWOOD, CALIFORNIA

I've made a list of some of the foods people do get puzzled about—bacon and broiled or fried chicken are on the list:

HOW TO EAT VARIOUS FOODS

ASPARAGUS   Canned asparagus is eaten with the fork. Usually this is the better procedure with frozen asparagus too. Fresh asparagus may be a finger food, although it may be eaten with the fork. In this case cut the tender part off with the tines, leaving the tougher end. Dip each manageable piece in the sauce. If the asparagus is to be eaten with the fingers, grasp the end between thumb and index finger, dip the tip in the sauce, lift the asparagus spear above the mouth and bite off the tender portions. Lay aside the tough end. Don't chew up and then discard (however delicately) these fibrous bits.

BACON Very crisp bacon may be eaten in the fingers, but bacon with any vestige of fat must be cut with fork or knife and eaten with the fork.

CAKE Sticky cake is eaten with a fork. Dry cake, such as pound cake or fruit cake, is broken and eaten in small pieces. Tiny confection cakes (served at wedding receptions, etc.) are eaten in the fingers. Cream puffs, Napoleons, and eclairs, all treacherous as to filling, are eaten with a fork.

CELERY, RADISHES, OLIVES, AND PICKLES These are taken in the fingers, placed on the side of the plate or on the butter plate (and see "Salt"). Olives, if small and stuffed, are put all at once into the mouth—otherwise they are bitten in large bites and the stone put aside but not cleaned in the mouth.

CHICKEN (broiled or fried) Chicken must be eaten with knife and fork except at picnics. Bones are not put into the mouth but are stripped with the knife while being held firmly by the fork. Joints are cut if one's knife is sharp enough and it can be done without lifting the elbows from the normal eating position.

CORN ON THE COB This is only for informal eating and is best eaten on the cob. A long ear may be broken in half, but only a row or so at a time is buttered and seasoned, never the whole ear at once. A mixture of salt and pepper may be made, unnoticeably, on the side of the plate, then spread a little at a time on the corn with a knife as you are eating it. If the corn is to be cut off the cob, the cob is held on one end with the left hand and the kernels cut off a few rows at a time with the dinner knife. The kernels are then seasoned and eaten a forkful at a time, as one eats peas.

FISH Small fried fish are usually served whole. The head is cut off first, then the fish is held in place with the fork and slit with the tip of the knife from head to tail and laid flat. The backbone is then gently lifted up with the knife and fork and laid on the side of the plate. The balance of the fish is then cut with the fork or knife a bite or two at a time. Any tiny bones taken into the mouth are taken in thumb and forefinger and are laid on the side of the plate.

FRUIT *Apples and Pears* Taken onto the fruit plate and peeled. The sections are then cored and eaten with the fingers or with the fruit fork.

Apricots, Cherries, Plums Eaten in one or two bites, and the stones, cleaned in the mouth, are dropped into the cupped hand and placed on the side of the plate.

Bananas When eaten at the table they are peeled, then broken as needed into small pieces and eaten with the fingers.

Grapefruit Eaten, halved, with a pointed fruit spoon. Sections should be loosened with grapefruit knife before serving.

Oranges Peeled with a sharp knife, pulled apart into segments, and eaten with fingers or fruit fork.

Stewed or Preserved Fruit The pits or cores of cherries, prunes, plums, apples, eaten in compote form with a spoon are dropped into the spoon, then deposited on the side of the plate.

Watermelon If served cubed in a compote, eaten with a spoon; otherwise eaten with a fork. Seeds are dropped into the cupped hand and placed on the side of the plate.

PIZZA This is usually a finger food. It is folded to make it more manageable. If it is served in a restaurant, it may be eaten with a knife and fork.

POTATOES *Baked* are eaten with a fork, and the skin may be cut up with a knife if one wishes. If the skin is unwanted, the mealy part of the potato is eaten right from the skin with each portion seasoned just before entering the mouth. Except for a child, do not scoop out all the potato, set the skin aside, and mash the contents all at once with butter and seasoning.

Chips are eaten in the fingers.

French Fried are halved with the fork, if necessary, and eaten with the fork.

Shoe String If really dry and impossible to eat with fork, may be eaten with fingers.

SALAD A quarter of iceberg lettuce may be eaten with knife and fork.

SALT If salt is needed for dipping celery or radishes or for corn on the cob it is placed on the edge of the plate, never on the tablecloth. If open salt dishes are used and no salt spoon provided, use a clean knife to take salt from a common container. If individual open salt dishes are at each place, salt may be taken between thumb and forefinger.

SANDWICHES Small tea sandwiches and canapés are taken in the fingers. Double- and triple-decked club sandwiches are eaten at least with the aid of the knife and fork. They may be cut into fourths and eaten in the fingers, or, if too unmanageable, they are eaten with the fork, after being cut into small bits.

SHELLFISH *Clams* (*steamed*) If the shell is not fully open, take it up and bend it back with the fingers. With the right hand lift out the clam by the neck, remove the sheath with the fingers and dip the clam body and cleaned neck first in melted butter or broth, or both alternately, then into the mouth in one bite. Empty shells are placed on butter plate or shell plate, if provided. Do not spoon up remaining liquid in soup plate—it may be sandy—but drink the broth separately provided in the bouillon cup.

Oysters and Clams (*Half Shell*) Hold the shell steady with left hand and, using oyster fork, lift oyster or clam whole from shell. Dip in cocktail sauce and eat in one mouthful. Oyster crackers may be dropped whole in sauce, extracted with oyster fork and eaten. The shell may be taken up with thumb and forefinger and the liquor tipped into the mouth.

SHRIMP COCKTAIL   Where shrimps are too large to be eaten in one mouthful, impale them on the seafood fork and bite off a manageable bite. Redip the remaining portion in the sauce, eat the balance. Do not attempt to cut the shrimp in half on the small service plate beneath the cocktail cup as this undoubtedly would be disastrous.

SPAGHETTI   The *aficionado* knows that the only graceful and satisfying way to eat real Italian spaghetti is to eat it with a large soup spoon and a fork. The spoon is placed in the left hand more or less upright in the plate of spaghetti. The right hand uses the fork to separate a few strands and then, with the tip of the prongs against the spoon, to wind the spaghetti into a manageable mouthful. As with any sauced dish, it should be eaten without stirring spaghetti, cheese, and sauce all together, infant style. The timid way to eat spaghetti is to cut it into small bits with the fork and eat it with the fork alone. Thick macaroni is better cut with the fork as one goes along. Remaining sauce of each dish may be eaten with a spoon or sopped up with small bits of bread, which are then eaten with a fork. The Roman way, considered by many Italians the only "correct" way, is this: With the fork, twist the spaghetti, lift it to the mouth, allowing the excess to dribble back onto the plate. Lean over the plate to prevent splatter.

TOAST AND HOT BREADS   Toast and the various hot breads—scones, English muffins, Parker House rolls, and so forth—may be buttered whole while they are hot, then broken or cut with the butter knife to be eaten in manageable pieces.

• •

Is it ever correct to have one's elbows on the table when one is eating? I was brought up to think it is not. L.G., BOSTON, MASSACHUSSETTS

It is not correct to put one's elbows on the table when one is eating but it is permissible to rest them on the table between courses.

Is it proper to apply lipstick at the dinner table? R.W., EL PASO, TEXAS

You don't do it in anyone's home. You may, however, apply lipstick and a dab of powder at a restaurant table. If you are traveling abroad, applying cosmetics at a restaurant table is often considered gauche. If you are with a party of Americans, on the other hand, you may wish to follow your own custom in the matter. It is wise to be discreet.

My husband buries his head in the newspaper at break-fast and doesn't say a word to me throughout. He just hands me the second section. Shouldn't a husband be expected to carry on some conversation with his wife at breakfast? MRS. F.D'A., NORWALK, CONNECTICUT

No one should be expected to carry on a conversation at breakfast. Many people don't really wake up until later in the day. Enjoy that second section. This is not a new rule, by the way; it has always been so.

I've never known quite what to do about an "accident" at the table. Just recently, while a weekend guest at a friend's home, I inadvertently spilled some jelly at breakfast. I tried to scoop it up with my napkin and managed after a fashion, but I wondered later if I had done the right thing. D.E., RIVERDALE, NEW YORK

The best way actually to retrieve a bit of jelly or sauce is to take a knife or fork, scoop up the substance, and place it at the side of your plate. If something is spilled onto your dress or tie, use a clean knife or spoon to get it off and then dip your napkin into your water glass and rub the spot lightly. Everyone has these unfortunate moments, the trick is to carry them off quietly, with a minimum of fuss.

INTRODUCTIONS

My husband has taken a new job in a different city, and I understand we will have to do a lot of entertaining. For some reason we're occasionally confused and embarrassed about making and acknowledging introductions. For instance, should men always shake hands when they are introduced? What do you actually say when you introduce a man to a woman? Do women shake hands? MRS. L.B.B., DURHAM, NORTH CAROLINA

When men are introduced to each other they shake hands standing, without, if possible, reaching in front of another person. They may smile or at least look pleasant and say nothing as they shake hands, or one many murmur some such usual, courteous phrase as "How do you do" or "It is nice to meet (or know) you." To which the other may reply, "Nice to meet you" or merely "Thank you." (Never say, "Please ta meetcha.")

In shaking hands, men remove the right glove if the action isn't too awkward because of the suddenness of the encounter. If they shake hands with the glove on they say, "Please excuse (or forgive) my glove."

Men who meet or are introduced to each other outdoors do not remove their hats unless a lady is present. When a man is introduced to a lady he preferably does not offer his hand unless she makes the move first, as it is quite correct for a lady merely to bow in acknowledgment of an introduction—in fact the usual thing. But of course no lady ever refuses a proffered hand and we should know that European men are taught to take the initiative in handshaking. Here, now, handshaking between men and women is becoming spontaneous. The words of the introduction between a man and woman go this way: "Mrs. Gardiner, Mr. Longstreth." Or, "Mr. Longstreth, I would like you to meet Mrs. Gardiner." Or, again, and more formally, "Mrs. Gardiner, may I present Mr. Longstreth." Never introduce the woman to the man unless he is a head of state or a head of church, or possibly an elderly and very distinguished man and the woman being introduced is very young. There is much less handshaking in this country between women, and between women and men, than between men. A hostess, however, always greets all her guests by rising and shaking hands, and all guests should seek to shake the hand of the host and hostess in greeting as well as in farewell.

When women are introduced to each other and one is sitting, the other standing, the one who is seated does not rise unless the standee is her hostess or a much older or very distinguished woman. The rising of one woman for another in this country indicates great deference. It is often a delicate matter to decide whether or not a woman is sufficiently older than oneself to be worthy of the gesture. If not, she may be offended rather than honored. Any young girl in her early teens, however, should rise when introduced to any matron and to any older man of her parents' circle, but she shakes hands only if the older person so indicates. Of course, any woman seeking employment rises when presented to her prospective employer, male or female, and permits the interviewer to make the move to shake hands, or not, as he chooses.

A woman or man introducing husband or wife to another person says, "This is my husband," or "May I introduce you to my wife?" A man's wife would, however, be introduced *to* a much older woman, to a woman of great distinction, or to an elderly and distinguished man, to her husband's boss's wife.

Neither spouse refers to the other socially as "Mr. Brown" or "Mrs. Brown." Nor does a man say "the wife" or "the missus."

No one properly says "Charmed," "Delighted," or "Pleased to meet you" when presented to anyone. In fact, under ordinary circumstances a casual "Hello," or "How do you do?" (to which no answer but a repeated "How do you do?" or a smile is expected) is sufficient. A spontaneous "It's so nice to meet you" or "I am *so* glad you came" or even "I have heard so much about you" is fine when it is really meant —but it is never obligatory. All introductions may be acknowledged with no more than a pleasant glance and a slight bow except those between men, where a handshake is usually expected.

• •

How do a man's bow and a woman's bow differ? Is it ever proper to refuse to return a bow if you're a woman? MRS. L.G., PORT CHESTER, NEW YORK

A man's bow is a modification of the deep bow he learned as a boy in dancing class. When presented to a lady, he bows first slightly from the waist, eyes on her face, then steps forward awaiting her tendered hand. If she makes no offer to shake his hand, he keeps his own at his side unless he is the host. (See Introductions, page 15.)

A lady's bow is a slight inclination of the head, usually accompanied by a smile. She follows her bow to a man with a handclasp if she wishes. No one properly refuses to return a bow.

• •

When ladies already seated at a luncheon table are introduced to each other, do they shake hands, seated, when they may conveniently do so? MRS. G.K., OAKLAND, CALIFORNIA

No, they bow. In this country there is very little shaking hands between women, although the hostess always shakes hands with her guests, male and female, and anyone acting in the role of hostess—say, a teacher at the school, a woman representative of a firm being visited by outsiders—would rise and shake hands with the visitors, women as well as men.

• •

My father, who was a widower, recently married. We are very fond of his new wife and wish to know the correct way to introduce her to our children and friends. My sister and I are both married and feel calling her "Mother" is incorrect. However, to say, "My father's wife" seems cold and impersonal. We would appreciate your help. MRS. L.M., TOLEDO, OHIO

Yes, I agree, "My father's wife" is a little cold, especially when such a bond of affection is between you. She is, after all, your stepmother, even though you and your sister are mature. I think it would be nice to introduce her that way. You probably call her by her first name, so you would say, "Molly, our new stepmother, of whom we are all so fond." Something like this would indicate your gracious acceptance of her.

• •

Should a clergyman's manners toward a woman be the same as those of a layman? Should a clergyman, for example, wait until a woman offers her hand before offering his? If he smokes, should he offer cigarettes to the women around him and light their cigarettes? H.G., TRENTON, NEW JERSEY

Generally speaking, his manners toward women are the same as a layman's. If he is at the door of his church, after services, he is in effect a host and therefore offers his hand to women parishioners without waiting for them to offer theirs. He is introduced *to* women rather than the other way around unless they are very, very young and he old and distinguished.

If he is smoking, he does offer cigarettes to those around him, men and women, but if he is a non-smoker and against cigarette smoking, he need not offer to light women's cigarettes.

I am a bachelor about to give an important party. Could you tell me how to introduce Mr. and Mrs. Jones to Mr. and Mrs. Smith? ROBERT K., CLEVELAND, OHIO

The simplest way to effect an introduction such as you have described is to say, "Mr. and Mrs. Smith—Mr. and Mrs. Jones." Or, if these are all people you call by their first names and who will presumably call each other by their first names at an intimate party, you would say, "Mary and John, this is Bill and Jean Smith. Bill and Jean, my good friends the Joneses." It is well, as you know, to avoid stiff formal phrases, such as, "Mrs. Smith, may I present Mrs. Jones and her husband, etc." While this is quite correct, it might make for an awkward pause. The simpler way would be better for the sake of the party.

• •

When one approaches a receiving line and is asked to give a name, does one say, "Mrs. Jones" or "Mrs. John Jones" or "Mr. Jones" or "John Jones"? F.F.C., NEW YORK, NEW YORK

You just say, "Mrs. Jones", "Mr. Jones", or more usual now, "John Jones." If you are a very special Jones, the person who introduces you finally to the guest of honor sometimes has the opportunity to define you, as it were. The receiving line should never be held up for lengthy conversations, however.

• •

Will you please describe the correct procedure for introducing one couple to another (1) when the couples are of approximately the same age, (2) when one couple is older or more distinguished in station than the other? J.L., ALEXANDRIA, VIRGINIA

When the couples are about the same age it doesn't matter whose names are mentioned first. When one couple is older or more distinguished—or perhaps guests in your town—you introduce the younger couple to the older one. You say, "Mr. and Mrs. Smith, I'd like to present Mr. and Mrs. Jones." Or if you are to be on a first-name basis, "John and Mary, Bob and Rosemary Hanson," and then to the Hansons, "The Smiths are here from New York" (or some other phrase in which you use the last name of the first couple if you are sure that the second couple does not already know it). You can also tell them the last name when you are on the way over to make the introduction. You can say, "I'd like you to come over and meet the Smiths."

• •

At an open house given by a Washington representative and his wife recently there was of course a receiving line, with the hostess first in the line and our representative next to her. As the guests entered I noticed there was some confusion as to who should be greeted first—the hostess or the representative next to her. What is the rule when the host holds such a prominent position? G.M., WASHINGTON, DISTRICT OF COLUMBIA

The rule is always the same. One greets first the person first in line, who is the hostess or the acting hostess, always shaking hands. Occasionally there is a line made up only of men, and in this case the first man encountered is the one one greets first. As a matter of fact, very often the most important guest, for whom the reception is given, is placed in the middle of the line.

COURTESIES OF EVERYDAY LIVING

THE MASCULINE GRACES

When a match is used, should a man light his own cigarette first and then his woman companion's? If a lighter is used is this still true? J.C., LEXINGTON, MASSACHUSETTS

A man lights his woman companion's cigarette first. In a high wind he lights his own cigarette first, then he lights his companion's cigarette with his own lighted cigarette if he does not have a lighter or if the lighter does not work in a high wind. In using a lighter he needs merely to hesitate long enough to be sure that the flame is adequate, then he lights his companion's cigarette.

• •

Should a man remove his hat to kiss a lady? B.R.J., BRYN MAWR, PENNSYLVANIA

A man kissing a lady on the street—in greeting or farewell (only)—should always remove his hat, no matter what the weather. He should be careful concerning this courtesy even—or perhaps I should say especially—with his wife or daughter.

• •

Do you approve of the custom of men keeping their hats on in the corridors and elevators of public buildings? F.J.L., BROOKLINE, MASSACHUSETTS

Yes—if the elevator is crowded a man is more considerate to keep his hat on his head, as holding it in front of him will require more space. If there are only one or two occupants in an apartment house elevator and there are ladies present, it is certainly courteous for a man to remove his hat.

• •

My wife tells me that a man accompanying a lady on the street always walks on the curb side. Is this still true when he is walking with two ladies? Does he offer his arm? B.J.M., SKOKIE, ILLINOIS

In America it is customary for a man to walk on the curb side when accompanying a lady on the street, but the rule is not so hard and fast as it used to be. In Europe the man walks on the woman's left, which may be the inside. When a man is accompanying two ladies he may walk between them, or, conservatively, on the outside, moving to the center position to assist both across the street. He does not offer his arm to a lady, except to an elderly or infirm one, in the daytime, although he does so at night or in bad weather. He offers his arm to assist her across the street but does not propel her by the elbow. He may never take *her* arm except to help her in and out of vehicles, to guide her across the street, etc. In this latter case, incidentally, a woman should bend her arm so that the man may pilot her efficiently.

• •

What do you consider the important "don'ts" for a man or boy to remember? E.N.B., ATLANTA, GEORGIA

Do not—

enter a room before a lady unless it is dark and you wish to make it ready for her

seat yourself while ladies are standing

smoke without asking permission of the lady you are accompanying or sit so near (as in a train) that the smoke might annoy her

call any but your contemporaries, servants, or children by their first names without permission

keep your hat on while talking to a lady (unless asked to replace it) or fail to touch your hat or to lift it when necessary

nudge a woman or take her arm except to help her into and out of vehicles or across the street

speak intimately of any girl or woman to other men

fail to pull out a lady's chair for her or fail to serve her or to see that she is served first

speak of repulsive matters at table

criticize another's religion, belittle his race or country, or refer unnecessarily to his color in his presence

enter any place of worship without removing your hat (if its removal is expected) and without speaking in reverent tones

laugh at the mistakes or misfortunes of others

fail to give due respect to a clergyman or clergy-woman of any faith, to a man or woman of any religious order

• •

How should a man refer to his wife to associates, to strangers? K.B., RICHMOND, VIRGINIA

A man refers to his wife as "my wife" to acquaintances, "Betty," to close friends, and "Mrs. Green" to strangers. He *never* uses the phrase "*the* wife" or "the Missus." To a waiter, she is "the Lady" except in a private club or a hotel where the couple is well known to the staff. Then a husband would say "Mrs. Green will have—"

• •

When a boy takes a girl to a dance in a public place where there is a checking concession, does he hand her the amount of the tip that she'll need to get her coat, or should he stand in line with her, get her coat, then stand in line for his own? Or should she handle her own coat herself and tip out of her own money? J.M.W., JERSEY CITY, NEW JERSEY

Where there are long lines at both checking counters, it is sensible and courteous for the boy to give the girl the expected tip and for her to get her own coat while he gets his. At any rate, they part, and a wise girl has her own tip ready, in case the boy doesn't think of this extra expense or she doesn't really want him to assume it. Where no waiting is involved the boy may, of course, go and get a girl's coat with her, leaving the tip.

• •

I ride a crowded city bus to work every day. I was taught that a gentleman should stand and give his seat to a lady but most of the women in the busses I travel seem to be going to work, too. Why should I give up my seat to them? Is it really considered necessary these days? J.A., CHICAGO, ILLINOIS

I agree with you that business women are used to standing on their own feet. A true gentleman, however, does rise for an elderly woman, for a woman laden with packages or carrying a young child, for a woman who is pregnant or obviously ill. When he does give up his seat he moves at least a few feet away and never attempts to start a conversation. The woman, however, always thanks such a man courteously though briefly for his kindness. An able woman may also offer her seat when it is needed by another woman or man.

• •

My husband thinks I am difficult because I expect him to wear his coat to the table. He says that a man should be able to do as he pleases in his own home and that wearing a coat at table isn't important. MRS. J.A.O'R., NASHVILLE, TENNESSEE

It is still the woman, the hostess, who sets the style in the home. Manners have become much more relaxed as most homes are without servants and most families, at least when they are alone, dine in a very relaxed fashion. You may wish to work out some new guidelines with your husband, at least when you are alone with the family. He might, for example, wear a sweater, a sports shirt, or jumpsuit, reserving coat and tie for times when you are entertaining. It goes without saying that taboo should be an undershirt or shorts without top unless you are dining around the pool in very hot weather and even then a proper sports top would be more attractive.

Must a man wait until a woman speaks first if they meet, or may he be the one to speak first? F.R., AUBURN NEW YORK

Frequently the two speak simultaneously. A man need no longer wait until a woman speaks first. He may even call a woman friend's name out softly in public if she has not seen him and he wishes to attract her attention.

Sometimes in a group my husband gets a little nervous and forgets to introduce someone he knows to me. I usually just stand there steaming. What should I do? MRS. F.X.H., NEW ORLEANS, LOUISIANA

You should introduce yourself, saying, "I am *Mrs.* Brown" (or, Joe's wife, or Mary Brown).

• •

When we go to parties, my husband leaves me almost inside the door and I don't see him for the rest of the evening until it is time to go home. It seems to me that this puts the burden of my entertainment too much on the other men present, especially when there is a buffet party. Don't you think he should pay some attention to me, even though we're married? MRS. G.N.K., TULSA, OKLAHOMA

Yes, he certainly should. He should not treat you differently than the unmarried girls he took out in his bachelor days. He should see that you have an opportunity for pleasant conversation, that you are given refreshments as needed, and that you are never left too long with what may seem to be an uncongenial companion. His neglect of you at these parties reflects on his own good manners with others.

• •

Yesterday my husband and I went to dinner with another married couple. After we had removed our coats, my husband complimented the other lady on the dress she was wearing. Since there were only two of us ladies present, don't you think the compliment should have been plural to include my dress? I believe the other lady's husband was embarrassed over it, but no one paid me a like compliment. F.J.R., DENVER, COLORADO

I think you are begging trouble if you demand compliments from your husband. If you make him feel guilty because he doesn't compliment you when you look nice, whatever compliments he then is able to force out of himself will be meaningless. You must build up a better opinion of yourself. If you have done the best you can about your appearance and you know you look nice, then compliments will come spontaneously. Whether or not they come from your husband is not important because men seem to think that their wives take it for granted that they think them attractive. Sometimes they are reticent about saying nice things just because their wives are their wives. Your husband's comment about your friend's dress may have been spontaneous or it may have just been an effort toward good manners. It did not mean that he thought her dress more attractive than yours or considered her more desirable than you.

• •

Every year at Christmas and birthdays my husband gives me an array of personal gifts, none of which ever fits me. Each year I accept them with thanks and later, when possible, exchange them. When I can't exchange them I must give them to somebody else. What should I do? MRS. J.M.R., AKRON, OHIO

Talk the problem over with him nicely, well before Christmas. Say nothing about his previous gifts not having fit you. Tell him you really like his taste in these personal things and how much you look forward to the gifts he is going to select. But give him a list of all your sizes, saying that some of them may have changed. If you find that what he normally selects is unbecoming to you and you have reason to believe that he'd like to be relieved of the need for making these selections, why not tell him specifically what you would like, perhaps hand him an advertisement from the paper or a magazine, marking the size and color you prefer. But in doing this don't exceed what you feel he would normally spend on you on these gift-giving occasions.

• •

When a headwaiter shows a couple to a table, who goes first, the man or the woman? What happens on the way out? Does the man lead or does the woman?

Where there is a headwaiter, the man steps back and allows the woman he is escorting to follow the waiter to the table. Where there is no headwaiter, the man goes first followed by the woman. He then seats her at a table that is available. It is well to hesitate long enough to be sure that the table is really free before sitting down. On the way out, the man leads if the restaurant is crowded to make a path for the woman. If it is not crowded, usually the woman goes first, followed by the man. She then steps out of the line of traffic, if any, while he gets his coat, then he steps ahead and opens the door if there is no attendant to do so.

Why is it that men always leave the toilet seat up. Women entering the powder room have to replace it. What can be done about this? MRS. B.E., LOS ANGELES, CALIFORNIA

Wives can tell their husbands. I know of one case of two girls who had an apartment. They decorated the under part of the seat with flowers and green leaves plus the message: "It's so nice to have a man around the house." They reported that most of the men got the idea.

You don't seem to see women carrying handkerchiefs anymore. They use tissues instead. I prefer tissues to handkerchiefs that are not perfectly fresh, and they are more sanitary when one has a cold. I wish you would say something, however, about men who take out handkerchiefs that are far from clean. And shouldn't they use tissues when they have colds? MRS. N.S., TULSA, OKLAHOMA

Fastidious men are careful to carry clean handkerchiefs but they also use tissues when they have colds. Man-sized tissues are available in sporting goods shops and some drugstores. There are even red ones for hunters. A man should never use a silk breastpocket handkerchief for utilitarian purposes. A man who travels a great deal uses tissues plus drip-dry handkerchiefs if necessary which are far better than using crumpled handkerchiefs which are not pristine.

I have recently become engaged. I notice that my fiancé is becoming rather relaxed about some of the social amenities. For instance, he hesitates just long enough when he stops the car for me to feel that I should open the door and get out myself. Should I make an issue of this now, or should I give in and expect much less manners from him once we are married? MISS V.B., DALLAS, TEXAS

There is no place where manners are more important than in marriage. We should all encourage husbands to maintain the traditional gallantry toward us, not so much for our own sakes but for theirs. It helps a man, I think, to maintain his status at a time when so much —I'm thinking of the independence of women— threatens him. It all seems a little sad if, when a man becomes a fiancé or a husband, he decides to skip the social graces. Modern women, however, do get out of cars by themselves except perhaps at night on special occasions. Young people's manners toward each other are increasingly egalitarian. Decide, together, what you both deem still important.

THE WELL-MANNERED WOMAN

When I call someone on the telephone—a neighbor whom I have never met and who doesn't know me— about some community matter, do I say to her, "This is Ann Little," do I say, "This is Mrs. Little," or do I say, "This is Mrs. John Little"? What if I have met her and we have many friends in common with whom we are on a first-name basis? MRS. J.L.L., MEMPHIS, TENNESSEE

In the first instance, you say, "This is Mrs. Little." Then quickly, as she may be confused, "I'm calling for the

Emmanuel Church Supper Committee." If you have met several times and you are sure she knows who you are, it would be more friendly to say, "This is Ann Little." Then you might follow it with, "We met at the Petersons' a few weeks ago." That should place you to her. Don't leave her in the dark, however, if she's to send you a contribution or do something which involves her communicating with you. Be quite clear and say, "May I give you my name and address again. As you may remember, I am Mrs. John Little of Kettle Creek Road." Generally speaking, where the contact is slight, you announce yourself as "Mrs. Little." Where there is some social element involved you may say, "This is Ann Little." However, if you were giving an order to a tradesman, say, "This is Mrs. Little of Kettle Creek Road," or, if there would be some possibility of mis-understanding, "This is Mrs. John Little of Kettle Creek Road."

• •

When I was a girl there were certain subjects that could never be mentioned in mixed company. For example, if a woman was going to have a baby, this was not considered a proper drawing room topic. Today things seem to be changed, and all around me I hear subjects discussed and words used that seem very discourteous, to say the least, to the women present. What is your feeling about this? R.L., HELENA, MONTANA

I feel that in today's society almost any topic in the world is discussible, if there is reason to discuss it and if the discussion of it is conducted with taste and discretion. I know that many men and women of a previous generation find the kind of talk they hear among young people intolerable, and I think young people should take this into consideration and moderate their conversation when older people who might be offended are around. However, the world has changed very much—women have gone into science, politics, the law, into advertising, business, and every other possible kind of endeavor and profession. They cannot continue to expect men's conversation around them to be geared to drawing room levels. The well-bred person does know the difference between vulgarity in conversation and permissiveness of topics discussed. He does not bring up things that have no possible relation to the conversation in progress just for shock effect. On the other hand, tasteful conversationalists have absolutely no compunctions against discussing such things as pregnancy, abortion, divorce, separation, political and other scandal, if such discussion is relevant to what is being talked over in the group. Not so very long ago, these things would have been considered very crass as subjects for mixed conversation, especially in a drawing room.

• •

What do you think of those meaningless clichés that some people seem to adopt as trade marks? I'm thinking of such gems as "Good-by now," "You can say that again," "like so," and "Out of this world." Do you think this sort of thing sometimes gets out of hand? K.E., TUCSON, ARIZONA

Yes, I do. Up to a point they can lend a color to your conversation, but they can easily become second nature, so that you seem to be a person of little imagination, one suffering from a sad poverty of language. These innocuous slang expressions sound particularly inept from a grown man or woman, unless one is using them quite consciously and in fun.

• •

We have been meeting a lot of new people since we have come to this community. Some of them put themselves immediately on an easy first-name basis, others seem more reserved. I don't want to seem overfamiliar with those who don't welcome the informality—how do you handle this? MRS. R.W.N., LAKEVILLE, OHIO

Be slow to use people's first names and try to let the other person take the initiative—as you seem to be doing. Conservatively, a man does not call a woman by her first name unless he is asked to do so. If she is willing to be on a more familiar footing, a woman may call him by his first name without any explanatory preliminaries, but she may say, "Do call me Joan."

• •

Recently my husband and I met a very attractive couple at a friend's house. We later invited them to dinner at our house, but didn't invite our host and hostess, for we had entertained them very recently. Later we heard that they were most offended. Were we wrong?
S.D., OKLAHOMA CITY, OKLAHOMA

Yes, one should always invite one's host and hostess the first time one entertains a friend first met at their house—or, as a matter of fact, in their company. The invitation must be offered at least, but if it is refused it is then quite correct to entertain the new friend without the others being present.

• •

I am one of those people who never forget a face but cannot master the art of remembering names. Is there a tactful way of handling a social problem like this?
MISS J.G., INDIANAPOLIS, INDIANA

If you are warmly greeted by someone whose name you can't recall, say something harmless such as, "Nice to see you" or "You're looking well." Then while looking quite attentive, let the other person do the talking until he or she gives a clue to his identity. Your own expression should always indicate that you remember him well and favorably.

No one is ever pleased if you say, "I know your face —but I can't recall your name." If you have trouble remembering the names that match the faces, always help out the other person who is probably suffering from the same thing. Never say, "Do you remember me?" Instead, in greeting people, identify yourself quickly and gracefully, "How do you do. I'm Joseph Bye." It is more tactful and modest to assume that you are not remembered than to presume that you are.

• •

How much may a lady make up in public? L.S., CLEVELAND, OHIO

Making up in public is much more relaxed of recent years. However, anything too technical in the matter of making up—hair combing, mascara-applying, or application of a liquid or cream make-up—are all taboo. A light dusting of powder and an unobtrusive reapplication of lipstick are acceptable—and usual—in a public place. But not at a private dinner table.

• •

I have a friend who seems to have no idea of anyone's privacy. She persists in asking questions about my age, the cost of everything she sees around the house, and she even had the nerve to ask me how much money my husband made last year. I think these things are none of her business, but I don't really want to offend her as I am sure it's just idle curiosity and that she really means no harm. What can I do? MRS. E.C.R., HARTFORD, CONNECTICUT

There are people who seem never to realize that they are offending and who continue their stream of personal questions to the discomfort of all their friends. The safe thing to do in a situation like this is to pretend that no offense was meant—as you say, your friend doesn't really mean to be malicious. If you don't want to advertise your age—and most women don't —you might answer "You know, the women in my family have always been ageless and I like to keep it that way." Women are expected to lie about their ages, anyhow, so, even if you told the truth, your interrogator would mentally add another five or ten years. When no tactful answer seems to suffice and the personal probing goes on, the only solution is to be quite frank. Say, without getting angry, "I know you don't realize it, but that is a personal question I don't feel willing to answer." If your friend then takes offense, she deserves to.

• •

I am allergic to cigarette smoke and I get asthma if I am exposed to it. Even sharing an elevator with someone who is smoking starts me coughing.

What bothers me most is that one of the girls at work smokes. She sits near me and must know that it bothers me, but she has never volunteered to go out to the rest room for her hourly cigarette. Also, many of the men who come to see my boss smoke. I would so like to be polite, but when one is allergic this is about as ridiculous as saying that one wants to be polite to a maniac who has his hands in a strangle hold on one's throat. E.C.S., SANTA BARBARA, CALIFORNIA

Your problem is difficult, one hard to work out with the full co-operation of other people—especially those whom you don't know well enough to ask such a favor.

Many allergics find ways to avoid things that bother them without too much social discomfort, or else they have medication they can take when they happen to run into foods or atmospheric conditions that are bothersome. True asthma, however, is another matter, and if the problem is very serious in your case perhaps the only solution will be for you to find employment where smoking is definitely not permitted. Certainly it is impossible to ask those who come to see your employer not to smoke in your presence. I assume that you have seen a competent allergist. In some cases, I understand, psychiatric help is valuable to asthma sufferers.

The important thing, I think, in your case, is not to feel that this is solely a matter of etiquette. Many people dislike very much getting into places where the air is blue with smoke. But they do not feel that they can ask other people to cease smoking just because they don't enjoy being surrounded by cigarette smoke. They understand that the adjustment usually must be on their own part. Only in their own homes or in private offices is it possible to press no smoking. Increasingly in doctors' offices, such a request is posted.

• •

I have the best next-door neighbor anyone could want. She is always doing something for me and always giving our eight-year-old daughter something. She takes care of my little girl and our dog whenever I have to go shopping or see the doctor. She does all this without pay, which would make her mad if I offered it. Should I get her a gift all her family can enjoy? Or what can I do to show my appreciation? MRS. H.E., FRESNO, CALIFORNIA

Your neighbor gives her services to you with loving affection. There must be many talents that you have that could serve to return her many kindnesses. If you are a good cook and she has a freezer, perhaps when you are baking a pie you can bake one for her, either for her freezer or for immediate use. If you have a way with flowers, perhaps you can make her a flower arrangement and give it to her, together with the container. If you sew well, perhaps she would enjoy a pretty apron or some potholders for her kitchen. If she is alone at night, you could invite her to your house for dinner or take her to the movies. I wouldn't wait for Christmas to return these kindnesses, but I'd try to do little things for her from time to time that will show how much you appreciate what she does for you.

• •

What is the proper procedure to follow when people insist that you visit at their home but will not accept an invitation to visit your home, no matter how many times it may be presented to them? I have a friend who always wants me to "come over," but when I ask her

to spend an afternoon with me she will reply, "Why don't you come over here?" I don't feel I should say, "I invited you first," but believe me, sometimes that is exactly what I think I should say. MRS. J.B.J., DETROIT, MICHIGAN

Some women are so housebound, so domesticated, that they lose track of the fact that in going out of their homes into those of their friends, instead of expecting everyone to come to see them, they are extending a real courtesy. In a case like this, this woman does seem to imply that she thinks her home is the one which, for some reason or other, is preferable for entertainment. No guest is comfortable being a perpetual one. We should all be permitted to reciprocate as we can for entertainment received. It does not have to be on the same level at all. You would be quite justified in saying sometime to this thoughtless friend, "I invited you first." If she still refuses to come, there is something very wrong in this relationship.

• •

What can I do about my mother-in-law's prying into our private life? She is a country woman and has no desire to learn about city life and cleanliness. When I take my two small children to her, her house is never clean, and when my husband wants to see his boyhood friends, she tags along. We are building a house of our own, and she even criticizes the fact that we want a fireplace, saying that it is "old-timey." I can't put up with this much longer, but I certainly don't want to have a fuss with her. I have just stopped going to see her. MRS. R.L., MESQUITE, TEXAS

It is hard for a mother to stop making suggestions just because her son has married. But if you can take these suggestions in good spirit and do just as you were planning to do anyhow, in time she may understand that it is you and your husband who must make the decisions about such things as whether or not you will have a fireplace in your house. I would not worry about whether or not her house is clean when your children visit her, as the important thing to them is the love and affection she shows them. So try not to project your feeling of criticism toward your mother-in-law to the children. They need to love and respect their grandmother, even if her ways are different from yours. In time, when she sees how comfortable you are and how attractive cleanliness and neatness are, she may try to imitate your way of living and even ask for your advice. Try to respect her as the individual she is and with the limitations she has. After all, the background she created produced your husband, whom you undoubtedly love very much.

• •

Now that my children are older, I am able to hold an afternoon job at the office where I used to work. My friends all know that I have quite a problem getting through my housework in the morning in order to do this. But one or two of the girls who haven't as much to do as I have will get on the phone when they know I'm home, and it seems to me that I just can't get rid of them without being rude. How can I handle this and still keep them as friends, because I do like them?
MRS. A.S., HOUSTON, TEXAS

Your friends have a social need for you, or they wouldn't call at such length. But your friendship will suffer if you don't deal honestly with the difficulty. Say something like this: "I'm so glad to hear from you, but you know I'm rushing to get through so I can get to work. May I call you tonight?" If this doesn't work just say: "Really, I can't talk now. I must finish up. I'll call you back just as soon as I can" . . . and hang up! If this is said in a properly reluctant tone of voice, no intelligent person can be offended—at least not after she thinks it over a little. As for you, you have no choice. Your home and your work must come first.

• •

When one person makes the telephone call, shouldn't she be the one to terminate it, not the one who's being called? MRS. P.E.J., PORT RICHMOND, NEW YORK

It's not too important, really. But usually it's the other way around. The one being called makes the necessary response, then, never too abruptly, hangs up.

• •

Since childhood I have been taught to say "Yes, sir" and "Yes, ma'am" to my elders. Recently in a family discussion, several members of my husband's family told me this is incorrect, that it should be simply "Yes" or "No," with no exceptions for age or position. B.D.W., CHARLOTTE, NORTH CAROLINA

In the North, "Yes, ma'am," and "Yes, sir," are unusual except among domestics. We think even then it is more democratic to say, even to one's employer, "Yes, Mr. Adams" or "No, Miss Jones." However, "Sir" and "Ma'am" are still very common in the South. A younger man even in the North uses "Sir" to older ones. Perhaps your husband's relatives are from the North where this is a less common custom. If saying, "Yes, sir" and "Yes, ma'am" to older or more distinguished people seems natural to you, I see no reason why you should change.

• •

Does the fact that you have a "green thumb" and love to work in the garden and take care of the lawn have any reflection whatsoever on your not being a refined person? I love the outdoors and plant shrubbery, trees, flowers, and maintain my entire lawn. Recently a neighbor remarked that this was rather unladylike. Is it? H.P., MIAMI, FLORIDA

Certainly not. It is a wonderful, creative hobby. Just join your local garden club, and you will see how many other "unladylike" ladies there are.

Is it proper for a single girl to have dinner in a bachelor's apartment without a chaperone? F.S., BANGOR, MAINE

Social conventions can do very little to protect the girl really bent on getting into difficulties. Girls having dinner in a man's apartment without chaperonage should realize they must themselves set the standard for the evening. Leaving before midnight is wise.

• •

By mutual agreement I stopped dating a fellow about six months ago, after going with him for eighteen months. Along with smaller gifts, I received a watch and a portable radio from him. I have been trying to decide what I should do about returning them. I know he probably won't accept them now, but I feel I should make the offer, although I don't want to offend him. MISS D.S., TOLEDO, OHIO

You shouldn't, you now understand, have accepted these expensive gifts in the first place. Then, without offending him, you could have said, "This is very kind of you, but I really can't accept such an expensive gift." Now the only thing to do is either to speak to him or write to him and say that you feel you really should not have accepted these gifts and that you would like to return them, although you want, of course, to remain good friends. He probably won't want them back, but at least you will know that you have made the proper gesture. And in the future, never put yourself in a position where a man can say, should a relationship break up in a less friendly fashion than this one did, "She was willing enough to take all kinds of expensive things from me, but when she got tired of me, that was that." Friendship between a man and a woman should be voluntary, not obligatory because of too many favors and gifts accepted. You must always feel yourself free in such a situation until and unless you have given your promise of marriage.

• •

There is a single man in my office whom I like very much and who has been nice to me but who hasn't asked me for a date. I live with my parents. Would it be all right to ask him to come and see me? A.M.M., FLINT, MICHIGAN

Yes, if you are rather casual about it and invite him first when there will be others of your age present. If he refuses your first invitation with obvious reluctance you may, after a discreet lapse of time, try again. If again he refuses, do not offer him a third invitation. However, by this time he may be sufficiently interested to offer you an invitation of his own. While you should never be overly aggressive in the pursuit of the male, you should realize that a man is more inclined toward a woman who shows obvious interest in him than toward one who seems completely indifferent. While many a man yearns desperately for the unattainable, he most often settles in time for girls who make him feel attractive and desirable, so long as there is no hint of desperation in their approach.

• •

I make a good salary, more than most of the men I go with do. I like to go to the theater but get tired of going "Dutch" with girl friends. Could I get seats and ask a boy? E.K., GREEN FARMS, CONNECTICUT

Yes, but don't repeatedly ask the same one to go to the theater with you when you are buying the tickets. Here again, be very casual in your invitation. Say, "I have two tickets for————next Saturday night. Would you like to go with me?" He will then understand he is not expected to pay for the tickets. If he accepts, however, he is responsible for your transportation to and from the theater and for any entertainment of you, before or after, he feels able to manage. Give him the tickets when he picks you up and avoid in every way seeming to be in charge of the evening. If you feel self-conscious about having had to furnish the tickets, it may help you to know that not so many generations ago it was considered ill-bred for a young lady to accept any such entertainment from a man—her parents or servants always made such arrangements or reimbursed him for anything of the kind. It has always been quite correct for a girl to invite a man to the theater, a concert, or the opera with the tickets presumably furnished by her parents.

• •

How and when is it ever "proper" to invite a doctor to our home? MRS. M.M., BATON ROUGE, LOUISIANA

This is a delicate matter. I assume you mean your own doctor. If, on your visits to him, you find that he himself engages you in some social conversation each time and seems anxious to prolong the visit for this reason, it is a quite proper thing to feel him out, as it were, to see if he would be interested in a social invitation. You might say, "Doctor, my husband and I hope that you and your wife will have time to come to our next cocktail party (or dinner party, whichever it may be)." If the doctor really feels that he has time—and interest —to pursue the matter, he will say, "I'm sure we'd love it. Just let us know." If he says something like this, "Well, that's very kind of you, but we have so little time for social activities," you will know that it is probably impossible for him to expand his limited social life and that this is no reflection on his feeling for you. Certainly, if he is married, you do not exclude his wife in invitations, and the invitation, when it actually is sent or given over the phone, should be directed to her.

• •

I am a doctor's wife. My husband's patients load him with all kinds of gifts, often extravagant ones, at Christmas. We wish they wouldn't. MRS. R.S.S., DETROIT, MICHIGAN

Our doctors at Christmas receive a great many presents from what they call "G.P.'s" (Grateful Patients) when in too many cases, I'm afraid, they'd much rather have their bills paid with greater promptness. People do feel a warmth and gratitude to their doctors and often feel impelled to give them gifts. Doctors themselves tell me that often they would prefer a little more restraint in the matter, especially where there is actually no social contact between patient and doctor.

• •

I had an argument with my girl friend about whether you should tell a strange woman you see that her slip's showing or that she has a run in her stocking. I always do, but my friend says it's none of my business. Am I right? A.M.W., MONTCLAIR, NEW JERSEY

This is a delicate matter. A woman who looks friendly and relaxed may welcome your calling such a thing to her attention if you can do it privately and casually so as not to embarrass her before others. The tactful time to tell a woman such a thing is when she's some place where she can do something about it, such as a dressing room where she is repairing her make-up and is obviously unaware that her costume needs attention, too.

INTERFAITH MANNERS

I am not a Catholic, but when I pass a Catholic church with my friend, he tips his hat because he is a Catholic. What should I do? MR. R.O'M., TAMPA, FLORIDA

Give your friend's church, when you are in his company, the same deference as you would give his mother, should you encounter her on the street. Raise your hat, too, out of courtesy to your friend's reverence. The same rule holds true if you should encounter a priest while in his company. Your gesture is social, only.

I have some friends who are Conservative Jews. They do not eat ham or seafood. Does this mean that if I have a buffet dinner I may not have either of these foods on the buffet if my friends are present? R.C.C., PITTSBURGH, PENNSYLVANIA

No, you may place these foods on a buffet, but you let your Conservative Jewish friends serve themselves from the buffet. They will avoid the ham and seafood. Do not attempt to serve them a filled plate that has either of these foods on it, as they then would not properly eat any of the foods with which the seafood or ham had come in contact.

• •

I have a friend who is a very strict Methodist. When he visits us, is it incorrect for us to serve wine at the table? MRS. W.L.J., MEMPHIS, TENNESSEE

You may serve it, but when it is passed he, of course, will refuse it. He cannot be offended at your following your usual custom. The wine glass at his place may be filled with the beverage of his choice—water, milk, cider, etc. He may have a small pitcher from which he may serve himself.

• •

I am a clergyman. I am expected to make regular pastoral calls upon my congregation, but as I live in a simple suburban community where there are few servants, I find that my call, no matter what time of day I seem to pick, interferes with the routine of young mothers. Do you think I should phone before calling? DR. J.W.M., MONTCLAIR, NEW JERSEY

Yes, I do. The clergyman's call is one that should be received in dignity. It is very hard for a young mother with a household and children to cope with to find that she is opening the door, even in the early afternoon, to her clergyman when she is not prepared to receive him.

If she has some forewarning of his visit, she can perhaps arrange to be free at that time and to enjoy the spiritual aspect of such an occasion without interruption.

• •

When I make up my list of friends to whom I am going to send Christmas cards, I never know whether or not to omit the names of Jewish friends. What is proper? N.A.D., PORTLAND, OREGON

It depends, I think, on whether your friends are deeply religious Orthodox Jews or perhaps those who think of Christmas only as a gift-giving holiday and celebrate it as such especially if they have children. It is, perhaps, better to avoid cards illustrating the Nativity if you desire to keep your Jewish friends on your Christmas card list. Many Jews themselves now send non-religious Christmas greeting cards, have Christmas trees, and give and receive Christmas gifts.

• •

I like the idea of bright and amusing Christmas cards, but I notice that they are increasing in number every year. However, I notice that most of my Catholic friends send me religious cards, and I wonder if there is any rule about it. L.A.O., FORT WORTH, TEXAS

No rule, really, but many Catholics are offended by the increasing commercialism of Christmas and by flippant Christmas cards, some of which are really in bad taste, no matter what your religious belief.

• •

Is it proper, when attending church, Catholic or Protestant, for a single girl or even a married woman to give a donation or offering when she is with her escort or husband? Or should she refrain from doing so and just let her partner contribute? A.M., CRESSON, TEXAS

The church service is not a social occasion. Therefore I would say that a single girl escorted by a young man makes her own donation to her church or to a church they are visiting. Where a woman is accompanied by her husband he would make the donation or offering for both, as head of the household.

ENTERTAINING

HOSTS

When a group of ladies meet at a home, is it proper for the hostess to smoke a cigarette and not offer one to her guests? Or should she not smoke when no one else does? J.B., NEW ORLEANS, LOUISIANA

She offers cigarettes to her guests if she plans to smoke, and, if they refuse, then I hope she will at least limit her own smoking. It would be courteous of her to ask the others if they mind if she smokes—just as a man would. Of course, if someone does mind, she should not smoke.

• •

How many drinks should the hostess figure per person at a cocktail party, and what are appropriate drinks to offer? M.P.M., BOSTON, MASSACHUSETTS

It is usual to figure three drinks per person for a cocktail party. Some guests will take one drink, some none, and some three or four, but it works out to an average of three. Most-liked drinks are martinis, manhattans, scotch, rye, or bourbon, with the usual mixers. It is often possible to arrange to have unused bottles returned to a hotel bar or to a liquor store furnishing the supplies.

• •

When friends and guests come to your home to spend the evening watching television or playing cards, is it expected of the host or hostess to serve refreshments? B.C.B., COLUMBUS, OHIO

It is usual to offer something informally, so long as the serving of these things doesn't interrupt the viewing or the card playing. On certain occasions a late supper is served.

• •

An older relative of ours visits us occasionally from another state. Naturally she pays her transportation here. We have planned a vacation trip to take this relative along in our car. Is it sufficient for us to pay the car expense and for the relative to pay her share of the food and lodging? Or, since she has spent money to come and visit us, are we supposed to pay all expenses of the trip? F.J.O., CARLSBAD, NEW MEXICO

In matters such as these, one needs to be frank. It seems unlikely that a couple such as yourselves should be expected to do more than pay the car expenses in such an event. But you should give your relative a chance to accept the invitation under these circumstances or return home before you make the trip.

• •

Sometimes, when we entertain, some guests bring us gifts more or less for the house. I never know whether to open them in front of the others, put them aside with murmured thanks, or just what. MRS. M.V., SOUTH OZONE PARK, NEW YORK

As "house gifts" are purely a matter of volition on the part of guests and are not really expected, the hostess does not open them ostentatiously if other guests who have come empty-handed are present. She thanks the donor quietly, puts aside the gift, and later privately opens it. She then thanks the giver in a way that makes him understand that she knows what she has been given and appreciates his thoughtfulness. In a party where one guest is from quite a distance and the others are all local people who see the hostess constantly, it would, of course, be perfectly suitable for the out-of-town guest who has come with a gift to enjoy seeing the hostess open it in front of the others. This is a matter for discretion. And certainly one cannot ask small children not to open the gifts guests bring. The important point is that guests sometimes bring gifts and sometimes they don't. Those who don't should not be embarrassed by those who do, when the occasion is not definitely a gift-giving one or even if it is.

• •

My husband occasionally receives an invitation for both of us. He frequently is puzzled about how to handle this gracefully. What should he do? MRS. L.S.S., GREEN BAY, WISCONSIN

When your husband does receive an invitation for you both, he must always say something such as, "I'll have Helen call you about this," or, if it is a telephone call, "Will you speak to Helen." This is not only a courtesy to the wife, but it prevents confusion in the matter of invitations. Whenever a couple is entertaining together, it is the wife who issues invitations and accepts them. She is, in effect, the family's social secretary.

• •

The husband of a woman we like very much often drinks too much at parties, then tells off-color stories that embarrass everyone present. We hate to cut them off our list because we like her so much. What can we do? MRS. K.N., CORAL GABLES, FLORIDA

Cease inviting them to parties. Entertain them alone and close the bar after one drink has been offered before dinner. Serve the meal promptly without wine. Do not offer after-dinner drinks. Choose a week night to entertain them. If the husband tells an unacceptable story, look blank and let a pause occur in the conversation.

• •

So often when I invite people in to dinner they break up into little groups after dinner and tend to stay in them until the party is over. How can I, as hostess, get people to move about and meet each other? MRS. A.J.O'C., WINSTON-SALEM, NORTH CAROLINA

As hostess you watch just such situations as these. If within small groups there is obvious congeniality, it is not necessary to break them up, but you can introduce from time to time other members into the group to keep it fluid. And perhaps from time to time you may remove a member from the group who doesn't seem to be partaking too enthusiastically in the conversation. He might enjoy another group better. One pleasant device toward the end of the evening is to try to bring all of the groups together in a general conversational circle. If this is done at some time, it doesn't really matter too much if much of the conversation has been in individual groups.

Our apartment is furnished in Early American pieces, many of which we refinished before our marriage. It was very hard work but gave us a great deal of pleasure. Now that we are married we entertain at least once a week and usually serve in the dining room. Time and again one or two persons out of a group make themselves exceedingly comfortable by placing their heels on the rungs of our ladder-back chairs and twisting their feet up and down while carrying on a conversation. I agree with my husband that this is very rude and inconsiderate, but I would rather not say anything about this to my guests, as I feel it might put a damper on the party as well as on my spirits. He, however, speaks right out and tells them to please remove their feet from the furniture. Can you tell us the most

tactful way to handle the situation without embarrassing anyone? I enjoy their company, but my husband refuses to invite these certain people once he sees how they act. MRS. L.R.J., ORANGE, NEW JERSEY

I remember a woman who was made absolutely miserable by her husband's friends. She loathed their relaxed manners and ran around after them, emptying ash trays even before they were filled, asking them to take their feet off the coffee table, putting coasters under their drinks, etc. Needless to say, she did not reform her husband's friends, but she did alienate her husband. And the friends eventually refused to come to the house. The moral is here: Either you accept, within reason, the manners of your friends, or you make new friends whose ideas of decorum concur with your own.

• •

I have guests who put their cigarettes out in my coffee cups. What can I do? MRS. S.C.H., LOS ANGELES, CALIFORNIA

Very firmly place an ash try within reach and say, "Would you mind using this, please."

When guests arrive at your house with a bottle of wine, or perhaps some article of food such as a ripe brie cheese, are you supposed to change the menu to include these things, or may you put them aside, with thanks, for service on a suitable occasion? MRS. T.W., BILOXI, MISSISSIPPI

You thank the guest and say something like, "The dinner wine is ready" (or, "I'd love to save the cheese for another time"), "I hope you will be here to enjoy it with us when we serve it." Of course, if the gift fits the menu it is nice to serve it.

We are trying in every way to save paper and are thinking of installing roller terry towels because they are so easily washed. Friends say that this is unsanitary,

that if I use roller towels they should be cotton or linen so that people using them can see the part that is still clean, but these have to be ironed. MRS. I.S., STATEN ISLAND, NEW YORK

Your friends are right. In public facilities roller towels in proper dispensers are always ironed, or of permanent press material, so that each user gets a clean section. If you decide to use terry towels within the family circle, they should be constantly laundered. No one wants to dry clean hands on dirty toweling.

When a guest gets boisterous, abusive, begins using foul language, and tells unsuitable stories, what can a hostess do at a dinner table? G.J., MADISON, WISCONSIN

Such a guest has probably been drinking too much. The hostess must always keep things going smoothly at her table for the comfort and pleasure of her other guests. If one guest behaves in this manner, it is her job to tell him or her quietly to stop what he is doing, or possibly she may ask him to leave the table, appointing someone to help. He should be taken somewhere to rest until he "feels better." The incident should not be allowed to disturb the other guests.

We are plagued by friends and acquaintances who are constantly dropping in unannounced. We live in a house so can't always pretend we are not home and we have very little free time. We hate to seem rude, but we need privacy. What should we do? MRS. J.C., LOS ANGELES, CALIFORNIA

Be honest. Say something like this, "I am so sorry we didn't know you were coming. We were just going to get some needed rest. We have had a particularly hard week and have early appointments tomorrow. It is nice seeing you, however briefly, but next time I hope you will let us know when you are coming over so we can really spend some time with you." Stay on your feet. If they don't get the idea, they are not true friends.

Don't feel guilty about handling these thoughtless

people in an honest way. They may never develop consideration, but everybody has a right to privacy and rest.

We live in a resort area and are plagued with unwanted guests. They turn up in the summertime without notice and say, "May we please spend the night?" If we accede then they are likely to spend a week. How do you say no under the circumstances? I know that people in winter vacation areas are equally plagued. MRS. M.A., NORTHAMPTON, NEW YORK

The only way is to be perfectly frank, though kind. Some people are indeed insensitive and will impose on their friends if possible. However, if you say yes when you really mean no, you can hardly be a good hostess. If you are willing to permit these people to stay overnight be careful to state the limitation and be prepared to move them out if necessary. People in winter vacation spots can fend off people they really don't want to entertain by replying when people write them, "I'm glad you are coming down. Right near us is a nice motel where some of our friends stay. It makes it simple for us to see them. If you like I will have the motel send you their brochure." Your friends should surely be able to read between the lines.

We moved into a new house. Our friends all are anxious to see it, and we like to show it off. I have been having a series of informal dinners for them. As I have no maid and the dinner preparation requires all of my attention, how can I courteously suggest that guests refrain from prowling about on their own until I can be with them? It is impossible for my husband or myself to show each guest around individually, and we'd like to do it together when all are assembled—and after the dinner hour is over. MRS. S.C., ALLENTOWN, PENNSYLVANIA

Simply say, "I know that you will want to see the house, but let's have dinner first and I'll show it to you later, all together. I think it will be more fun that way."

My children go to a private school. I find that it is more or less expected that sometime during the term the teacher is invited to visit the homes of the children in her class. Sometimes she is invited to tea or sometimes to dinner. Would it be all right to ask a teacher like this just to a party? T.J., TERRE HAUTE, INDIANA

No, not unless you know her well socially. Visiting the parents of a child is part of such a teacher's work, although a voluntary part. She is often invited to dinner, but she goes to get to know the parents better in relation to their child. She couldn't very well accomplish this mission if she were invited to a general party.

• •

I would like to know the proper approach to a friend who insists upon blotting her lips on my best linen napkins when she is dining at my house. This leaves a large lipstick imprint. What can I do about it? F.C.R., AUSTIN, MINNESOTA

Lipstick marks are inevitable on linen napkins, but for a guest to deliberately blot her lips on a linen napkin is thoughtless, to say the least. The lips should not be rubbed with a napkin, they should be gently dabbed. Nevertheless, the napkin will gather lipstick traces. Your solution is either to use large-size dinner napkins in paper (many of which are very attractive these days) or to go over the napkins immediately after the table has been cleared and put some lipstick remover on the soiled napkin so as to loosen the stain before the napkins are laundered. Meat tenderizer in solution works, too, on any soil or grease, or often undiluted Woolite will remove the stain. I don't see how you can speak to your friend about this habit without offending her, unless some day you just happen to bring up the subject of the difficulty of getting lipstick out of napkins and ask her what method she uses. Perhaps she'll take the hint.

• •

Will you please say something about the preposterous incorrectness of a host and hostess collecting a fee from their guests to help defray the cost of the party to which the guests were invited? This recently happened to us, upon our arrival at an open-house party celebrating moving into a new home. Nothing had been said at the time the invitation was extended to indicate that it would be required of each guest to contribute for food and drinks. It seems to me that no one should be expected to have a party that will topple his budget, but if one cannot afford to extend ordinary hospitality without collecting a substantial fee from each guest— enough to buy a good dinner at a restaurant—it can't be feasible that the party is essential. When will some people learn? MRS. J.C.R., OAK PARK, ILLINOIS

I can't imagine this myself. I can imagine that among quite young married couples, at a co-operative party, people might be asked to bring their own drinks and food. Everyone knows everyone well and understands the financial situation. But for someone to invite people such as yourselves and not mention that a fee is going to be charged at a private home is, I agree, indefensible. Better a party with hot dogs and coffee than one like this.

• •

We are going to give a large "at home" without outside help. We are three boys in our late teens, but the party is also for the friends of my mother and father. My question is, "Who should open the door for guests and who should welcome the guests?" P.R., DECATUR, ILLINOIS

Any one of you boys or your father may open the door as guests approach. Your mother stays in the living room, rises and greets each guest as he approaches. The hostess always rises and greets each guest, male or female, as he or she approaches, extending her hand. At the end of the afternoon or evening, whichever it is, you and your brothers and father will help the guests into their coats and show them to the door after they bid your mother good-by in the living room. As the party tapers off, of course, she may wish to approach the door to say good-by to several at a time. If taxis are needed, one of you boys or your father will summon the cabs or see unescorted ladies into their cars.

GUESTS

Is it proper to smoke a pipe of any kind at a formal dinner when cigarettes and cigars are passed? C.J., MASON CITY, IOWA

Yes, if one of the small dress pipes is used and if the tobacco is mild. Even then, it is always polite to ask the hostess if she minds a pipe.

• •

The invitation reads 8 p.m. What time should the guests arrive? MRS. Y.E., PROVIDENCE, RHODE ISLAND

It depends on where you live. In New York City, guests would never think of arriving promptly but would get there anytime from 8:15 to 8:30. Beyond that one is "late." In the Midwest an invitation for 8:00 often sees the guests arriving at 7:45. In Washington, D.C., particularly at diplomatic functions, if the invitation says 8:00, the guests arrive promptly—never early, never late. It all depends on the custom of your community.

• •

I have been invited to a dinner party. What is the proper time to leave when no special entertainment has been offered and you are just sitting around talking? B.G., DETROIT, MICHIGAN

Usually you do not leave for an hour. However, sometimes it is necessary to leave before then, for example if you are catching a train. If you must leave early, be sure to tell the hostess either before your arrival or upon arrival so she will be prepared. Then others in the group won't feel they must leave when you do.

• •

At a formal dinner, must the men and women separate when coffee is served as they used to in Victorian times and still do in England, the ladies having their coffee together and the gentlemen remaining at the table? T.A.A., BAKERSFIELD, CALIFORNIA

In this country we usually have our coffee together, either in the dining room, living room, or library.

• •

When a guest enters the room at a party, whom does he or she greet first? T.K.W., NEWARK, NEW JERSEY

The hostess, then the host, then the guests. The host and hostess always rise when a guest approaches for this traditional greeting.

• •

The dinner party is in progress, and one guest comes late. Must all the men rise for introductions? P.L., MEMPHIS, TENNESSEE

No. In the case of a woman guest she slips quickly into her seat indicated by the hostess after brief greeting, and the man to her right, alone, rises and seats her. The hostess does not rise because then all the men would have to rise with her. The host rises half as she is seated—or seats herself.

• •

If you are a house guest and want to help, is it proper to make the family's beds as well as your own? I have

been told that this is impolite. L.S., CHICAGO, ILLI-
NOIS

A guest should not attempt to make the beds of the
host family. She shouldn't even offer to do so unless
she is on a very intimate basis. Otherwise, she makes
only her own bed if she knows how to do it when there
is no household help. Or, when she is leaving, she should
strip the bed, fold the used sheets and pillow cases and
leave them with the folded blankets neatly on the bed.

If I am an overnight guest in a house where there is no
maid, should I strip the bed in the morning before leaving or leave it as it is? S.F.P., BROOKLYN, NEW YORK

Ask your hostess which she prefers. If you are a good
bed-maker and have the time, you might ask her for
clean sheets and make up the bed yourself in order to
save her work. At the very least you could considerately
remove and fold the linen and blankets.

• •

My wife and I and my sister were informally at a
friend's house the other evening. Our host and hostess
were a married couple without servants. During the
evening, in the living room, the hostess brought in coffee and ice cream. My sister says that I should have
gotten to my feet as my hostess approached my chair
and taken from her hand the cup of coffee and ice
cream. I have argued that this is not necessary and
that I was not discourteous and did not show bad form
when I remained seated. Who is right? D.E.C., AUGUSTA,
GEORGIA

Your sister. As soon as the hostess had finished ap-
portioning out the ice cream and coffee, you should
have risen and assisted her in passing it to the guests.

• •

**The other evening my husband and I had to have din-
ner with some very important clients of his. The client
and his wife proceeded to drink entirely too much and
were obviously intoxicated in the restaurant in which
we were eating. I was afraid that if we sat it out
through all the courses of the dinner some episode
would occur that would make it impossible for my husband to have proper relations with them again. So after
the meat course I suggested that we skip dessert and
just have coffee before leaving. My husband felt that
perhaps I was rude. Do you think so?** C.N., ALBU-
QUERQUE, NEW MEXICO

No, I think you did the right thing. You undoubtedly
saved a very difficult situation. If the client and his wife
had made a serious disturbance in the restaurant, they
would have somehow blamed your husband and you
for it, and your husband might not have been able to
go on with his business relations. Your tactful ma-
neuver prevented this. It is not always possible to
anticipate when people are going to drink too much,
but when they have, the best thing is to cut off contact
with them as quickly and as diplomatically as possible,
even when a business situation is involved. They remember very little the next day, anyhow.

• •

**I am a young man who is frequently invited to be an
extra man at dinner parties, theater parties, etc., in our
city. I know many men acept these invitations without
ever attempting to return them or even bothering to
thank their hostesses, except at the time of the entertainment. Could you set me right?** J.M.W., PASADENA,
CALIFORNIA

The eligible young man is certainly at a premium today
in many cities. He is likely to become spoiled by social
attention of the kind you mention being showered upon him. Still, however, courteous young men phone
their hostesses a day or two after a party, or even write

a brief line of appreciation. Some even send flowers, preferably before the function, telling the hostess to expect them. While hostesses do need attractive bachelors to fill in on such occasions, they come eventually to resent even the most attractive ones who continuously take and never reciprocate in any way.

• •

I was recently asked to a party given by a young couple and the invitation read B.Y.O.B. which I discovered meant Bring Your Own Bottle. I did, and served my date and myself as everyone else had his own bottle. At the party's end, everybody took back unfinished bottles on which they had originally written their names. Was this correct, or should they have left the bottles for the hostess? W.T., CHICAGO, ILLINOIS

It is usual for young people to whom the cost of liquor can be considerable to take home their own bottles from a party like this.

• •

When a couple takes a bottle of wine to friends with whom they are going to have dinner, who makes the presentation and to whom? MRS. P.L., OAKLAND, CALIFORNIA

The man gives it to the hostess.

I know that traditionally newcomers to a neighborhood wait for the established people to call on them but it seems to me that it can be very lonely waiting for this courtesy. Why can't they do as is done in some parts of Europe, that is, initiate the calls? A.I., ENGLEWOOD, NEW JERSEY

Here is a change I heartily advocate in neighborhoods of single-family houses, but usually not in apartment buildings where in big cities, at least, anonymity is still the rule. But even in tenant-owned buildings, however, there is now much more opportunity for apartment dwellers to get to know each other and work toward their common good. Be careful as a newcomer not to be "pushy." But if the wait for neighbors to call is too long, you might try tendering an invitation to something simple like a cocktail party to people in the neighborhood who look attractive to you. They may be very grateful for the overture.

When you attend a function where there are individual flower arrangements on each table, is it all right for one of the guests at each table to take home the centerpiece if it seems obvious they are not going to be used again?
MRS. C.C., MADISON, WISCONSIN

Guests should not take them unless asked to do so. Often at a club lunch, for example, it is announced that centerpieces may be taken home. Either the guests agree at each table as to who will take home the flowers, or a drawing is arranged for each table which of course is fairer. Sometimes the winning number is under a place plate. The suggestion, however, should always come from the hostess at a private party.

My sister claims it is impossible to thank anyone for a meal. For instance, if a friend takes you to lunch, you must not thank her for the luncheon, or if you are invited to a home to dine, you must not thank the hostess for the nice dinner. What is your opinion?
G.J.S., LOS ANGELES, CALIFORNIA

Today, people do thank their hosts and hostesses for the "nice luncheon" or for the "lovely dinner." They even comment on the food itself if it has been unusual. Most hostesses are flattered by such attention from their guests. But the idea behind your sister's remark goes back to the days when it was considered somewhat indelicate for a lady, in particular, to concern herself about eating. She had to pretend an elaborate disinterest in food. Days might have been spent on the preparation of a great dinner, but guests were considered ill-bred if they mentioned it specifically in thanking their host for entertainment. What should be avoided is what might be called the "overly hungry" attitude toward such entertainment. A guest should never give the impression that he comes only to eat, that the food is a prime consideration in the acceptance of the entertainment.

• •

Recently I was a house guest, and my host and hostess had made reservations at a restaurant for dinner. As I was dressing, friends of theirs arrived. My host and hostess explained that we were getting ready to go out, but the friends made no move to go. How should this situation have been handled? My hostess felt that she should stay and entertain her friends as long as they remained. MRS. G.M.B., LOS ANGELES, CALIFORNIA

Your hostess should have said to her friends, "I'm so sorry. We didn't know that you were coming. We have made a reservation for dinner and are due there in an hour. In the meantime, it will be very nice talking to you." Friends who don't realize that their host and hostess owe them no obligation when they drop in casually like this, when prior arrangements have been made, are thick-skinned indeed. Certainly your friends had no obligation, either to stay home and entertain the "drop-ins" or to invite them to join you at the restaurant at their expense. Their obligation was to you as their properly invited guest.

• •

When I was a girl the only proper guest towel was a linen one. However, when I go to my friends' houses I find in the bathroom for guests, towels of paper and fingertip towels of turkish toweling, as well as the more familiar small linen towels. Do you approve of this?
F.J.L., CHICAGO, ILLINOIS

Very much so. It is very nice to have a full complement of small guest towels in the bathroom in linen, but it is wise to have a pile of the pretty, individual paper towels that are soft and pliable as well as decorative. Men in particular like to use the little turkish fingertip towels because of their easy absorbency. A roll of paper toweling is fine for children.

PARTIES, SPECIAL OCCASIONS, AND CELEBRATIONS

Please advise me concerning entertaining at Christmas. This being our first year settled in our home, my husband and I wish to begin to have open house at Christmas for our friends every year. What day would be best? I hope to have approximately fifty guests. MRS. R.W., KANSAS CITY, MISSOURI

Many people like to entertain on Christmas Eve, New Year's Eve, or New Year's Day at an open house. It is nice for a young couple such as you are to pick a day the first year of your marriage and plan to make it a regular occasion. The custom of social calling has been greatly neglected the last generation, but many people throughout the country consider New Year's Day one on which a call should be made on as many close friends and acquaintances as possible. So whether or not you have an open house at some other time during the holidays, it is probable that on New Year's Day, if you are at home, you will receive some calls.

• •

Sometimes people give me Christmas gifts well before Christmas. I save my gifts and feel that I should also save my thanks until I know what is in the package. During the year when I get gifts, is it more polite to open them in the donor's presence or may I open them later? N.H., CLEVELAND, OHIO

Most people do wait until Christmas to open Christmas gifts at which time they thank the donors. At other times in the year whether or not you open the gifts depends on the circumstances. If they are meant for a certain day such as your birthday, you will probably want to wait and then thank the donors. If they are brought as hostess gifts, don't open them if other guests have not brought gifts. You should merely put them aside for opening later. In the case of hostess gifts, which are usually very simple, you may thank the donor without opening the gift. In some cases you may wish to phone or write a note later.

• •

We have moved into a new neighborhood and are going to have a housewarming. Should we invite neighbors we haven't met yet? MRS. G.T., TRENTON, NEW JERSEY

Usually you invite just your friends, though especially if you are quite young you might wish to include your immediate neighbors even if you have just seen them in passing and find them attractive. They may not even know the convention that they should call first, or they may not even be conscious of the fact that you are new neighbors. Don't necessarily stand on tradition. We are much more free about these things today.

• •

May you issue invitations to dinner and parties by phone or in person? If so, how do you go about it? E.S., BROOKFIELD, CONNECTICUT

Yes. You say, "Will you come to dinner on Tuesday, the eighth, at seven? It will be quite informal."

• •

Soon my husband and I will be moving from a three-room apartment to a new six-room house. We would like very much to give a housewarming sometime after we are all settled. Just how long after is it permissible to give such a thing? What refreshments are served, and most important, is it possible to put in our invitations, "No gifts, please"? I have heard there are gifts for the new home generally brought to housewarmings, and I don't want anyone to feel obligated to bring us a gift. Also, as we are young and just starting out, we won't be able to have rugs in all of the rooms right away. Should we hold up our housewarming because of this? MRS. F.R.M., BOUND BROOK, NEW JERSEY

Have your housewarming, rugs or not, and at any time that is convenient for you. The housewarming may include a buffet supper or may be a tea or cocktail party —in fact, any kind of entertainment you wish. Say nothing about gifts. Some people will bring them to the house, and others may not know of this custom. Where some bring gifts and others do not, it is courteous of the hostess to put aside the gifts some do bring, for later opening. Gifts should be acknowledged by a brief note or a telephone call if guests are not thanked at the time.

• •

My three sisters-in-law and I would like to show our affection for our father-in-law by entertaining for him on his eighty-fifth birthday. "Open house" here in our Nebraska town is an informal afternoon tea, with anyone who would like to come invited. As our father-in-law is an early settler, we hope nearly everyone in the community will do him honor. Occasionally we see announcements for such things in the newspapers here, but someone has raised the question, "Is it proper?" Sometimes the announcements say, "Please do not bring gifts." MRS. J.B.K., LEXINGTON, NEBRASKA

Yes, it is proper to give an announcement to the society editor of your local paper concerning your "open house," and while I think you should let the news get around that you do not expect gifts, I would rather not see it in the announcement in this way. Most people know that gifts are not expected on such occasions except perhaps from those very near and dear.

• •

My daughter's family lost all of their belongings in a fire a year ago. Now they are moving into a new house by Christmas. May they have a housewarming, or should some member of the family give it for them? R.U., CHATTANOOGA, TENNESSEE

They give it themselves in most communities.

• •

My fiancé is hoping to be granted his naturalization shortly. If and when he becomes a citizen, I plan to invite a few friends to my house to celebrate the occasion. Will you please let me know the procedure for the invitations and the party? Would it be proper for his friends and myself to present him with a gift and if so, what would be appropriate? MISS L.P.E., SARASOTA, FLORIDA

It is nice to want to give a party for a newly naturalized citizen. You just do this as you would make arrangements for any other informal party, inviting his close friends and yours. At the party you could have someone propose a toast to the new American. I wouldn't specify the reason for the party, necessarily. You would invite people by phone, by note, or, if it's a cocktail party, you could use little cocktail cards. You could give your friend a gift—something that would make his life smoother here might be nice—our flag, a good dictionary or an American etiquette book, for example.

GIFTS

When you are a week-end guest, are you supposed to take a gift to the hostess, to the family as a whole, to the children, if any? D.S., SALT LAKE CITY, UTAH

If you are a frequent guest in the household, you take gifts from time to time, not necessarily on every visit. When there are young children they are often disappointed not to receive something from a guest—and the gift may be very modest indeed to please a child—colored pencils, (especially with his name on them), a rubber ball, a little toy. A gift to the whole family may of course include the children and is often something like candy. A gift for the hostess may well be something for the house or a book that appeals to her reading tastes. A woman may give wearing apparel to the hostess but a man guest should not (unless he's a relative) give anything so intimate as pantyhose or lingerie. A woman guest who does not know her hostess well also avoids gifts that are intimate. Gourmet foods are always a safe choice.

• •

My husband and I and our two small children are planning on visiting friends whom we have not seen for three years in another part of the country. There are also several other families with whom we will be staying, and we would like to compensate them for their hospitality. They are all hard-working people and we wonder would it be bad to send a gift of appreciation after we come home, buy them something for their home the second or third day of our visit, or should we simply leave a gift of money in an inconspicuous spot? We have never been able to entertain them overnight. MRS. Z.H., PHOENIX, ARIZONA

You may take them each some gift from your own home town which might be unusual to them, or, as you suggest, get them some gift you see that they might enjoy the second or third day of your visit, or you may send them something after you reach home again. By no means leave them a gift of money. This is only appropriate when there are domestics to be compensated for extra work guests cause on overnight, or longger, visits.

When you put a card enclosure in a gift, is anything written on the envelope if it is going to be placed inside the package? Is it just left blank? Does it make any difference whether you mail it, or deliver it? MRS. E.T., PITTSBURGH, PENNSYLVANIA

If you hand deliver a gift with a card enclosed in its own envelope, it isn't necessary to write anything on the envelope. If the gift is sent by mail, and it is obvious for whom the gift is intended, nothing need be written on the envelope. If it is sent to a new mother for the baby, it is fun to write "Miss Simms" or "Master Simms" (no first names). If you write a gift card and put it in an envelope at a store to be enclosed in the gift, it is obviously necessary to put something on the envelope so that if the card is mislaid, it will get put with the proper order. Just the last name is used "Mrs. Smith," "Miss Jones." Gifts to a baby are addressed on this little card, "Master" or "Miss Smith." The shop's tag or label, of course, will bear the full name and address.

• •

I have been dating a girl for ten months. I plan to give her a Christmas present, but should I include her father and mother too? I have been entertained in their home many times, and they are very friendly toward me. T.R.S., PASADENA, CALIFORNIA

It would be nice to give the girl's mother an impersonal gift or give some small gift to the household which the father and mother will both enjoy. If Christmas giving is a strain financially, you could do this at any time during the year. You would, of course, very probably send a Christmas card to the girl's parents.

• •

I am a man invited to spend Christmas Day with a family in the country. There are three small children,

a husband and wife. I am an old friend of the wife's but know the husband slightly. What gifts am I expected to take? M.R.K., ERIE, PENNSYLVANIA

If the children are so young that they dislike sharing presents, you might take a small gift to each, not necessarily expensive. You could then take an impersonal gift of some kind to your hostess, the pleasure of which her husband would share. Perhaps salted nuts, a box of candied fruits, a bottle of wine, or any one of a number of things for the house. In this category come bar accessories, basic books, such as new cookbooks, books that fit in with the family's hobbies if you know them, flowers, house plants, or games.

MEAL SERVICE

The subject of demitasse has always confused me. If guests prefer coffee with their meals is it proper to serve demitasse afterward? Is it served at the table after the completion of the dinner or after the guests have been seated in the living room? In the latter case is it correct to serve a liqueur with the demitasse? K.W.T., NEW ORLEANS, LOUISIANA

If all guests have had coffee at dinner, you are certainly not expected to serve demitasse after dinner, although it would be nice if everybody is particularly enthusiastic about coffee. You may serve a liqueur, of course, after dinner even when demitasse is not offered. Where you have served demitasse, guests may be offered liqueurs after demitasse has been served to everyone present. As some people like to add liqueur brandy to their demitasse, the liqueur service should not be delayed too long after the coffee has been passed. It is correct today, by the way, to offer cream with demitasse, as many people like it that way. It is considerate to have a decaffeinated coffee available should anyone prefer it.

• •

We frequently entertain buffet style for supper or dinner. I am expecting a new baby and already have two others. Most of my guests are eager to help me, but some never offer to. In this instance, could I go ahead and start cleaning up alone? I wouldn't want them to think I would rather wash dishes than be with them. MRS. G.A.G., FORT WORTH, TEXAS

Don't worry about them. Think about yourself. It is good for you to have guests, but not if they make too much work when you have no help. If you know yours are the non-helping kind of guests, serve them as informally as possible—use paper cups and plates—and don't apologize. And enlist your husband's aid in the serving and cleaning up of the meal.

• •

A friend tells me it is bad manners to serve vegetables in individual vegetable dishes at a home table the way they do in restaurants. Is that right? MRS. B.B.G., CHARLOTTE, NORTH CAROLINA

Vegetables aren't served this way in first-class restaurants. Instead, the waiter serves them onto the diner's plate from a serving dish. At a family dinner, something like stewed tomatoes could be served in separate vegetable dishes to be eaten with the fork, but in more formal service the vegetable is always taken onto the dinner or luncheon plate. Of course you can always serve a vegetable as a separate course, European style. Asparagus hollandaise is nice this way and so is creamed spinach with croutons. They are served before the meat.

• •

Recently a friend gave me a lace tablecloth which is very beautiful. This particular cloth is machine-made as distinguished from a handmade type. I would like your advice on the proper times to use it. Would it be appropriate for all or some of these four occasions:

1. **Everyday dinner—just for the family.**
2. **Everyday luncheon.**
3. **Dinner with guests invited.**
4. **A buffet table setting.**

MRS. S.K.F., HOUSTON, TEXAS

A lace cloth is always much more formal than a plain one of any kind. Therefore, it is suitable for dinner with guests and for a buffet table setting and should be accompanied by fine silver, china, and crystal. It does not lend itself well to informal table accessories such as earthenware, wood, and stainless steel. It should always be laid on a bare table (see page 75).

• •

Do salad bowls and iced-tea glasses require service plates beneath them? T.W., LONG BEACH, CALIFORNIA

A salad bowl does not require a service plate beneath it, nor does an iced-tea glass, although in the latter case, if you wish, you may have one, and then the spoon may be placed upon it rather than left in the glass while one is drinking, necessary when there is no service plate beneath it. In the latter case, one uses the index finger to hold the spoon against the side of the glass as the tea is drunk or small metal or ceramic spoon holders may be at each place.

• •

I have parfait glasses and sometimes like to serve a parfait for dessert. I have no parfait spoons. Would it be all right to use iced-tea spoons instead, and do you think a parfait makes a nice company dessert? MRS. G.W., LYONS, NEW YORK

Yes to both questions.

• •

May candles ever be lighted on a dining table in the daytime? A.V.L., MAPLEWOOD, NEW YORK

No, except late in the day and if the curtains are drawn. Candles placed on the table to be lighted at a later hour, as the tea or reception wears on, should have their wicks charred.

• •

When just our family eats together we seldom put water on the table except at Sunday dinner when we are a little more formal. The children have milk and my husband and I have coffee and, as we don't drink the water even if we do put it on, I like to save myself trouble. When we serve wine when guests are present, should I put on the water glasses, too—and what is the appropriate glass? G.M.B., BALTIMORE, MARYLAND

You may, French style, as do many people serving wine at home, omit the water goblet if wine is to be opened. The hostess should note, however, if a guest refuses the wine. She should then offer another beverage to be served in the wine goblet. If water goblets are on the table with wine glasses, or alone, water is poured before the guests are seated. The glasses are replenished as needed throughout the meal from a pitcher of ice water on the serving table or sideboard— or even on the table itself if there is plenty of room. When the water pitcher is on the table, the guests serve themselves additional water as desired. When there are no servants and the water pitcher is on the sideboard, the hostess watches to see when guests may need more water and passes them the pitcher so that they may serve themselves.

• •

I'm writing you for information regarding the serving of frozen foods which are packaged in foil tins. I am referring particularly to individual meat pies which are purchased and baked in foil containers. Should they be removed from the containers or served in them? Is it proper to place the baked pie, still in its foil, on the dinner plate to be eaten from the container? Would it

be better to place the pie in the foil on a bread and butter plate beside the dinner plate with a serving spoon for one to serve himself? MRS. F.E.A., BRATTLE-BORO, VERMONT

No, you do not remove the baked pies from the foil containers when you serve individual pies. Because the pies are served hot, it is easier to place them individually on dinner plates and then place the dinner plates in front of the diners. The vegetables are then passed separately.

In the case of individual dessert pies, again, I would heat them in the oven, place them on dessert plates, and serve them that way instead of asking the diners to try to manipulate them with serving spoons and forks, as this might prove disastrous.

• •

We are going to entertain the parents of my daughter's fiancé at dinner. How should I seat the six of us at table? MRS. L.R., NORWALK, CONNECTICUT

You seat the father of your daughter's fiancé at your right and your future son-in-law at your left. To your husband's right sits the mother of your daughter's fiancé and to his left sits your daughter.

• •

I know it is supposed to be proper for one to seat the next most honored male guest to the hostess's left. But I have a very small boy, age three, who, with our older daughter, has dinner with us. I like to have the little boy next to me so that I can supervise his eating and keep him from being a nuisance. Is this all right? And if a man and his wife are our guests, how should I seat everybody at table? MRS. J.K., SYRACUSE, NEW YORK

As a mother myself, I understand your dilemma. I think you are wise to keep your smaller child next to you, on your left. You would then seat your male guest to your right and his wife to the host's right, with your daughter to her father's left. However, if your woman guest is rather unfamiliar with the ways of children and seems a little nervous at sitting next to the baby, you might ask her if she prefers to sit at your husband's left and have the two children sit together at the same side of the table. I know some of my readers might suggest that the children eat by themselves at an earlier hour. This is the better solution, of course, but doesn't always work out in a household where there is no servant, especially if the children are used to eating with their parents. I recommend that children eat with both parents and guests as soon as they are able to do so without unduly upsetting the guests, for this is the best social training for them. However, one must pick one's guests, under the circumstances, very carefully.

• •

When you have no maid, where is the best place to put the dessert silver? I find that if I put a dessert spoon with the soup spoon and the dinner knife sometimes people pick it up when they mean to pick up the soup spoon. Then when the dessert course comes, I have to replace the dessert spoon, which sometimes embarrasses the guest. MRS. L.O., PROVIDENCE, RHODE ISLAND

The best way I think to place dessert silver informally when there is no maid—and sometimes when there is one—is to place it above the dinner plate. If a spoon and fork are both needed (when the dessert is at all liquid) they are placed in the manner shown in the illustration. The dessert silver, of course, may also be brought in on the filled dessert dishes, spoon (if needed) on the right, fork on the left. Or if the hostess is serving the dessert from her place she may bring in the dessert silver and place it in a pattern at her right, adding it to the dishes as she fills them.

INFORMAL PLACEMENT OF DESSERT SILVER, informal lunch and dinner: This is a convenient way to place dessert silver above the place plate. Without first course (or with first course served after guests are seated): Dinner napkin may be on dinner plate (or on service plate if one is used) when guests sit down, as at a formal dinner. Note optional placement of dessert silver, easy when service is limited or when serving is done by the hostess.

• •

On a properly set table for dinner, where does the napkin go (1) When there is already a course in place when the guests sit down? (2) When there is a service plate but no first course in place? MRS. J.J.M., TULSA, OKLAHOMA

When there is a course in place as the guests sit down, the napkin is at the left of the place setting. When there is no first course on the service plate, the dinner napkin is laid on the plate itself with the fold optionally to the left or to the right, but with the left fold more traditional. Or, it may be folded in any of the ways that permit it to stand upright. See illustration.

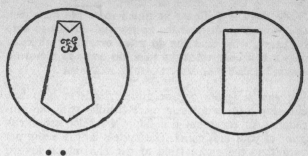

I would like to be able to serve tea more often. But it always seems so complicated. Could you tell just how to go about it so I'll have more confidence? R.C., JAMAICA, NEW YORK

I think the best way is to give you this information in the following illustration. The great secret in successful tea serving, of course, is to let the water boil actively three or four minutes. It is then poured immediately over the tea leaves—one teaspoon of tea for each cup. And the pot should be scalded first. Some dry it out before adding the tea. For the tea tray setting see the illustration. A spirit lamp keeps the tea hot but is not essential if a tea pot which retains the heat well is selected.

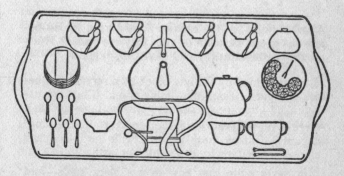

When there is a dinner at which there are both men and women guests and the hostess has no one to help her serve, what does she do when everybody offers to help her at once when the time has come to remove a course? MRS. J.V.L., MONTGOMERY, ALABAMA

She can designate one or more friends to help her, choosing those who seem more familiar with the procedure. An eager but dish-happy bachelor can break a lot of your best china. The hostess is firm about not permitting the entire table to rise and march toward the kitchen, as this breaks up all semblance of conversation. I feel strongly that a hostess without help should make her parties as simple as possible, and in this instance an efficient hostess can clear the table herself with the help of a serving table, often, actually, without even leaving the table if she has managed it well. She lets her guests pass their soiled dishes to her and she places these on the lower shelf of the table, scraping where necessary very unobtrusively. She then takes the next course off the top of the serving table, if it has been possible to arrange it there. At any rate she cuts down her trips to the kitchen to an absolute minimum. If she prefers to clear alone she may always say so, and guests should follow her request. The host and hostess should not both leave the table at once.

• •

At what point are the candles lighted on a table—before the guests sit down or after they are seated? When are they extinguished? L.D., PORTLAND, OREGON

They are lighted by the hostess or by a servant just before the guests enter the dining room. They are extinguished after the guests have left the table and it is about to be cleared.

• •

I am never quite sure how to use place cards—and when. How are names properly written upon them? L.E., TROY, NEW YORK

Place cards are a convenience to the hostess who is seating more than eight guests. They may be used at any time—at a festive breakfast, at luncheon, at seated buffet suppers, and, of course, at large formal dinners. For family affairs, birthday or holiday parties, the familiar decorated cards are quite permissible, with first names, if desired, written in black ink, "Julie" or "Tom," but formal place cards follow a prescribed pattern. For example, titles at diplomatic dinners are abbreviated, "H.E." [for His Excellency] (an Ambassador) Mr. Sorensen, and other place card names are written simply "Mrs. Roberts," "Miss Sweeney," etc. Place cards, if flat, are propped against a standing dinner napkin or laid on a folded one. Or they may be placed above the place plate, possibly in a holder. If the double cards are used they are set above the place setting.

• •

When you use a lace tablecloth do you lay it directly over the table or on a table pad? Is a lace tablecloth ever used with a colored lining? MRS. M.MCN., OZONE PARK, NEW YORK

You use a lace tablecloth directly over the bare table. As the lace design is decoration enough, it is better taste not to put it over a colored lining.

• •

Often when I entertain, my table or buffet is quite crowded with platters of food and I don't have room for a bread dish. Since I do want to serve rolls with dinner, would it be possible for me to have rolls and butter already on the butter plates before the guests are seated? MRS. B.R., YOUNGSTOWN, OHIO

Yes. This is a solution used even in formal service.

Should water be poured before guests sit down? If wine alone is being served, should it be poured before the

guests are seated or after? If the wine is on a coaster on the table, should the cork be removed before guests are summoned or after they are seated? Does it matter whether it is white wine or red wine? M.H., ALBANY, NEW YORK

Water is poured before the guests sit down to approximately ½ inch from the top. Red wine is uncorked approximately an hour beforehand and allowed to come to room temperature. On a hot day, French fashion, red wine may be served cold. It is poured after the guests are seated to within ¼ inch from the top. White wine may be uncorked at the table but should be allowed to "breathe" a little before it is poured, again to within ½ inch of the top. Sparkling wines are chilled and are opened and poured when guests are seated. Wines served from decanters are considered to have "breathed" in the transfer from the bottle.

Do you put the napkin back in the ring at the conclusion of a meal if you are not a house guest? I notice that many people are now using old napkin rings with drip-dry napkins to save paper. Even guests' napkins are put in these rings, I suppose, to give uniformity to the table. L.A., CHATTANOOGA, TENNESSEE

It used to be that napkin rings were furnished only to family members, or to house guests, and napkins were to be replaced in them after use. Now, many hostesses with napkin ring collections do use them even for guests who will be there for that meal only. Such a guest does not return the napkin to the ring at the end of the meal, but merely leaves the napkin loosely placed to the left of his place setting.

ENGAGEMENTS AND WEDDINGS

ENGAGEMENTS

I understand that when an engagement is announced, the boy's parents call as soon as possible upon the parents of the girl. But my case is very difficult. My daughter, who is announcing her engagement, lives with me, and I am divorced from her father, who lives in the same town. We are fairly friendly. Would it be expected of us to receive this call together at my home? Should they ignore my daughter's father or call on him separately? D.W.W., COLUMBUS, GEORGIA

Receive their call without your former husband. They may call on your daughter's father separately if he is still very much part of all of your lives. If they do call, they call jointly, or the boy's father may call alone on your former husband and perhaps, during the call, arrange for him to come and meet the new family. Even if your relations with your former husband are friendly, you should not make the traditional return visit a joint one.

• •

How does a father announce the engagement of his daughter to a gathering of relatives and friends at home? Is a toast in order? C.B.C., ST. PETERSBURG, FLORIDA

Yes. After all have assembled and the party is well under way, the father, first catching everyone's attention, proposes a toast. Sometimes if champagne has not been served up to this point it is brought out and ceremoniously poured. When everyone has been served, the father raises his glass and says something like this: "To my daughter Margaret and my future son-in-law John. Let us drink to their happiness."

• •

My daughter, who is in her first year of college, has just become engaged to a boy in the service. He has three years more to go, the first half to be spent overseas. They plan to marry in three or four years. We like the boy very much but, in view of the length of time involved, I feel that no announcement of the engagement should be made now. Am I right? A.C.R., DULUTH, MINNESOTA

A great deal can happen in three or four years, especially with young people separated. What they both think they want now may not be at all what they want at the end of that time. Therefore, do not announce the engagement, and try to persuade them to leave each other free until it is practical to speak of a wedding date.

• •

My girl friend at college has an apartment with the man she expects to marry when they both finish college. They say it seems silly to announce their "engagement" formally, although they feel deeply committed and plan marriage. Do you agree? D.C., DENVER, COLORADO

I agree. When the time comes they may have any kind of marriage ceremony they desire.

• •

My daughter is going to marry a man who cannot afford to give her an engagement ring. Should she announce the engagement when she has no ring, and should her friends give showers for her? A.L.H., PENSACOLA, FLORIDA

Yes to both questions. Sometimes engagement rings are not given and other gifts are given by the boy instead. Or the girl may choose a wedding ring that is a combination engagement and wedding ring—perhaps it will have some stones in it, not necessarily diamonds, or it may be decorated in some other way. Above all, she should not apologize for not having an engagement ring nor imply that the boy cannot afford one.

• •

Our daughter has just become engaged, and we would like to announce the event through the newspapers. Are there any special rules to be followed? Do you suggest we send pictures? MRS. C.MCK., PROVINCETOWN, MASSACHUSETTS

Be sure your story follows the basic rule of journalism so that when completed it answers the questions, "who, what, when, where, and how?" Here is an engagement announcement that answers the editor's questions:

CYNTHIA ANN TALBOTT
TO WED ASA G. SANTOS

Mr. and Mrs. Loring Talbott, of 10 Low Place, announce the engagement of their daughter, Cynthia Ann, to Mr. Asa Griggs Santos, son of Dr. and Mrs. José Santos of Mexico City, Mexico.

Miss Talbott is a graduate of The Hewitt School and of Vassar College. Mr. Santos is a senior in the Yale School of Medicine and a member of Phi Beta Kappa. He will intern at Lying-in-Hospital, Boston. The wedding will take place in June.

If you wish, send a picture of the engaged girl with the announcement. It should have a caption attached with the typed information, "Miss Cynthia Ann Talbott whose engagement to Mr. Asa G. Santos has been announced," on a piece of 8″ by 10″ typewriter paper. Enclose picture, with a protective cardboard and the release, in a mailing envelope and send "first class" to papers or have delivered by hand to either city or society desk as the news seems to warrant.

• •

I am planning to be married soon. It will be a second marriage for me—his first. We are planning a small, quiet ceremony with only close members of the family and one or two good friends. However, there is little or no information available about announcing the wedding. Is any sort of engagement notice proper in the newspaper? I believe, after the wedding, announcements should be sent to people directly concerned. Can you help us? MRS. D.L.E., WAUKEGAN, ILLINOIS

Brides who have been previously divorced usually do not announce their engagements, except informally to close friends and relatives. The exception might be in the unusual newsworthiness of one or the other of the parties or in the case of a very young divorcée, divorced without scandal, remarrying. Then the new engagement is sometimes announced by the parents of the bride. Announcements are sent after the ceremony.

• •

We are having a party—not at home—to be held in honor of an engagement. We have been advised that we should have a receiving line, as many of the guests have not met either set of parents personally. If we should have a receiving line, what is the proper order? L.K.M., HAYS, KANSAS

An engagement party, when given at all, is essentially an informal occasion. It does not call for a receiving line. Although it is to be held away from home, presumably in a public place, the matter can be handled very simply. The party will probably be given by the parents of the engaged girl, and the announcement of the engagement will be made by the father during the evening in a toast to the young couple. If all of the guests know the occasion for the party, the young couple may choose to receive together, just inside the door —the girl first, then her fiancé. They will greet their guests informally, just as they will in their future home. As the opportunity arises, they introduce their guests to the two sets of parents, or, if many people arrive at one time, guests may always introduce themselves to each other and to the parents.

• •

When does my fiancé give me my engagement ring— while we are alone, or in front of our guests at the engagement party? M.B.R., PITTSBURGH, PENNSYL-VANIA

He should give you your ring in private.

• •

What sort of gift should I give my fiancé? I have a better-paying job than he has and wish I could add to the sum he can spend for my ring so I can have one that's a little better. Do you think it would be right to suggest such a thing? L.S.E., PUEBLO, COLORADO

No. If you feel two rings would be a real problem financially, suggest the kind of jeweled wedding band that will double for engagement ring and wedding ring. Tell your friends that this is your preference, but do not wear the ring until your wedding day.

• •

I am planning on becoming engaged soon. When I was sixteen, I inherited a diamond ring. Would it be proper for my fiancé to have the diamond ring reset for me to wear as an engagement ring? J.R., BUFFALO, NEW YORK

Yes. It would be quite all right for you to wear your family's heirloom. Your fiancé, however, should pay for the resetting.

• •

What is the current attitude on the type of stone which is suitable for an engagement ring? Must it be a diamond, or can a man give a different type of stone and still not be accused of ignorance? M.L., JR., READING, PENNSYLVANIA

A diamond is the traditional engagement stone, but any other stone is suitable. A girl with a large hand and long fingers might be much happier with a square-cut tourmaline than with a miniscule diamond. And many modern girls like the idea of a gem-studded wedding band which combines engagement and wedding ring in one. Some girls even forego an engagement ring in favor of some other keepsake, such as a bracelet or a pin. The important thing in the matter is that the ring, if given, should not be so costly that it is all out of proportion to the man's income. An heirloom ring, however, can be very valuable, and any girl should be proud to be given one. But no girl should place a burden on her fiancé in the purchase of a ring which he cannot really afford.

• •

I have just become engaged, and my mother says I should be engaged for a year before I get married. Do you think this is necessary? MISS M.T., PHOENIX, ARIZONA

Today the usual engagement runs approximately three months but may be shorter. Long engagements are inadvisable.

• •

I have just broken my engagement. What do I do about gifts and money that I have received from friends and relatives? Should I return them? How should I explain about my broken engagement? MISS V.G., SANTA BARBARA, CALIFORNIA

Yes, you should return the gifts and money. It isn't necessary to make any explanation of your broken en-

gagement except that you have broken it by mutual
consent.

• •

**My son recently gave a diamond to a girl who lives in
another state. I have met her parents but once. Will
you please answer the following questions?** MRS. R.M.,
HOLLYWOOD, CALIFORNIA

1. Do I write to the parents, the girl, or neither? A:
   You write to the parents and to the girl separately.
2. The girl has attended college for two years in the
   city where my son has lived his entire life. Is it
   proper for me to plan an affair for all his friends
   and relations so they may meet this new bride when
   they are married? A: If you mean that she is to be
   married in her home state and will return to yours,
   yes. It is proper and cordial of you to sponsor
   some occasion at which she will meet all of the immediate friends of the family and relatives. Unless
   she is coming directly from her wedding she should
   not wear her wedding veil. She may wear her wed-
   ing dress.
3. Should this affair be at the home of the groom or
   in a clubhouse or church? A: At the home of the
   groom or in a clubhouse or anywhere else you would
   be likely to entertain.
4. Are presents expected or displayed? A: No, the bride
   will have received her gifts at her own home.
5. Should there be a receiving line? If so, who should
   be in it? A: It depends on the formality of the
   occasion. If you have an actual reception, you as
   hostess should be first in line, followed by the
   bride, her mother, her father, and if the occasion
   is very formal, the groom's father. The groom, presumably knowing everyone present, would circulate
   as host, and, except under formal circumstances,
   so would his father.
6. What kind of invitations or announcements are sent?
   A: No announcements are sent by you, but you
   may invite people by phone, personal note, or by

fill-in cards. The engraved ones, if the reception is at all formal, are best and the ink should match the engraving.

• •

My daughter's engagement was just announced, and we are planning to send the information to our local newspaper. Her fiancé is an excellent amateur photographer and has taken some rather lovely formal photographs of her. Would one of these be suitable to send to the papers or must these pictures be taken professionally? MRS. L.T., CORAL GABLES, FLORIDA

Any picture taken for use as an engagement or bridal picture should be a professionally-taken formal pose. The candid pictures often taken at wedding receptions should also be taken by professionals so that friends may enjoy themselves and not worry about "working" during a wedding. This way, too, the bride can be sure she will have her wedding recorded in good pictures.

SHOWERS

Should the bride-to-be, after opening all the gifts at a bridal shower, go on to the envelope gifts (money) and read the amount or not? Many of us think she should, because when a gift is opened all the people see it and almost everyone can guess, or already knows, what it costs. Therefore, I think the bride should say, "Three dollars, five dollars, or ten dollars from so-and-so," instead of "Money from so-and-so." Lots of people get offended that way if they don't tell the amount. What do you think? MISS M.S.T., READING, PENNSYLVANIA

Whether or not a money gift to the bride-to-be is in the form of a check or in cash, the rule remains the same: The donor is disclosed conversationally: i.e. "Father gave us a check." But later in any display of wedding gifts it is proper only to say, perhaps on a card propped up, "Check, $100.00," without the name of the donor.

(Actual checks are not displayed.) This is done to save the feelings of those who cannot in any way meet the amount named in their own giving. Besides, any very obvious discussion of money under social circumstances is considered bad taste.

• •

I have been asked to be maid of honor for a friend and would like to give her a shower. However, a large party was given for her by her family to announce the engagement. Many of her friends took beautiful gifts to her at that time—some of them quite expensive. She is going to have a large wedding with a reception, and the majority of these same people will send presents. I feel it would be an imposition to ask them all to contribute a third gift, and I myself being in modest financial circumstances would like to avoid the expense I would have to go to in giving her a shower, the cost of a special dress, etc. May I have your opinion? MISS L.T.S., DALLAS, TEXAS

You are not obligated to give her a shower, especially as it would be a strain on you and perhaps upon her already generous friends.

• •

I work in an office where, when a girl gets married, we collect money and give her a gift which is sometimes presented to her at a shower. Now, if she invites me to the wedding with an individual invitation, does this mean another gift from me? J.L.H., PROVIDENCE, RHODE ISLAND

Yes, but the gift may be modest.

• •

A friend of mine has been reared by her paternal grandmother who wants to give a bridal shower for her. But the girl's sister, who will be maid of honor, also wants to give the shower. The grandmother is willing to share

expenses. Who should give it? MRS. R.G., PITTSBURGH, PENNSYLVANIA

Neither. No member of the family should give a shower for the bride. A bridal shower should be given by a friend rather than a relative because, if a relative gives it, it looks as if the family actually is asking for gifts for the bride. However, there is no reason why both sister and grandmother could not quietly share in any of the shower expenses, either by supplying some of the food or in defraying some of the cost. In some ethnic groups, for example among the Poles, it is quite usual, however, for family members to give showers for the bride.

• •

My girl friend and I received an invitation from two girls we know to a shower they are giving in a restaurant. We were shocked when we read the invitation. At the end it went something like this: "Buffet Supper —$2.50 fee." I have never seen anything like this. Is it proper? K.W., PATERSON, NEW JERSEY

No, it isn't. A shower is properly given in the home of a friend of the bride-to-be. It should not be commercialized in such a manner as this.

• •

Both my little girl, eleven and a half years old, and myself have been invited to the shower of a young cousin by marriage. I have also been invited to the wedding and have ordered a gift to be sent. I feel that neither my daughter nor I should have been invited to this shower as there is such a difference in our age relation to that of the engaged girl. Should I send a gift to the shower if we don't go? D.L.S., CHICAGO, ILLINOIS

I agree that neither of you should have been invited to the shower because of the difference in your ages from that of the bride and her friends. You are not obliged to send a gift, although you should let them know if you are not going. The wedding gift you are sending is certainly sufficient.

ARRANGING THE WEDDING

Our local church is fairly huge, but I am having a simple wedding with few guests. Must the church be completely decorated with flowers? Should I have the aisle carpeted? Do I need a canopy out to the street? A.C.M., LANCASTER, PENNSYLVANIA

You may limit the flowers, if you wish, to suitable ones for the altar. Even very formal weddings frequently do not use the canopy any more. It is not necessary to have the church aisle carpeted, but, if you decide to do so, this is taken care of by the florist who decorates the church.

• •

Is it possible to have a widow or a divorcée as a matron of honor? Is it all right if some of the bridesmaids are married? And if they are married, must one have their husbands as ushers? L.S.W., WICHITA, KANSAS

The matron of honor may be a widow or a divorcée, but it is preferable that she not be very much older than the bride. Bridesmaids may be married. Their husbands need not be members of the wedding party, but they should, of course, be invited to the wedding and reception although they do not usually sit at the bride's table. Conversely, when a married man is invited to be part of a wedding party, his wife is invited to the wedding although she does not usually sit with the bridal attendants at the reception.

• •

Someone told me that it is not good taste to get married on Sunday. If it isn't, why isn't it? A.R.R., SOMERVILLE, NEW JERSEY

Ministers tell me that it is less customary for people to be married on their own Sabbath because their clergymen are fully occupied on that day. Aside from this, there is nothing really against being married on the Sabbath. Jews often marry on Sunday, which is not their own Sabbath. Sunday Christian marriages are almost the rule in some parts of the South.

• •

I am planning to be married in our own small church where the minister has known me since babyhood. I understand that under ordinary circumstances my fiancé and I should visit the minister to discuss the details of the ceremony and any church regulations that must be fulfilled. Also so the minister can see if he approves of my husband-to-be. But as they have met many times socially, couldn't my mother make the church arrangements, as I work every day? G.A.T., PHOENIX, ARIZONA

Yes, under these circumstances your mother could make the arrangements. Try to have a conference with the minister, however, sometime before the marriage, taking your fiancé with you, so that the minister may be fully satisfied that you are both taking the right step.

• •

Who should I choose as my best man? I live with my married sister and her husband. My future wife, my sister and her husband, and I have gone out socially many times. Considering my fiancé has only one brother and I have none, I wonder if he should be my choice, although I don't know him well. Who would be a logical choice? R.P., WACO, TEXAS

Your sister's husband, unless you have a very close friend whom you would prefer to have and providing there is not too great a difference in age. Very occasionally, especially if he has no brother, the groom asks his father to be his best man. If the father is very young-looking this does not seem too incongruous, but it is best to keep the wedding party at the same age level as that of the bride and groom.

• •

My husband and I are invited to an out-of-town wedding, but he will be unable to go. Would it be correct for my son, a college freshman in school near the city where the wedding will take place, to meet me and go as my escort? MRS. W.J.M., BERWYN, ILLINOIS

Yes. You would reply to the invitation this way:

Mrs Ronald Gordon Smith
and Mr. Ronald Gordon Smith, Jr.
accept with pleasure
the kind invitation of
Mr. and Mrs. Jones
for Saturday, the third of November
at eight o'clock
Mr. Ronald Gordon Smith
will be unable to attend.

• •

A few days ago I received an invitation to a wedding containing a stamped, addressed response card. Quite honestly, I was insulted that these people didn't think I would answer their invitation on my own. Were they correct? F.M.P., JUNEAU, ALASKA

Response cards should be limited to business and charity invitations and debuts.

• •

I am going to be a bridesmaid and have never been one before. Am I expected to buy my own dress? And how do I get to the church? G.C.F., GARDEN CITY, NEW YORK

Today's bridesmaid nearly always buys her own clothes, but she wears what the bride selects, of course, so that all the bridesmaids may be dressed alike. Bridesmaids assemble at the home of the bride a full hour before the ceremony. They may arrive dressed, or dress after they reach the bride's home where they receive their bouquets. Transportation is provided for them from the bride's home to the church.

• •

I am going to have my little sister, aged fourteen, as a junior bridesmaid. Must I have a maid or matron of honor as well, and where does she stand in the processional? MISS L.G., PITTSBURGH, PENNSYLVANIA

I would prefer to see you have a maid or matron of honor as well as a junior bridesmaid. Such a young girl might feel nervous acting as your only attendant. However, if you feel that she can do it, she walks directly in front of you. If you decide to have a maid or matron of honor as well, the junior bridesmaid precedes the bridesmaid.

• •

My daughter is to be married soon, and we are considering how large a wedding we can afford. Could you give me some idea of the expenses involved for both bride and the groom? MRS. R.W., DETROIT, MICHIGAN

Traditionally the bride's parents assume the following expenses:

Engraved invitations and announcements
The bridal outfit and, though it is no longer expected, the costumes of the bride's attendants if money is no object
Bridal photographs
The bridal consultant and social secretary, if needed
The bride's trousseau
Gifts for the bride's attendants

The household trousseau

The bride's "maiden dinner," if any

All the cost of the reception

Cost of the bride's premarital blood test for the license

Flowers for the church and the reception

Corsages for the bride's mother and grandmothers, if they wish to wear them

Flowers for the bride (see NOTE), her attendants, her father's boutonniere

Gratuities for off-duty traffic policemen or others asked to direct traffic at the wedding

The groom's wedding ring if they are to have a double ring ceremony

Fee, if any, for the church rental

Music at the church and at the reception

Bridesmaids' party (although this may be given by the attendants, relatives or friends)

Sexton's and organist's fee. Choir fee

Carpets, ribbons, awnings, tents—anything of the kind often rented for large weddings and receptions

A limousine for the bride, at least, and other cars for the transportation of the bridal party to and from church

A wedding gift of substance, usually silver

Hotel bills for out-of-town attendants when they can't be accommodated by the bride's family, relatives, or friends

The groom assumes the following expenses:

The wedding ring

The marriage license and the cost of the groom's premarital blood test

The bride's flowers (see NOTE)

His own and the ushers' boutonnieres

Corsage for his mother and grandmothers (see NOTE)

The ushers' gloves, if worn, and ties

Gifts for the ushers

The minister's fee

A wedding gift for the bride—something for her to treasure, usually jewelry

His bachelor dinner

The entire cost of the wedding trip

His own wedding and wedding trip clothes

The home into which they will move and the equipping of it with its major furnishings

Hotel bills for his best man and out-of-town ushers who can't be accommodated by family, relatives or friends

NOTE In large formal weddings the bride's flowers and those of the bridesmaids are considered part of the entire wedding expense and thus borne by the bride's parents. It is becoming customary however for the groom to send the bride's bouquet, though she selects it, and to provide his own, the best man's, his father's, and the ushers' boutonnieres. In some communities the groom pays for the entire bridal party flowers as well as for corsages for both mothers. Sometimes the mothers and the grandmothers decide not to wear corsages.

• •

When my husband and I were married, almost five years ago, we did not have a double ring ceremony. Now he has expressed the wish to have a ring, providing it would be good taste to start wearing one at this later date. Would this be proper? Certainly I would very much like to give him one. And if it would be all right, should I just present it to him as a gift or should we arrange for some sort of church ceremony (Espiscopal) for his putting it on? MRS. R.L.T., SALT LAKE CITY, UTAH

As you know, in the Episcopal service there is a blessing of the ring. So you may take the ring to church and, by pre-arrangement with the rector, have it blessed. There is, too, a little publication called *The Book of Offices* (published by the Church Pension Fund, New York, N.Y.) which your rector undoubtedly has in his library. In it is a simple service designed for the blessing of married couples who have had only a civil ceremony. Within this service is the ceremony of the blessing of the ring, and perhaps your rector could expand this to offer a brief service of thanksgiving for your happy marriage, the blessing of the children if you have any. Certainly your husband's asking for a wedding band now, after five years of marriage, is a great tribute to you and to the institution of marriage itself.

I was married in an Orthodox Jewish ceremony in which the marriage ring is placed on the right hand, as you know. My mother, who was born in Europe, objects to my removing the band and placing it on my left hand as is the custom in this country. She continues to wear hers on the third finger of the right hand. Don't you think I should conform to the American tradition in this case? MRS. H.W., LOS ANGELES, CALIFORNIA

Yes, it is usual for Jewish brides in this country to transfer the ring to the left hand. In our culture here the wedding band on the third finger of the left hand indicates a married woman. Worn on the right hand, the ring has no special significance here.

• •

My fiancé has asked me to go to a wedding with him, to which I wasn't invited. The wedding is his brother's sister-in-law's. Would it be proper for me to attend it without a written invitation? "TROUBLED," MACON, GEORGIA

If the wedding is to be in church, you may go without an invitation. You may not go to a reception following the wedding without one but your fiancé could ask for an invitation for you. This privilege, however, applies mainly to engaged people. Others should not ask to bring "dates." Most receptions are very expensive and the cost of each guest must be considered. Last minute additions are usually impossible.

• •

My son has just returned from overseas with a foreign bride. What is expected of me as to entertainment or a

dinner so that relatives and friends may meet my new daughter-in-law? C.E.F., SPOKANE, WASHINGTON

You may give a tea or any other gathering that is convenient for you and invite to it relatives and friends who would be interested in meeting your daughter-in-law. You may invite them by telephone, by note, or personally. Stand inside the door of the room in which you are receiving.

• •

There is to be a big wedding in our town, and the groom's father has been married twice, the first time to a very difficult alcoholic. The father and the first wife are very unfriendly and even a chance encounter usually causes fireworks. We know she will insist on coming to the wedding. Could we properly ask her not to? What is your solution? W.P.R., MERIDEN, CONNECTICUT

Have some trusted member of the family, known for his tact, visit the mother and explain the situation. Say her son wants her to witness his wedding but that he does not want the occasion spoiled in any way. Say that someone will call for her and take her home immediately after the service. Alcoholics differ greatly, psychologically, but perhaps such an appeal to her pride and motherhood will help.

• •

Is it proper to autograph wedding photographs when we send them to our friends and relatives? D.C.C., MUNCIE, INDIANA

Yes, but it isn't necessary.

THE RECEPTION

I am having a large reception following our wedding, and here is our problem. Some of the ushers are married, and I would like to know whether it is necessary to seat their wives with us at the bride's table. Will you

also tell me who proposes the first toast to me? D.A.,
WEST ORANGE, NEW JERSEY

It would be unusual to include the mates of married
attendants at the bridal table. The best man rises and
proposes the first toast to the bride and others may follow
suit—not forgetting to toast the groom, too. The bride,
seated, may also propose a toast to the groom by turn-
ing her head toward him, lifting her glass and smiling.

Here is a diagram of the bride's table.

THE BRIDE'S TABLE, *seating optional, see text. Reading from*
left to right: Usher, bridesmaid, best man, bride, groom,
maid or matron of honor, bridesmaid, usher.

• •

We are really an enormous family, close-knit and with
many friends. One of us is going to be married, and we
would like to be able to invite all our family and close
friends to a reception as well as to the church. But to do
this in the traditional way, with a caterer, would cost
too much. Would it be all right if we hired a large hall
with kitchen facilities and, more or less pitching in our-
selves, prepared the day before the things that we would
like to serve at our wedding dinner? We could hire
waitresses to serve it. If we do this, what in the world
would we serve, handling it this way? J.P., BROKEN
BOW, NEBRASKA

Your solution is a good one. It is not necessary to have
professional help at a wedding dinner or reception. You
may well do all the work yourselves, and it isn't necessary either to have professional servers. I suggest that
you prepare roasts of various kinds—beef, ham, turkey
—and hearty salads, such as cooked vegetable salad or
potato salad, with the usual relishes. You then handle

it much as you would a church supper, letting people serve themselves from a buffet. Your wedding cake may be homemade or bakery made, and as a beverage you may serve anything from fruit punch or cider to champagne, as your pocketbook and tastes dictate.

We are going to have a parents' table at our wedding reception but would like to know who sits where. Can you give me directions? U.C.M., ST. LOUIS, MISSOURI

When a parents' table is provided, guests are placed as follows: father of the groom to the right of the bride's mother. Opposite her sits the bride's father with the groom's mother to the right. Other guests may include the clergyman and his wife, perhaps the grandparents. Here is the diagram.

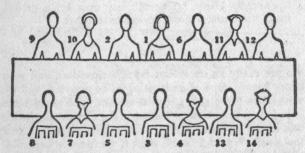

SEATING AT PARENTS' TABLE, *table optional*. 1. Bride's mother, 2. father of groom, 3. father of bride, 4. mother of groom, 5. important officiating clergyman's wife, 6. officiating clergyman (*or see text*), 7, 8, 9, 10, 11, 12, 13, 14, friends of parents or possibly grandparents.

• •

My son is about to be married, and his future parents-in-law have asked us to keep down our guest list to approximately fifty for the reception. However, this number will not even cover the members of our own family. Could I ask her family's permission to submit a larger list so that I may include some intimate friends,

agreeing to pay for all over fifty? MRS. C.A.B., CON-CORD, MASSACHUSETTS

If you make your own guest list over fifty, offering to pay the difference, I think you may tend to make the bride's family feel uncomfortable. As you realize, the bride's family is responsible for the cost of the reception, and they could not properly accept your offer to pay for additional guests. You could, however, give a second reception or even a cocktail party after the couple returns home from the wedding trip for as many guests as you wish.

• •

In the cutting of the wedding cake, where does the bride stand? L.C.N., SHREVEPORT, LOUISIANA

The bride stands to the groom's right. She places her hand on the cake knife, and he places his right hand over hers for the cutting of the first slice.

• •

At the reception, does the bride's father dance first with his own wife or with the mother of the groom? Does he wait until all the guests have started dancing to do this? J.K., ESTES PARK, COLORADO

Dancing begins after the bride and groom have had the first dance—usually a waltz—alone on the dance floor together. Then the bride's father leads out the mother of the groom, and the groom's father dances with the mother of the bride. Attendants join in, and finally the guests enter the dance floor as they desire.

After the initial dance with the groom, the bride is claimed by her father-in-law, and the groom dances with his mother-in-law before asking the bridesmaids. The bride then dances with her father, next with the best man, and then with each of the ushers.

• •

At a reception, must the guests stay to see the bride off or do they leave sooner? E.F., QUEENS VILLAGE, LONG ISLAND

Just before leaving to dress for going away, the bride usually throws her bouquet to the bridesmaids. Sometimes she sees to it that a grandmother, unable to attend, receives it. Dancing may continue, but usually it begins to come to a close and the guests start leaving. It is only the late-stayers who remain to see the bride off.

• •

We are having a buffet reception after my wedding and do not plan to have a bride's table. After the groom and I receive, should we be seated for the collation or just stand around with the other guests, eating? M.A., BOSTON, MASSACHUSETTS

Usually at a buffet reception the bride and groom are seated alone at a small table for this first meal together after their marriage. They usually do not serve themselves but are waited upon from the buffet.

• •

I just received an invitation to attend a formal wedding. Please tell me the correct greeting to those in the receiving line. R.C., LEBANON, PENNSYLVANIA

As the receiving line moves fairly swiftly, there is little time to say much. You may not have more than time to say, "How do you do" to the bride's mother, or, if she detains you, you can say anything nice and spontaneous you feel like saying. Remember that the reception is a social occasion, one for smiles and cheerful remarks. You do not "congratulate" the bride. You "congratulate" the groom and "felicitate" the bride. To say anything like "Congratulations" to the bride is perhaps to indicate that you think she was lucky to find a husband at all! It is my theory that people don't really listen to what you say as you pass down the receiving line. It's not necessary to say much so long as you look warm and gracious, pleased with the bride, and happy for the groom.

• •

My sister, who is thirty-seven, will be married at a nuptial mass, and I will be her attendant. I am married and head of our family. At the reception should I be at the door receiving the guests with my gloves off or on, or does the bride come in later with her party when all are seated? C.L.F., BUFFALO, NEW YORK

Yes, you receive just inside the door as hostess for your sister, but the bridal party should arrive before the guests and form its receiving line beyond you before the guests start arriving at some focal point in the room. You keep your gloves on.

RECEIVING LINE AT WEDDING, *Optional Arrangement:* Bridal party before fireplace banked with flowers, or possibly in front of picture window. 1. Mother of bride, 2. father of groom (*optional*), 3. mother of groom (*optional*), 4. father of bride (*optional*), 5, 6. bridesmaids, 7. maid or matron of honor, 8. bride, 9. groom, 10. bridesmaid, 11. bridesmaid. NOTE: Whatever arrangement, the bride is on the groom's right except when he's in uniform. The best man is *never* on the line. Exceptions: Occasionally in the receiving line the bride must stand on the groom's left for convenience sake. In this case the line must be routed so that the bride is reached first by the guests. If the groom's father acts as best man, he then may be in line.

ENTERTAINING BEFORE THE WEDDING

As I am getting married soon, I want to give a bachelor dinner. However, here in Chicago there have been some fashionable weddings where the bachelor dinner was given by the best man or by the ushers—in the latter case, "Dutch." Is this proper? If I give the dinner, where do I seat the best man? J.P.R., CHICAGO, ILLINOIS

It is traditional for the groom to give the bachelor dinner, but, with the increasing simplification of weddings, very often the bachelor dinner doesn't take place at all any more. However, it does usually take place before very large, formal weddings. I have never heard of its being given by other than the groom, but as we know, etiquette customs change and if in Chicago this one has, you may choose to follow the new custom or adhere to the old. If you give the dinner, you seat the best man to your right.

• •

Should I ask my house guests from out of town who are staying with me for the wedding to my wedding rehearsal dinner? S.A, NORFOLK, VIRGINIA

The rehearsal dinner is for the participants in the wedding. If those in your house party are not going to be in the wedding party itself, you need not include them, unless the rehearsal dinner is to be at your home and the guests for the house party have already arrived. Then it would be necessary to plan the party to include them.

DRESS

BRIDE AND HER ATTENDANTS

With a bridal gown, what kind of shoes are worn and what kind of jewelry? When I go to the altar should I

leave my engagement ring at home or wear it? P.C.O.,
BUFFALO, NEW YORK

Bridal shoes are white silk or satin sandals or pumps.
Jewelry should be limited to either that which is func-
tional, such as a pin needed to hold the dress together,
to a strand of pearls, perhaps small gold or pearl earrings. A watch or bracelet should not be worn. The engagement ring may be worn on the right hand until after
the ceremony.

• •

I am being married at home. Should I wear a hat and
gloves? Is music necessary? Would I simply wait with
the families until the ceremony begins? L.M., BOSTON,
MASSACHUSETTS

You need wear nothing on your head. Today gloves
would be unusual for such a home ceremony. Music
is not necessary, but if you have a piano or a record
player it is nice to have THE WEDDING MARCH, at
least, played at the right moment. You stay upstairs or
in another room until the ceremony begins, when you
enter with your father or whoever is going to escort
you to the altar.

• •

My wedding is to be simple and small. It will be in our
Episcopal church with no music and only a few close
relatives. However, I would like to dress as a bride and
have a large reception at our country club. Is this in
proper taste? MISS N.C.H., DULUTH, MINNESOTA

Yes, you may have your church wedding witnessed by
just a few and then have as large a reception as you
wish. Of course, you may wear a wedding gown.

• •

I am being married at home soon. I am forty. Is
beige antique silk, short length, all right, or would a

coffee color be smarter? I don't want to look like an old girl trying to look young. Beige is becoming. My mother is trying to hold out for white with all the trimmings. Please try to help me convince her to the contrary. MISS D.W., DALLAS, TEXAS

Explain to your mother that while you are a very young forty and would probably look fetching in a bridal gown with veil, this youthful costume might not be flattering to the contemporaries who will act as your attendants. While you have a perfect right to wear a wedding veil, I believe your decision not to is better. Wear either beige or coffee, short or long, whichever you prefer, but at forty don't try to be a blushing bride, no matter what your mother tells you.

• •

I'd like to have my bridesmaids dressed exactly alike. Is this correct? What about my maid of honor? V.C., NEW YORK, NEW YORK

Yes, your bridesmaids' dresses may all be exactly alike, with different headdress and/or slightly different dress distinguishing the maid of honor. All their dresses should be the same length as the bride's, and they may wear flower headdresses, hats, or Juliet caps. The brides-maids' slippers are all alike, but the maid or matron of honor may have slippers to match her dress. In the formal wedding party, the bride may be gloveless (if her sleeves are long), and bridesmaids rarely wear gloves now.

GROOM, BEST MAN, AND USHERS

We are getting married at a formal daytime wedding at high noon. I am wearing a formal wedding gown. Is it all right if the groom wears a director's jacket with striped trousers instead of a cutaway which he thinks is unbecoming to him because he isn't very tall—five feet, eight? D.P.A, PHOENIX, ARIZONA

Yes, if he wishes, he may wear the director's jacket—or stroller (a double-breasted sack coat)—which is now also considered formal daytime wear. He wears it with striped trousers, gray vest, white shirt, French cuffs, turned-down collar, and any combination of black, white or gray four-in-hand tie, black shoes and socks. He may go hatless. He optionally wears gray gloves and black pearl or onyx jewelry. If he prefers, he may also choose to wear one of the conservative Edwardian outfits now available with his ushers and best man attired the same way. Fathers would choose traditional formal daytime wear. At a late spring wedding or in summer, ushers in morning coats (either the cutaway or the director's jacket) are hatless. They may also wear Edwardian attire (see above).

I am not going to have a really formal daytime wedding as I am planning on only one attendant, and my marriage will take place at home. I am going to wear a short veil, and my fiancé is worried about what he should wear. H.E.H., WINNETKA, ILLINOIS

The groom may wear a business suit, black or oxford gray, or he may wear a blue blazer. His shirt should be white with a white fold collar, his tie conservative. His shoes and socks black. His jewelry black or gold.

My husband, the father of the groom, is not fat but he does have a bay window. I know you say that the father of the bride and the father of the groom should dress alike and in the same manner as the groom and his attendants. But the groom has decided that he wants the attendants and himself in Edwardian suits, nipped in at the waist, ruffled shirts, tight flared trousers. My husband says never! What should he wear? L.F.R., GREAT NECK, NEW YORK

He needn't wear that costume. He and the bride's father should wear formal dress suitable to the time of day: for example striped trousers and a cutaway or a director's jacket (they should both dress alike, however), for a daytime wedding twelve noon or after. At an evening wedding they should wear white tie and tails or, alternatively and much less formally, black tie (tuxedo). They should avoid colored jackets.

Is it proper for me to wear a director's jacket and striped trousers at my afternoon wedding to a divorcée who will wear a dressy silk suit? R.M.H., LAS VEGAS, NEVADA

Yes. But you could also wear a blue blazer, gray flannel trousers, white shirt with a fold collar, conservative tie, black shoes and socks, black on gold jewelry. A dark business suit would also be appropriate with conservative accessories.

• •

At a formal daytime wedding, must all the ushers and the best man be dressed alike? And what if one of the ushers is in the armed services? G.L., NEW HAVEN, CONNECTICUT

The rule here is that if the groom and his best man wear dark clothes, the ushers don't wear, for example, white linen suits, as there must be unity in the wedding party. A member of the armed services, acting as an usher or an attendant, wears his uniform, or, if regulations permit and he so desires, he wears the same civilian clothes as the others. A uniform of the armed forces is considered perfectly formal and appropriate for all social occasions.

• •

Should the male members of a formal wedding wear white handkerchiefs in their breast pockets? If so, how should these be arranged? T.O'C., NASHVILLE, TENNESSEE

Ordinarily a handkerchief in the breast pocket of a man's suit is always a finishing touch. White handkerchiefs are always correct for any formal occasion, mono-

gramed if desired in black, white, gray or maroon.
They are not worn, however, by an usher when he is
wearing a boutonniere. A man's handkerchief, incidentally, is usually shaken out and and then put casually
in his pocket, not arranged in little points. The square
fold is equally acceptable, though probably not as popular.

• •

**My fiancé's wish is to wear his uniform at the wedding.
He is in the Army. I would like to know what the best
man and the groom's father should wear. It will be a
morning wedding and I will be wearing a semi-formal
gown.** S.H., OAKLAND, CALIFORNIA

The best man and the groom's father should wear dark
business suits, white shirts, conservative ties, dark socks,
black shoes.

PARENTS OF THE BRIDE AND GROOM

**My daughter is getting married in June and has planned
what she is going to wear and what her attendants will
wear but has no idea of what her mother and I should
wear. The wedding is going to take place at four in the
afternoon.** "FATHER," TOLEDO, OHIO

The fathers of the bride and groom dress as the groom
does, but see reference to Edwardian attire on page 103.
The mothers of the bride and groom wear soft long
or short pale or pastel colors for a wedding at this hour
but both mothers wear the same length. The mother of
the bride has first choice of color and determines the
length of the mothers' gowns. Guests at such a wedding
wear the sort of clothes that they would wear to any
formal afternoon function.

• •

**We are having a formal evening wedding. My groom
will wear white tie and so will his best man. Is it all
right if the ushers wear white dinner jackets, as the**

wedding will take place in July? MISS B.S., CHARLESTON, SOUTH CAROLINA

I suggest that the groom, his best man and the fathers involved all wear white dinner jackets and abandon the idea of tails this late in the season. It would not be correct for the ushers to be dressed so differently from the principals.

• •

My daughter is being married out of doors in our orchard. She will wear a long cotton dress, no veil and will be barefoot. The groom will wear blue cotton trousers, sandals, white linen embroidered Mexican shirt. What should the guests wear? What should the mothers of the bride and groom wear—and the fathers? The "reception" will be a picnic on the grass complete with hot dogs and watermelon. MRS. H.H., FORT WORTH, TEXAS

The guests and the parents of the bride and groom should wear informal cottons or linens that make them feel comfortable. Over-dressing would be as inappropriate as too much informality on such an occasion.

A friend of mine says that if you go without a hat, you should also go without gloves. I plan to go to a church wedding where there is no insistence on headcovering so I will not wear a hat. Should I then not wear gloves? The wedding will take place in the early fall. MRS. E.W., SAN FRANCISCO, CALIFORNIA

There is no rule that says if you go without a hat, you must go without gloves. Many women, especially those in the suburbs, no longer wear gloves when the weather is pleasant, but at a church wedding I would like to see you wear gloves no matter what the weather.

GUESTS

I am invited to a Sunday wedding at 2:30 p.m. Should I wear a cocktail dress or something less formal, such

as a suit? Is a hat necessary? MRS. R.K.L., PITTSBURGH,
PENNSYLVANIA

As this is probably a dressy occasion and the wedding
followed by a reception, a dress would be more suitable
unless you have a very dressy type of suit, say in velvet,
faille, or slipper satin. In most communities now and in
most churches, headcovering is optional.

• •

Everyone writes so much about the bride's clothes, but
who gives any thought for what guests at an informal
daytime wedding should wear? I am never sure whether
I am dressed up enough or overdressed. Is there some
rule about it? MRS. L.J., RICHMOND, VIRGINIA

The best rule is to wear attractive somewhat festive
clothes suitable for the time of day. Hats in most
churches are an optional matter. I like to see gloves
here.

• •

I am invited to a Jewish wedding at a Conservative
synagogue, and although I am not a Jew myself, I
understand a man is supposed to wear a hat. It happens that I rarely wear a hat, so if I should go without one, would I be wrong in following my own custom? N.B.B., EL PASO, TEXAS

Yes, you would. It is proper for a man, on entering
a Conservative synagogue, to take up one of the prayer
caps, or yarmulkes, available to you. Sometimes these
are of paper and sometimes of fabric. You would also
wear a yarmulke in an Orthodox synagogue but not in
a Reform one.

I know when I go to a church wedding that if I am
invited by the bride or know that I am indebted to her
for the invitation—I say to the usher who comes to
escort me, "Bride," and that he places me on the left

in the pew reserved for the bride's guests and family. The groom's guests of course sit on the right—but I understand that this is different in Jewish synagogues. As I expect to go to a Jewish wedding soon, will you please set me right? R.K., MONTGOMERY, ALABAMA

In Reform temples, the custom is the same as it is in churches—the bride's guests to the left, the bride's side of the church. However, in Orthodox and Conservative synagogues, the groom's guests receive the left-hand seats, the bride's the right.

• •

Would it be all right for me to wear a suit to a five o'clock wedding? S.J.G., HARRISBURG, PENNSYLVANIA

Yes, if it is a soft, dressy one. Wear dressy shoes and hat if you wish. In most churches now headcovering for women is not obligatory, but it is wise to check the custom of the particular congregation. A tailored street suit would be inappropriate.

• •

My nephew is getting married, and I am not to be in the wedding party, although I will be a guest. My daughter insists that I should not wear my best black dress— that black isn't proper at a wedding. I'd like to wear it and brighten it with a little pink. Would this be all right? C.C.A., CHICAGO, ILLINOIS

Yes, you may wear the dress you describe, and brightening it with pink would make it more festive. It is only the women who are in the wedding party who may not wear black—guests may do so, of course, especially in big cities.

• •

I am going to a large, formal wedding to be held at 8 p.m. in a hotel in a near-by city. I intend to wear a dark, street-length dress. Should my husband wear a dark suit or something more formal? MRS. E.D., CHARLESTON, SOUTH CAROLINA

It would be correct for your husband to wear a dinner jacket at the wedding you mention. However, if possible, check with others who are going to see what the men plan to wear. If other men guests plan to wear dark suits, your husband would prefer to dress as they do. If you know no one going but can find out what the groom is going to wear, that can help you decide. If he is going to be in tails, the male guests wear dinner jackets unless they are part of the bridal party, in which case they, too, wear tails.

• •

Are a street-length dress, small hat, and white gloves suitable attire for a church wedding taking place at 6 p.m.? In a Protestant church, is a hat necessary or out of place at that particular hour? At the reception at a club, does one remove gloves and carry them with purse or tuck them in purse? I do not wish to buy new formal clothes and hope the cocktail-type outfit will be proper. JANE A., PROVIDENCE, RHODE ISLAND

The costume is suitable for a wedding at such a time although the hat is not required. At the reception you may wish to remove your hat, if you wear one, especially if there is dancing. Once you have gone down the receiving line wearing your gloves, you may then put them in your purse. Never eat or drink anything with your gloves on.

SECOND MARRIAGES

I expect to marry a widower (I am a widow) this year. He would like to give me a diamond ring on my birthday in the spring. Would this be proper? Would it be in good taste for my mother to announce our engagement in the paper? We are both forty-three. If this is not correct, how should it be done? We live in a small community where we are well-known and

plan a small, quiet wedding in our church. Does this sound proper? A.F., NIAGARA FALLS, NEW YORK

Yes, your fiancé may give you an engagement ring. However, such engagements are usually made known only informally among one's friends and relatives rather than announced in the newspapers. You may issue news of the marriage jointly in the following manner:

Mrs. Harry Holden, of 8 East 10th Street, and Mr. Rutherford Tyng, of Princeton, New Jersey, announce that their marriage took place Saturday, April 3rd, at the Church of the Ascension, Baltimore, Maryland. Mrs. Holden, the former Elsbeth Finn, is the daughter of Mr. and Mrs. Clarence Finn, of Baltimore. Mrs. Holden is the widow of the late Mr. Harry Holden.

Mr. Tyng was married to the late Elizabeth Johnson of this city. He is the son of Professor and Mrs. Rufus Tyng of Princeton and is an instructor in mathematics at Princeton University. The couple will make their home in Philadelphia.

• •

I am marrying a widower. Is it correct for me to wear a wedding gown and veil? K.D.W., EUGENE, OREGON

Yes, indeed. The status of the groom has nothing to do with the matter. The bride who has never been married before may wear the wedding veil, although if she has reached her mid-thirties or more she usually prefers not to, no matter how youthful she may look.

• •

I am a widow and am getting married again. I understand it is not correct for me to wear anything that looks like a wedding dress even at a church wedding, which I am planning. I am going to wear a pale gray silk suit and a pink flowered hat and will wear a corsage of sweetheart roses. What should my groom wear? T.G., CLEVELAND, OHIO

When the bride does not wear a veil, the groom wears a dark blue or gray business suit, white shirt with fold collar, conservative tie, may go hatless or wear a Homburg, and, optionally, gray gloves. He could also wear a well-cut blue blazer, white shirt, conservative tie, gray flannels, black shoes and socks. If the wedding is to take place in the summer, he might wear a lightweight wool suit in gray or blue with white shirt and black shoes, or a white linen suit or any light colored summer suit with white shirt, black shoes and socks. In the country, he might choose to wear a navy jacket with white flannel trousers, white shirt, black socks, conservative tie, and black shoes. Optionally, he might wear the Victorian-era inspired Prince Edward with a white or possibly colored ruffled shirt, black shoes. Most men's wedding garb is rented today, and some of the costumes suggested are in bad taste. It is wise to follow conservative guidelines. Although of course some of these outfits carefully put together can be attractive if rented from a quality organization.

I am a widower. I plan to marry a widow. We are prominent, and our wedding will be covered by the newspapers. In furnishing them with information, must I necessarily state the name of my former wife? This is complicated, as before I became a widower I was divorced, and I would rather skip the whole matter. MR. W.L.B., PHILADELPHIA, PENNSYLVANIA

It is not necessary for you to mention your former wife's name in the release to the press. As you are prominent, it is possible that the newspapers' "morgues" have full information concerning your prior marriages and will print the information.

I would like to know if it is good taste for a divorcée to be the honoree at one or more small parties before her second marriage. She did not live in this area during her first marriage, and her prospective bridegroom was not previously married. L.P.B., SEATTLE, WASHINGTON

I see no reason why she couldn't have some parties given for her so long as they are not showers. Showers are not usually given for second marriages.

• •

For a second marriage is it permissible for me to have a close relative (matron of honor) stand with me and for the groom to have an attendant? What kind of invitation, if any, should I use? K.R., MACON, GEORGIA

You may have a close relative as a matron of honor and your husband-to-be may have a close friend as his best man who both, incidentally, may act as your witnesses. As both of you usually must have witnesses—adult ones—it is nicer if they are close friends or relatives rather than strangers. (For example, at a civil wedding in a courthouse or elsewhere any adult witnesses are often used, whether or not they know the bride and groom.) This is also the case when a couple goes alone for a quiet ceremony in a church or in the vestry.

• •

I am a young widow and I am planning to get married again in the fall. Naturally I have a great many household things from my previous marriage, many of which were wedding gifts. I am wondering if it is proper to specify, on wedding invitations, that it is to be a "purse wedding." If so, how is it done? F.A.B., GREENWICH, CONNECTICUT

Formal invitations are usually not sent for second marriages. And you wouldn't engrave on an invitation any such information as you would like to impart. You can let it be known through close friends and your family that you would prefer gifts of money from those close to you. However, quite often those friends who have sent gifts for a first marriage do not do so for a second and should not really be expected to.

INVITATIONS, ANNOUNCEMENTS, AND REPLIES

What is the traditional form for formal wedding invitations and when should they be sent out? MISS L.M., HOUSTON, TEXAS

Wedding invitations are sent as much as four weeks in advance and never less than two. Here is an example:

Dr. and Mrs. Grant Kingsley
request the honour of your presence
at the marriage of their daughter
Penelope
to
Mr. George Frank Carpenter
on Friday, the tenth of June
one thousand nine hundred and seventy-three
at twelve o'clock
Saint Mary's Church
San Francisco

Mention of the year is optional on an invitation but obligatory on the announcement of the marriage. The word "honour" is always spelled in the old way. The phrase "honour of your presence" is always used for invitations to the church. When the marriage takes place at home or somewhere other than church, the phrase "pleasure of your company" is used. No R.S.V.P. is used where the invitation is for the ceremony alone. The R.S.V.P. is used if the invitation includes the reception.

• •

What is the proper location for a zip code when writing an address? Should zip codes be used when addressing wedding invitations? MRS. I.R., FREEPORT, NEW YORK

Zip codes should be used whenever you write an address—even on wedding invitations. They are placed immediately following the state with no punctuation in between. Here is an example:

Mrs. Robert S. Miller
19 Barclay Street
Douglaston, New York 11363

• •

My daughter plans to be married in the church by the priest and at the altar. However, only the families of the bride and groom will attend, and there will be no reception afterward, just a small dinner party. Is it proper for us to send wedding announcements? Should they be sent out before or after the marriage? Could you give me some kind of form so I could have them made up? MRS. C.S.T., FORT WORTH, TEXAS

Yes, send out the announcement immediately after the wedding. They should be ordered a month to six weeks before the wedding and should be all addressed, ready for mailing, as soon as the ceremony has taken place. Here is the form:

Dr. and Mrs. Grant Kingsley
have the honour of announcing
(or have the honour to announce)
the marriage of their daughter
Penelope
to
Mr. George Frank Carpenter
on Friday, the tenth of June
one thousand nine hundred and seventy-three
(must give year)
Saint Mary's Church
(optional to mention)
San Francisco

• •

I have been on my own for many years and have no close relatives or friends to issue my invitations and

announcements for me. May I do this myself? A.L.C,
LOS ANGELES, CALIFORNIA

Yes, you may, and quite properly too. Here is the form
you would use:

> The honour of your presence
> is requested at the marriage of
> (or "wedding reception of")
> Miss Cordelia Kingsley
> (note "MISS")
> to
> (or "and")
> Mr. Winthrop Cass Bowers
> etc.

Your announcement would read:

> Miss Cordelia Kingsley (note "MISS")
> and
> Mr. Winthrop Cass Bowers
> announce their marriage
> at the Church of All Saints (optional)
> at Greenwich, Connecticut
> on Tuesday, the eighth of March
> one thousand nine hundred and seventy-three

• •

**I am having a large church wedding with a reception
following, to which I plan to invite about a hundred
guests. Could you give me the proper form for the reception card?** R.N., ALBANY, NEW YORK

When not all those attending the wedding are to be invited to the reception, a reception card of the same
stock as the invitation and about half the size is included with its tissue if the invitation itself is a folded
one. It should not bear a crest, shield, or motto and
may read:

> Dr. and Mrs. Grant Kingsley
> request the pleasure of your company

at the wedding breakfast
following the ceremony
at
"The Gulls"
Belvedere

R.S.V.P. (or "The favour of a reply is requested")

Note "pleasure of your company," as this is now a social occasion.

• •

Should the tissues that come with engraved invitations from the stationer's be left in place when the invitations are placed in the inner envelope, or should they be removed? L.P., HARTFORD, CONNECTICUT

Unless the invitations have been ordered very far in advance so that you are sure the ink is well dried, it is safest and usual to leave the tissue in place.

• •

Is it necessary to reply to a wedding invitation? What is the correct form? MISS L.B., WICHITA, KANSAS

Formal, engraved invitations to a church wedding alone do not require answering. But if a reception card is received, one answers in the traditional form in response to R.S.V.P. on the invitation. The reply is written in the third person, in longhand on one's best conservative paper in blue or black ink, with the wording and spacing taking the form of engraving.

Mr. and Mrs. Morrow Tuft
accept with pleasure
Dr. and Mrs. Kingsley's
kind invitation for
Friday, the ninth of June
at noon

A regret follows the same form. It reads:

Mr. and Mrs. Morrow Tuft
regret that they are unable to accept
Dr. and Mrs. Kingsley's
etc.

On a regret, the repetition of the time is unnecessary.

● ●

I am sending out formal invitations to my forthcoming wedding. Are there any rules about the addressing of envelopes that should be adhered to? K.R., AKRON, OHIO

Yes, the addressing of wedding invitations and announcements is rigidly prescribed. Black ink must be used. Abbreviations are not permitted except in "Dr.," "Mr.," "Mrs.," and "Jr." (or "Lt." when combined with "Colonel," etc.). The names of cities and states are written out and zip codes are used. For instance:

Mr. and Mrs. Cedric Moore McIntosh
1886 Shore Road
Chicago, Illinois 60600

Where there are several members of a family to be invited avoid the phrase "and family." On the inside envelope is written:

Mr. and Mrs. McIntosh
(no Christian name)
Belinda and Gordon
(if the children are under age)

If there are other adults in the family whom you wish to invite, they must receive separate invitations.

It is also traditional for the handwriting (in black ink) on the envelopes to be obviously feminine and, if possible, of a round, clear style. The address, of course, may never be typed.

● ●

I am planning an informal, morning church wedding to be followed by a wedding breakfast. Most of the groom's relatives and friends live in a city considerably distant from this. It is likely that only one or two will attend the ceremony. We would like to know whether it is necessary to send wedding invitations to relatives at such a distance and whether close friends who we know can't attend should receive invitations. MISS A.S., SPRINGFIELD, ILLINOIS

Send invitations to all relatives and to close friends even if you know they cannot attend. To friends who do not receive invitations, send announcements.

• •

In addressing wedding invitations, how do you address the envelope to two sisters, both single? K.V.C., SAN JOSE, CALIFORNIA

Address them "The Misses Clark," both on the outer and on the inner envelope. Optionally this may read "The Misses Angela and Mary Clark."

• •

I am having a small informal wedding. Do I send out engraved invitations? R.C.M., GALVESTON, TEXAS

No. This type of wedding does not call for formal invitations. Invitations can be extended either by telephone or by short informal notes to your friends. However, announcements usually are sent after the wedding to as large a list of friends, relatives, and acquaintances as you care to cover.

• •

I would like to have my wedding invitations engraved in gold ink. Is this correct? What color stationery do you recommend? A.F., AKRON, OHIO

For wedding invitations, only black ink should be used.
Silver or gold inks are frequently used however for the
twenty-fifty or fiftieth wedding anniversary invitations
if one wishes.

• •

I work for a large company where I'm not personally
acquainted with all the employees and have only a
speaking acquaintance with others. Of course, I know
those with whom I work each day very well. Would it
be permissible for me to send one wedding invitation to be placed on the bulletin board, or should I send
invitations only to those I think would like to come?
Some girls I know have sent just one invitation in the
past, and those in the company who wanted to attend
went and vice versa. N.W., BANGOR, MAINE

I would send an invitation to those with whom you
have a warm social bond in business—if such is the
case—and I see no reason why you cannot send your
wedding invitation for the bulletin board for others who
might know you slightly and wish to see you married
—if, of course, your wedding is to take place in a
church.

• •

My daughter eloped—with our approval, I may add
—but should we send formal announcements or leave
them out and just tell our friends about the marriage?
MRS. W.B., HOUSTON, TEXAS

It is not necessary that you send them, although you
may. If you do send them, state the place of the marriage and the date. If a civil ceremony was performed,
only the name of the city or town appears. If the couple was married in church, it is optional whether the
church is mentioned or not.

Etiquette blithely ignores the fact that sometimes divorce isn't as final as it should be and could be, and

that often the participants are in the somewhat un-
certain position of wondering how they should tell their
friends who are out of town (and certainly wouldn't
know otherwise) that they have been remarried to each
other. This isn't such an unusual situation after all. Of
forty-one marriage licenses recently listed in our local
paper, thirteen were remarriages of divorced couples.
Please do let me know what to do. MR. J.M.H., HOT
SPRINGS, ARKANSAS

The good news that two people have come together
again despite divorce is proclaimed to their friends and
relatives by telephone, telegram, and, of course, by
note and word of mouth. Formal announcements are
not sent out.

My fiance and I would like to have both our parents'
names on our wedding invitations and announcements.
We have seen this done but are told that it is not
"etiquette." S.S., DENVER, COLORADO

It is "etiquette" in many parts of the world and has
been used here by some ethnic groups for generations. I
recently worked out two forms as there has been increasing interest in the idea. I feel that the two ex-
amples I give are perfectly clear and may be used instead of the traditional style of invitation and announcement which uses the parents of the bride solely. Here
are the two optional ways, good because they make
clear exactly whose child is whose.

Mr. and Mrs. Andrew Brown
request the honour of your presence
at the marriage of their daughter
Marianne
to
Mr. John Preston
son of
Mr. and Mrs. Robert Preston
on (date) at (time)
(place)

R.S.V.P.
Mrs. Brown
Address (including Zip Code)

or optionally,

Mr. and Mrs. Andrew Brown
Mr. and Mrs. Robert Preston
request the honour of your presence
at the marriage of
Marianne Brown
to
John Preston, etc.

GIFTS

Is it expected that the bride put her wedding gifts on display? O.M.E., ROANOKE, VIRGINIA

A formal display of wedding gifts is less often seen now, but it is still in good taste to exhibit them. Cards are removed from the gifts displayed, and gifts of like value are grouped together. The amounts of checks are recorded on propped-up cards reading "Check, $100," with the donor's name *omitted*.

• •

The people with whom I work will be unable to attend my wedding without loss of pay, since it is to be on a weekday. However, there are several close ones who should be invited. But does an invitation imply a wedding gift is expected? I do not want it to appear as such. J.T.B., THOMASVILLE, PENNSYLVANIA

Invite your friends, even though you know they cannot attend. An invitation to a wedding does not obligate anyone to send a gift if the wedding is at church. Wedding guests included in the reception usually do send gifts if they accept and even when they regret, if they feel particularly close to the principals.

• •

In sending a check as a wedding gift, to whom is the check drawn—bride or groom or both? The check will be sent before the day of the wedding. R.C.H., CHICAGO, ILLINOIS

Before the wedding, a check is drawn to the bride in her maiden name. A check presented by some member of the family or a close friend after the wedding has taken place, perhaps just before the reception, is properly made out to the bride and groom, "Anne and Richard Brown."

One of the girls in our shop was recently married, and we men gave gifts that were beyond our means. It isn't that we regret this, but we now have another problem. The girl is now in her own home and has invited us to visit her. Is it proper for us to go empty-handed? W.S.H., PORTLAND, MAINE

It is never actually necessary to take a "house gift." I am sure your friend is already very appreciative of your generosity.

• •

Is it all right to use informals in giving thanks for a wedding present? B.G., NEW YORK, NEW YORK

Yes, so long as there is no printed phrase such as "thank you" that substitutes for the written words of thanks and if the informal is conservative and of good quality paper. If the informal is plain, the note begins on side one. If it is printed or engraved—in the bride's name only, Mrs. Robert James Smith, or the bride's new initials or monogram—this would be on side one. On such an engraved or printed informal the note begins on side three, continuing if necessary to side four. Any "note" longer than that deserves correspondence size paper. It should be sent, of course, first-class mail, sealed.

• •

I am leaving immediately after my wedding for six months abroad, where my husband is stationed. I am thanking as many people as possible before my wedding for gifts they have already sent. But I won't be able to see the gifts that arrive after my departure, and they won't be sent on to me. Shall I wait until I get back to thank the senders, or may my family handle the acknowledgments for me? MARILYN L., ATLANTA, GEORGIA

There is a card available now at all good stationers who do wedding invitations and announcements. It may be used under the circumstances you describe or where there has been a very large formal wedding where hundreds of gifts have been received. It is sent immediately on receipt of the gift and merely states that Miss So-and-so has received your gift and will acknowledge it personally at an early date. In your case, your family should send you a list of the gifts that have arrived after the wedding so that you can make each note quite personal and appreciative.

• •

When I write my thank-you notes to my husband's relations, should I write "Dear Aunt Sally," etc., even when I haven't met them? My husband is very close to his family. K.V.C., SANTA BARBARA, CALIFORNIA

Yes, address them as "Dear Aunt Sally," etc. They are now *your* relatives, too. Try to make your letter spontaneous and friendly, just as though you were talking face to face to the person who has sent you the gift. Thank-you notes are signed, "Sincerely," "Cordially," "Love," or "Affectionately."

• •

We find that brides are more and more using Mr. and Mrs. informals in giving thanks for wedding presents. We feel that this is not correct and wonder what your opinion is? STATIONER, ROCHESTER, NEW YORK

It would be awkward for a bride to use the Mr. and Mrs. informals in giving thanks for wedding presents. This piece of stationery is designed for the issuing of invitations and for inclusion with flowers or other gifts, with an unsigned line or two—"A happy birthday!" "We hope you like it." To use it for notes means that it has to be written in the first person plural and be signed by both people, an awkward procedure. Properly, the bride writes her own acknowledgment, on her own stationery or informal, and if she wishes to mention her husband in it—as is usually done—that is, of course, all right. But she should not sign the note jointly with her husband, or even as some girls do "Sincerely, Pat and Bill."

• •

Recently I gave a very nice wedding present to a young girl of whom I was very fond. The acknowledgment was so long in coming that I finally had to write her to ask if she had received my gift. After an even further delay she wrote that of course she had and that she and her husband were very pleased with it. Can't you say something about the necessity for prompt acknowledgment of wedding gifts? MRS. L.V., WESTPORT, CONNECTICUT

Yes, a bride should acknowledge her wedding gifts as soon as possible, if only with a few lines. Where a great many gifts have been received and the bride is a working girl, this is very difficult, I know, but nevertheless it is a prime social obligation. Three months should be the outside limit even if there have been hundreds of gifts.

• •

Could you give me suggestions for suitable gifts for my bridesmaids and also some ideas of what my fiancé can give his ushers? Are there any special rules? W.S.B., ESSEX, CONNECTICUT

The only important rule is that the gifts be something that will be lasting mementos of the occasion. The gifts are usually silver or gold, engraved with the date and the initials of the recipient. The ushers' gifts—cuff links, key rings, silver ash trays, bill clips—should be all alike, as are those of the bridesmaids. The chief attendants receive the same kind of gifts—bracelets, charms, compacts (usually something to wear or carry) —but they vary a little in design and size to give a little more importance to the chief attendants' gifts.

• •

My daughter recently married a service man at a registry office. Her father and I sent out announcements and "at home" cards to relatives and friends. Within a matter of weeks the couple have separated and have started suit for divorce. What should my daughter do about the gifts she has received and is still receiving? What do I do about those friends who inquire about my daughter and ask for gift suggestions? Must I explain that divorce is pending? I feel this is much too personal a problem to discuss, and frankly I'm not up to it. MRS. H.E.K., ASHEVILLE, KENTUCKY

Your daughter is quite entitled to the gifts she has received and needn't worry about the necessity for returning them. Wedding gifts are returned only if the marriage is called off. She should send the usual thank-you note, without explanation of her problem, to those who send gifts. You can handle the situation on your end as delicately as possible by explaining that, as your daughter married a service man, her plans are rather indefinite and that she would prefer to wait before receiving any more gifts. I think that you show great sensitivity in not discussing the difficult problem you all face. Even when a situation has become so drastic that divorce proceedings have been started, there is always the hopeful possibility of reconciliation. Those around them should give the couple every chance to come together again. Try to get your daughter and her husband to seek professional aid, if possible, to save their marriage.

ANNIVERSARIES

What do you consider the major wedding anniversaries and what are the proper gifts for them? N.A., DETROIT, MICHIGAN

The most celebrated anniversaries are the first (paper, plastics, possibly furniture), the fifth (wood and decorative accessories for the home), the tenth (tin or aluminum), the twenty-fifth (silver or silver-like things, even silver-wrapped articles), the fiftieth (gold or gold-like things, or gold-wrapped ones) and the seventy-fifth (diamond, or diamond-like stones, or gold). Many substitute beautiful gifts in gold color, for example yellow roses.

When one receives an invitation to a golden wedding anniversary, must one send a gift? We have had several invitations during the past year and are elderly people with a small retirement income. MRS. R.N.W., ANN ARBOR, MICHIGAN

You are not obliged to send a gift under the circumstances, especially if you do not attend. If you do send a gift, you send something that is well within your means. If this cannot be done, write a warm letter of felicitation, send a telegram, or take yellow flowers from your garden or a potted plant you have grown (and gild the pot), or bake a batch of cookies with golden icing. No worthwhile friend asks the price of the gift you give. And if you have given of yourself in loving labor such a gift is beyond monetary valuation.

My wedding anniversary comes in the middle of winter. We would so much prefer to celebrate it in the spring or summer. Must you celebrate an anniversary on its actual date or would you say it is a movable feast? MRS. E.R., ST. PAUL, MINNESOTA

It is a movable feast. Celebrate it when it is convenient for you to do so any time during the anniversary year.

I am in doubt about my anniversary date. I lived with my husband for two years before we were married. Now we are going to celebrate our twenty-fifth anniversary but should we count it from the time we moved in together or from the time of the actual marriage? MRS. T.M., MEDFORD, OREGON

From the date of the actual marriage.

FUNERALS

FLOWERS

Can you tell me exactly how to send flowers to a funeral? How do I sign my name and do I address the flowers to the deceased or to his family? A.F., NEW ORLEANS, LOUISIANA

When flowers are sent to a funeral a plain white card is attached with the name of the sender, "Miss Helen Murray" or "Mr. and Mrs. Frederick Wallace," or a visiting card (a husband-and-wife card) may be used with a line drawn through the names in the case of intimate friends, and the message, "Deepest sympathy from Jean and Hugh," written in ink. The envelope is simply addressed to:

> The funeral of Mr. Lawrence Karl Volkman
> Silvan Funeral Home
> Greenpoint.

When the funeral is at home, is it correct to leave the name cards on flowers that have been sent and are banked against the casket? MRS. E.B.C., CHARLOTTE, NORTH CAROLINA

No, usually these are taken off by some member of the family or a funeral director's staff member who records "spray of carnations from the Gordon Joneses," so that the family member who acknowledges the flowers may make a specific reference to what was sent. It is always proper, if anyone asks, to say from whom a particularly lovely floral offering has come.

• •

When a death notice reads "Please omit flowers," does this mean you should send flowers under no circumstances? If the death notice suggests sending a check to a charity, how do you let the family know? MRS. R.M.H., BROOKLYN, NEW YORK

When the death notice reads "Please omit flowers," this request should be scrupulously respected. At some Protestant funerals the family prefers that the casket have one floral offering—that of the family. It is a growing custom for close friends to send flowers sometime during the weeks following the funeral (except to Orthodox Jews). The accompanying card should avoid reference to the bereavement. It may read: "Kindest thoughts from us all, Peggy and John." When a request that a check be sent to a charity is given, you send the check to the charity and write a note to the family without, however, specifying the amount you have given. The charity notifies the bereaved family.

When an engraved acknowledgment folder is sent out by a family after a funeral, is it necessary to send them to people who signed the funeral chapel register but did not send flowers? MRS. N.C., ALBANY, NEW YORK

Funeral calls are not returned so it is not necessary to send the foldover cards to those who have signed the registry.

I recently received a printed acknowledgment of flowers I had sent to the funeral of a friend. I know that these can be supplied by morticians (at extra cost) and that sometimes people have them engraved, but shouldn't some personal words be added? F.L., MEMPHIS, TENNESSEE

Yes, there should be some personal acknowledgment if only a few words for flowers, letters of condolence, telegrams, special services. These need not be written by the most bereaved (for example, the widow) and may be done by any member of the family or possibly a friend. Here is an example:

My friend, Mrs. Warren, has asked me to acknowledge your very kind gift of yellow chrysanthemums. They were of great comfort to her.

(signed) Annette Drew

DRESS

Do you feel it is essential for at least the family of the deceased to wear black at the funeral? And what about the children and the men? B.M.F., KANSAS CITY, MISSOURI

There is no insistence today that even immediate members of the family wear black to a funeral although many still do. Conservative clothes in quiet colors are acceptable. The black chiffon veil is still often worn by bereaved women at a funeral, but under most circumstances there is no requirement any more for headcovering. Stockings need not be black but can be in any neutral color. Men in the family wear dark business suits, preferably with black shoes and socks, white shirts, black or gray ties. Others wear conservative street clothes. In most communities even conservative pantsuits are not a good choice for a funeral. In most congregations now the wearing of a hat even to a funeral is optional. Men of the family sometimes wear cutaways for large church funerals as do men at state funerals.

Pantsuits have become a way of life with me. I wear conservative ones to church and feel quite comfortable, although I am in the minority. The question has arisen whether I would be suitably attired in a pantsuit at the funeral of someone in my immediate family. I will abide by your advice. MRS. F.H., CINCINATTI, OHIO

I agree that pantsuits are here to stay and most practical, especially for travel. It would be unwise, however, to wear such a relatively unconventional costume to a funeral for a member of the family. A dress or a suit would be much more acceptable.

FUNERAL CALLS

When a mortuary chapel is used, where does one make funeral calls? Must the family be represented at home as well as in the funeral chapel in order to receive calls? R.MC Q., TUCSON, ARIZONA

Now that the mortuary chapel has so much replaced the home in the laying out of the dead, people are often confused as to where they are expected to make their funeral calls. If they are close friends or relatives they may call both at home and at the chapel if they wish, leaving their cards or signing the register at the funeral chapel. If calls are received at the funeral chapel some family representative should be present, if possible, at least during the afternoon and early evening, when calls are likely to be made.

• •

Recently, having read the notice of the death of an old friend in the newspaper, I attended the funeral service. My daughter says it was incorrect for me to do this—that I should not have gone without an invitation. What is the etiquette in this case? MRS. J.H., RED BANK, NEW JERSEY

You were right. Unless the words "Funeral Private" appear in the death notice, any friend or acquaintance of the deceased or his family may attend the services, as do interested strangers if the funeral is in church. Close friends or relatives may ask the person in charge of arrangements for permission to attend the interment if they are able to provide their own transportation or if there seems to be adequate room in the funeral cars. They should be very certain that their presence at so difficult a time will be of real comfort to the immediate family, which usually prefers to be alone with the clergyman at the last brief rites.

• •

Will you please tell me the correct signature for a married woman when signing the register in a funeral home under the following circumstances:

1. If accompanied by husband, are both signatures signed on one line (like Mr. and Mrs.), or are they signed one beneath the other?
2. If husband and wife visit the funeral home at different hours (separately) does the earlier one visiting sign for the later one? P.S.F., OAKLAND, CALIFORNIA

1. They sign one line, "Helen and John Jones."
2. They sign for themselves separately as "Helen Jones" (or "Mrs. John Jones") and "John Jones."

PRESS NOTICES

How is a paid death notice inserted in newspapers? And who does it? O.T., NEW ORLEANS, LOUISIANA

The person in charge of the funeral prepares the death notices and may insert them himself in the local paper or have the mortician do so. A paid death notice may be phoned to papers selected, but it should always be *read* from carefully checked information. Where it is given over the phone, the newspaper's classified department usually calls back for recheck, to be certain the notice is legitimate. The form is:

Volkman—Lawrence Karl, on November 23 (year optional), husband (or beloved husband) of Helen Schroeder Volkman (his wife's maiden name is always given to aid identification) and father of Louise and Peter Schroeder Volkman (the daughters are listed first). Funeral at (name of church and address, if necessary), at 2 P.M., Tuesday.

Sometimes, especially when there was no generally known preliminary illness, the word "suddenly" may be added after the names of the immediate family. If a man was married his wife is always listed first, not his parents, whose names, in this case, usually do not appear in the paid notice but who are mentioned, of course, in news stories.

LETTER OF CONDOLENCE AND REPLY

How do you address a sympathy card to the married daughters and sons when the mother dies? Is it proper to sign it "Mr. and Mrs. Bowen and family"? A.S.M., HIGHLAND PARK, MICHIGAN

You address not a sympathy card but a personal note to the eldest daughter, who is now technically the female head of the family. In the letter, you refer in some way to the others. If a married couple is extending its sympathy, it is the wife who writes and in the body of the note refers to the sympathy also extended by the husband. It is she who signs the letter. She does not sign it "Mary and John."

Social letters of condolence, always handwritten on conservative paper, need not be long. In fact, "Deepest sympathy" may be written on your visiting card in black ink. You always address your letter to the nearest relative, whether or not you are acquainted. It is better to avoid the words "died," "death," and "killed" in such letters. It is quite possible to write the kind of letter that will give a moment of courage and a strong feeling of sympathy without mentioning death or sadness at all. For instance:

Dear Jeanette:
It is several years since I have seen Larry, but it was with a real sense of loss that I heard the news. He will always be with us in spirit.

Most sincerely,

Mary

• •

The death of a loved one occurred in our family a short time ago. Different members of the family have received numerous letters, notes, and cards of condolence.

Should these be acknowledged by us? J.J.M., HEMP-STEAD, NEW YORK

Those members of the family who have received letters of condolence answer them possibly on the family's foldover acknowledgment cards if only with a few words written inside. Cards of condolence are not properly sent but if received may be acknowledged verbally or by personal notes on personally engraved cards or folders, if they are used.

In reply one may write at any length one wishes, but it is quite understandable that the note be brief, even to a close friend. Today it is usually on plain white paper. Black-bordered mourning paper is rare.

CUSTOMS OF DIFFERENT FAITHS

May a non-Catholic arrange for a mass card to be sent to a bereaved Catholic family? May he have a mass said for a Catholic friend who is ill? If so, how is this done? A.M., DES MOINES, IOWA

Yes, this may be done by anyone. The person who wishes the mass said calls upon any Catholic priest, either in his friend's parish or in his own locality. He asks that the mass be said and he sometimes indicates the exact time he wishes it celebrated. The priest then gives the mass card to the donor, who may send it to the family or deliver it when making a funeral call. These masses may be arranged, too, for a year after the death, on its anniversary, or any time immediately after death has taken place. Recovery masses are often said for Catholics who are ill or facing operations. In this instance, a mass card may be taken by the donor to home or hospital when the sick call is being made or may be mailed. The person who arranges the mass makes a voluntary contribution to the church in which it is said—the amount varying, according to his own particular circumstances, around $5.00, depending on the kind of mass said.

• •

Should a Protestant send flowers to an Orthodox Jewish funeral? J.A., LOUISVILLE, KENTUCKY

No. To Orthodox Jews flowers are a sign of joy—they should never be sent to a funeral. Often, too, flowers are not desired at a Conservative or Reform funeral.

• •

I sometimes see Catholic funerals with masses of flowers in the cortege—although I understand it isn't customary for other than the family's flowers to be allowed in the church at a Catholic funeral. Is this correct? M.J.W., MONTCLAIR, NEW JERSEY

Many Catholics seem to prefer mass cards (see preceding) to flowers. In some Catholic parishes only the family's flowers are permitted in the church, although, of course, other flowers may be sent to the home or funeral home and be taken to the cemetery.

SPECIAL PROBLEMS

Please tell me what the correct name is for the grave marker of a widow. For example, Mary Elizabeth Smith married George Dwight Reilly. When she passes on, does her grave marker read: Mary S. Reilly or Mary E. Reilly? MRS. I.J.P., MINOT, NORTH DAKOTA

There is no very definite rule about this, and it is done both ways, either with the baptismal name—Mary Elizabeth—or with the maiden name, Mary Smith, combined with Reilly, her married name. However, my preference and that of top church authorities I have discussed this with is for the retention of the maiden name for the sake of clearer family records. Therefore, it seems preferable for the marker to read Mary Smith Reilly.

• •

When you have been invited to attend a funeral in a friend's family what is the proper reply? MRS. S.F., WATERVILLE, MAINE

You say, "Thank you for telling me. I'll be there." You obviously avoid any phrase that makes your acceptance sound like one to a social occasion. You cannot be "happy" to attend a funeral.

My husband, when I married him, was a widower. He had his wife buried in a family plot. When he died, he was buried at his request along side of his first wife. I would like to have a marker set for me now. The marker for his first wife says "beloved wife". May I use this phrase too? We had a very loving marriage. MRS. J.F., PROVIDENCE, RHODE ISLAND

You may certainly put your marker in now with just your date of birth, your name and "beloved wife of" in the same style as was used on the first marker. Such monuments are often put in place by the living with just the name and date of birth inscribed. Later, at the proper time, the final date is added.

When a funeral service is held in church, does the minister receive a fee? Is this taken care of by the funeral director of the family? J.K.T., COLUMBUS, OHIO

It is usual (but not universal) for the minister to be given an honorarium for his services. Sometimes an appropriate amount is sent to him by the funeral director, who includes this expense on his bill. More often it is sent by a member of the family in a letter of appreciation for his comfort and help.

The amount should be based on the family's ability to make a contribution. Simplicity of the funeral is today no indication of lack of funds. Certainly if the funeral has been large and expensive the clergyman should not receive less than seventy-five to one hundred dollars. From the average family he usually receives from five to twenty-five dollars. Checks should be made out to the clergyman rather than to the church, as these fees are expected to contribute to his own expenses.

The sexton in a large church is on the church payroll and devotes full time to church business affairs. He receives twenty-five dollars or more for his work at a large funeral. In a small church the custodian, paid by the church, fulfills the sexton's duties. He appreciates a small fee of say ten or fifteen dollars, as does the organist.

• •

We had a death in our family some nine months ago. With Christmas approaching I feel I would like to send Christmas cards to my friends, but my mother feels that it would be disrespectful to our father. I don't know why my mother couldn't send cards, too. R.C., OAK PARK, MICHIGAN

The modern feeling is that we do not shut off warm contacts with our friends during our period of mourning. Now, after three months of social restriction, most people gradually resume a normal way of living. I agree with you that you may send Christmas cards to your own friends, but they should be very conservative ones. Insofar as your mother is concerned, it depends on how she really feels about it, but there again she may now send conservative Christmas cards, or, if she prefers, little notes of Christmas greeting to her close friends.

• •

I am divorced. My former husband's death seems rather imminent. If he dies, should I accompany my children to his funeral? My children are between the ages of ten and fifteen. There has been considerable bad feeling as a result of the divorce, and perhaps my presence at the funeral would be open to criticism on the grounds of insincerity, to say the least. R.J., BIRMINGHAM, MICHIGAN

I feel, too, that you should go for your children's sake. They will need your support. This is no time for bitterness. Keep in mind the happiness you must have had at some time with your former husband.

YOUR MANNERS
AWAY FROM HOME

DRESS AND CUSTOMS
ON SHIPS, PLANES, AND TRAINS

I am going to Europe by ship in the early spring. What sort of clothes should I take for wear abroad? What sort of things should my husband take? M.T.S., ROCHESTER, NEW YORK

Clothing aboard ship is casual during the daytime—the sort of clothes worn at a country club in any good resort. At best they are conservative, with shorts and bathing apparel confined to the swimming and sports area. Slacks on women are seen on all decks, to some extent in the dining room for breakfast and at lunch. Men wear coats at all meals, too, on first-class liners. They do not wear sport clothes at night except under certain circumstances—for example, the night of embarkation and the night of debarkation and for certain informal parties aboard—in the public rooms or dining room. Women may or may not wear sport hats or scarves, as they please, on deck or at daytime meals. In the evening, except in tourist and cabin class, there is some attempt at formality, depending, of course, on the ship on which one travels. On the great transatlantic liners dinner jackets are the general, though not obligatory, rule. It is never bad taste to appear in dinner dress, and on ships where a Captain's or Gala Dinner is given, formality is expected, with men wearing dinner jackets and women appearing, if they wish, in full evening dress. On some ships this special night is made into a fancy dress affair, which permits considerable leeway in costumes. These are usually available from the ship's stores, but if you know a costume affair to be the ship's

custom you may take along your own costume. Those
that win the prizes, however, are usually the ones that
are extemporized out of whatever happens to be on
hand in one's baggage. But quite a few diehards attend
such evenings in their usual clothes and enjoy themselves nonetheless, with perhaps a paper hat added to
give the right festive note.

• •

**My husband and I are taking a cruise. Are there any
nights that we don't dress? We are taking dinner
clothes for the really festive nights we know are
planned.** E.H., SALT LAKE CITY, UTAH

On the first night and the last night aboard people
usually don't dress for dinner but wear their ordinary
travel clothes. This is because on the first night one is
just unpacking and on the last night one has just packed
up. The nights following shore excursions are "don't
dress" nights. Bulletins distributed to staterooms each
morning make dress suggestions.

• •

**If a woman is traveling alone (divorced, widowed, or
just traveling without her husband), is it proper for her
to dress formally on dress nights on a cruise?** MRS. A.C.,
ALBERT LEA, MINNESOTA

Of course. She dresses the way the others do. Most
ships' bulletins indicate what dress is expected at night.
People usually don't dress when the ship is in port
unless they are going to some special place on land, for
example, a gambling casino (but not necessarily even
then).

**My travel agency tells me that on the ship I'm going on,
you don't dress the first night or the last because you
are presumably packed up and should be wearing travel
clothes. Would there be anything wrong in taking a
dress bag containing a silk dress (long or short) which**

I would prefer to wear to dinner, rather than the suit in which I am planning to travel? MRS. H.W., DALLAS, TEXAS

Nothing wrong. In fact many experienced travelers among women do exactly that. Because there is dancing on cruises the first night and the last, dresses are more comfortable to dance in than travel clothes. Men, however, usually wear their travel clothes on embarkation night and debarkation night, but they may also change into more comfortable clothes if it suits them.

Our whole family is going to Europe for the summer. Should we let our friends know that we'd like them to see us off? If so, are there any special arrangements that need to be made with the steamship company? If they ask us if we would like gifts, what do you think is suitable? Our family consists of two almost grown up teen-age children, a boy and a girl, my husband, and myself. C.D.G., LARCHMONT, NEW YORK

International traveling is becoming so very common for Americans that there is much less elaborate "seeing off" of people on boats than there used to be. However, you may certainly tell your friends the date and time of your embarkation and invite them to come aboard if they would like to. It is advisable to ask the steamship line what the permissible visiting hours are, then, if you expect friends, get aboard with your family in plenty of time to receive the earliest comers. If friends actually ask you what you would like as a bon voyage gift, try to suggest something that you would have included in your regular luggage. The meals aboard the great liners are so varied and sumptuous these days that the old-time huge baskets of fruit given to departing voyagers often go to waste. Too many flowers, too, crowd a stateroom, and few women these days wear corsages aboard ship or elsewhere. The best gifts for the ship's passengers are magazines, pantyhose, paperbacks, travel tissues, films, gum, cosmetics, scarves, underwear, compact kits of various kinds. One of the very nicest is for the visitor to make arrangements with the steamship company to serve a bottle of wine or champagne during the voyage with the compliments of the donor.

• •

I have some friends who are going to Europe by air. As their closest friends, should my husband and I give them a going-away present? Are we expected to see them off? MRS. N.G.B., CHAPPAQUA, NEW YORK

It is much more convenient to see friends off on such a trip by plane in your own home town rather than at the airport. There, visitors are rarely allowed beyond the gates, and farewells are very brief. As for gifts, you know that there are severe weight restrictions on luggage. Take nothing to your friends, if you do go to their point of embarkation, that will add to the weight of their luggage. If well in advance of their packing you want to give them articles of clothing in nylon and the other miracle fibers, these are always welcome to the plane traveler. Pantyhose, tiny packets of detergents put up for travelers, airplane luggage, paperback books, plastic-packaged toiletries should all be welcome.

• •

Under what circumstances is it all right for a man to talk to a woman when traveling? I am a friendly person and I know there are rules about this, so perhaps I am being overcautious. J.G.R., FAR ROCKAWAY, NEW YORK

On short train and bus rides there is rarely any conversation between seatmates. People read their papers and books and do not encourage conversation from strangers under these circumstances. On long bus rides and long train rides, some conversation is usual but should be kept on a highly impersonal level and names are not usually exchanged. Airplane travel is so very usual these days that sometimes one can travel halfway across the continent without saying a word to a seatmate. On the other hand, limited conversation may be welcome. On boats one speaks to fellow passengers and enters into conversation that seems welcome without special introduction. A passenger who does not wish to engage in conversation can always answer in a monosyllable and take up reading matter which he providentially has brought with him.

• •

When you have a compartment or a roomette on an Amtrak train, is it proper to tell a porter when you want to retire? And where do you go while he is making up the berth? What is the function of the stewardess on the train? L.A., NORWALK, CONNECTICUT

You may tell the porter at what time you would like to retire. As he has many other berths to make up, however, give him plenty of advance notice. While he is making up your berth you may sit in other unoccupied seats, go to the lounge, observation car, or the dining car. If a mother and small child occupy a whole section, it is perfectly proper to have the lower berth made up at any time during the day if you prefer to recline during the trip. Elderly or ill people often do the same thing.

The stewardess is in effect the hostess on the train to answer questions. If you want room service instead of going to the dining car, the porter brings you a menu and takes your order.

• •

In passing a woman in a narrow corridor of a train, what should I do so that she may pass without coming into close contact with me? D.J., MAMARONECK, NEW YORK

You step into an empty compartment if there is one, or if there isn't, you flatten yourself, face inward, against either wall.

TIPPING ON SHIPS, PLANES, AND TRAINS

I am about to go abroad for the first time. Can you give me the rules for tipping aboard ship? G.M., NEW ORLEANS, LOUISIANA

Just before debarking, a passenger tips the following personnel: room steward, table steward, headwaiter, wine steward, if he's been used, the deck and bath stewards. The steward who has taken care of your cabin receives seven-fifty to ten dollars per person as does the table steward and head waiter. Ladies are attended by both steward and stewardess. The tip of seven-fifty to ten dollars is divided between them at the end of the voyage. Deck stewards receive one dollar or more depending on the amount of service they have rendered. Passengers without private bath tip the bath steward one dollar at the end of the voyage, and the "boots" receives one dollar for keeping shoes shined. Cabin boys are usually tipped at the time they perform their small services, if at all. Bar attendants are usually tipped at the time of service if the bill is settled at the time. If the check is signed by a regular frequenter of the smoking room, he might prefer to tip at the end of the voyage. On some ships the card-signing custom prevails, on others payment is required at the time of ordering. On most ships the chief steward is classed as a ship's officer and, as such, is never tipped.

• •

How do you tip a Pullman porter for a short ride, and for an overnight one? R.N., DETROIT, MICHIGAN

For a very short train ride in a Pullman, say two and one half hours, it is usual to tip the porter twenty-five cents—even if he has performed no service for you such as brushing your clothes or handling your luggage. Overnight it is usually a minimum of fifty cents per night and as much as a dollar if there has been much baggage that he has had to handle in making up your berth and in getting you off the train.

• •

I never know how to tip aboard a train when I am having a meal and whom to tip. For example, does the head steward who comes out and seats me expect a tip or just the steward who waits on me? What about the steward in the observation car who serves drinks? D.L.C., NEW BRUNSWICK, NEW JERSEY

A dining car steward is tipped 15 per cent of the bill, never less than a quarter per person if a meal has been served. An observation car steward who has served drinks is tipped 15 per cent of the total bar bill, not less than a quarter. The head steward is not tipped unless he has performed some very special service.

• •

I am making my first airplane trip in a number of years. I can't remember whom you tip and I've heard that the planes don't serve meals free anymore. Can you help me out? J.H.H., PATERSON, NEW JERSEY

You do not tip anyone aboard an airplane, as all the crew have a professional status. When you pick up your luggage at the destination the airline provides porter service from the plane into the checkout area. Some lines have porter service for ticketed passengers at their entrance doors so luggage can go right on the planes. Tip the sky cap 25 cents per bag. Staff porters within the luggage area are not tipped but porters (sky caps) who take over from them and carry your luggage to waiting limousines or taxis are tipped approximately twenty-five cents per bag. On some planes now (particularly on the tourist flights) no real meals are served, but coffee and other beverages and frequently little snacks are served free. On regular flights it is sometimes advisable to ask whether they are luncheon or dinner flights before taking off. Meals are always served on the international planes. These regular meals are free. There is a charge for alcoholic beverages in tourist class.

• •

I have not traveled frequently for many years, and I understand the regulations regarding the tipping of redcaps in railroad stations have changed and that they are often different in different localities. Can you set me right? MRS. M.T.D., EL PASO, TEXAS

In most terminals redcaps get a standard price per bag, as much as thirty-five cents per bag in city areas. A tip on top of this fee is usual where the service has been prompt, courteous, and efficient. In areas where redcaps do not receive a set fee, a minimum of a quarter per bag is expected possibly, plus a tip of a quarter or more, depending on the amount and weight of the bags. In some of the big terminals self-service porterage is available. The patron pays a quarter for the cart and conveys his own luggage.

HOTELS

When a man and wife are registering in a hotel, who signs the register and how does it read? MRS. B.C.E., YORK, PENNSYLVANIA

It really doesn't matter who signs, but the register should read Mr. and Mrs. John B. Barrett. If there are young children, their names should be added as Lucy and Thomas. A daughter over eighteen is registered as Miss Elsie Barrett. A boy eighteen or over is Mr. James Barrett.

• •

What is the best way to reserve a hotel room? MRS. G.K., NASHVILLE, TENNESSEE

If the hotel you plan to stay in is part of a chain, the local outlet will make a reservation for you in any of its other hotels, usually by teletype, giving you an immediate confirmation. You can do this by phone to the hotel near you. If space is available, you are usually requested to send a deposit equal to one day's charge to the hotel where the reservation has been made. Travel agents will also make hotel reservations for you at no additional cost.

• •

I am puzzled by the travel brochures which say in the hotel ads "European plan" or "American plan." Can you explain the difference to me? G.P., MAYSVILLE, KENTUCKY

European plan means room alone without meals. (Continental breakfast—coffee and rolls—is included except in tour packages.) American plan means room and meals.

• •

What is the proper procedure in checking out of a hotel? T.K., EL PASO, TEXAS

If you have luggage with which you need assistance, you pick up the phone and say, "I'm checking out. Will you send a bellman." If you have, say, only one small bag you wish to carry yourself, you may carry it to the lobby where you may, if you wish, refuse the services of a bellman while checking out at the desk.

TIPPING IN HOTELS

Are you supposed to tip the chambermaid in a hotel, even if you don't see her? M.S.T., QUINCY, MASSACHU-SETTS

In hotels where one is a transient the tip for the chambermaid is twenty-five cents to fifty cents for an overnight stay, depending on the quality of hotel. The tip is best left under a pillow on the bed if one leaves before the beds are made up; otherwise it may be left in a marked envelope at the desk, or given to the housekeeper who will see that she receives it. In a hotel where one is a resident the chambermaid receives a dollar a week, more or less, depending on the quality of the hotel. Where a guest stays a week or two the chambermaid receives a dollar per week for each bedroom in her charge.

• •

How do you tip a hotel porter? MRS. H.D., MIAMI, FLORIDA

A hotel porter receives fifty cents per trunk carried up to a room. If there is other heavy baggage as well, a dollar or more. If he performs special services, such as making reservations or securing theater tickets, he receives anything from fifty cents to two or three dollars, depending on the difficulty involved.

• •

What's the difference in tips for a bellman who brings up your bags and for one who just delivers a package or brings up your mail? S.T., EL PASO, TEXAS

The minimum standard tip for a bellman carrying up luggage for a newly registered guest or couple is a quarter per bag if he is able to bring all the luggage in one trip. Bellmen who deliver packages, a newspaper, or other small things to the room receive a quarter.

• •

How much do page boys in hotels get for summoning guests? C.A.P., WASHINGTON, DISTRICT OF COLUMBIA

Page boys usually receive a tip of a quarter from the person paged.

• •

I noticed a lot of hotels have Servidors so that the valet can pick up your clothes and leave them for you, but you never see him. What happens if a valet brings

pressed clothes back to you—to the door? Do you tip him? C.T., CHARLOTTE, NORTH CAROLINA

Hotel valets, usually operating their own shops within a hotel, do not expect tips, except for rush jobs or those done outside of the usual hours.

• •

I live in a residence hotel and wonder whether I am supposed to tip the elevator starter after I have been here for a few months. J.A.M.C., MIAMI, FLORIDA

A resident in a hotel usually tips the elevator man regularly, giving him a dollar a month, approximately, and remembers the starter, too, at regular intervals.

• •

I live in a hotel and frequently have my meals sent up. I get confused when I order something like a pot of tea, because 10 or 15 per cent of that order would be very little for the waiter's time. Can you help me out? N.L., TOLEDO, OHIO

Room waiters are tipped not less than a quarter—for an individual small order such as a pot of tea and toast. For a dinner order it is 15 per cent of the bill. If wine has been served there should be an extra tip for the handling and serving of it. Guests may add a notation at the bottom of the bill concerning the amount of the tip they wish given the room waiter. Resident guests tip room waiters for each service, too, but usually see that head room waiters receive a tip about twice a year, the tip depending on the amount of room service the guest requires—a minimum of five dollars each time and possibly as much as ten.

• •

It certainly seems to be that a disproportionate amount of my income goes for tipping, as I travel a lot in my work. For instance, should I tip a hotel doorman just

for opening the door of my cab? J.A., JAMAICA, NEW YORK

No, not if he performs no other service. If, however, he helps to unload the cab with a great deal of your luggage, even though he just takes it to the entrance of the hotel, he expects a tip—perhaps a quarter. If he must go out in the rain to find you a cab in the midst of traffic, you gauge the tip by the amount of trouble he has had. You might give him twenty-five cents, or even fifty cents, or in a stormy night or very late, as much as a dollar if he has a hard time finding a cab. Those who seek shelter under a hotel marquee in the rain (especially if they are not guests at the hotel) tip the doorman anything from a quarter to a dollar for summoning a cab, depending on the difficulty he has had in procuring one.

RESTAURANTS

Who goes first into a restaurant, a lady or her escort? J.H., ST. LOUIS, MISSOURI

On entering a restaurant door a lady goes first if there is an attendant to hold the door open for her, otherwise her escort provides this service. Once inside, the man moves his companion out of the traffic, checks his things, then moves at her side, or slightly in advance, to the entrance to the dining room. There, if the captain comes to meet them, the man indicates their wishes, the lady steps forward and follows the captain to the table indicated, allowing herself to be seated. If there is no captain, her escort leads the way into the dining room, locates a table, and seats his companion himself. On leaving the man goes first, if the restaurant is crowded, making a pathway for the lady. If the captain comes forward to see them out, the man then steps back and lets the lady follow the captain. But an escorted lady is never left to make her way through a crowded restaurant alone.

• •

Another couple often goes with us to restaurants. They are about our age and I wonder what is the proper way for the women to be seated. What happens when we are dining with a couple that is very much older? L.N., QUINCY, MASSACHUSETTS

When two young couples seat themselves at a table, the women take chairs opposite each other. If one man is the host, he tries to seat himself so the woman to be honored is at his right even if it is his wife—for example, on her birthday or their anniversary. No great point, however, need be made these days over the seating at a banquette (built-in wall seats). If a younger couple is dining with a much older one, the older couple is offered the wall seats and the younger couple sits together on the aisle so that the younger man is opposite the older woman. When two women are seated together opposite the two men, they sit opposite their own escorts—husbands or not.

• •

When dining in a restaurant, does the hostess give the entire order for the guests or are individual orders taken by the waiter or waitress? When just two—man and woman—dine together, who gives the order? MRS. D.A.N., EVANSTON, ILLINOIS

When quite a few people sit down together in a restaurant, it is much simpler if individual orders are taken by the waiter or waitress, unless the host or hostess has ordered the entire dinner, the same for everyone, in advance. When just two, a man and a woman, dine together, the man asks the woman what she would like to have—perhaps makes some suggestions—and gives the order to the waiter. If the dinner is table d'hôte the waiter asks the woman what she will have and takes the order from her. Even in a fashionable restaurant waiters now expect a woman to give her order direct to save time at a busy period.

At an intimate restaurant dinner where the host or hostess's voice can clearly be heard the length of the table, a guest may accept the card from the waiter and make a selection, but he then waits for his host to ask him what he would like and permits his host to place the order. At a table of women where there is no question of there being a hostess but all plan to pay for themselves, orders are always given individually, even in a very small group such as four.

• •

When two couples or more have dinner out, is the bill afterwards to be split evenly or is each couple to pay for what they ordered? For instance, if one couple orders hamburgers and the other sirloin steak, one couple does not order drinks and the other does, when the check comes do even the drinks have to be paid for by the non-drinker? This has caused hard feelings. My husband feels that if he orders less he should not be expected to pay a split bill at the end of the evening.
E.R., OAKLAND, CALIFORNIA

If there is a large discrepancy between the amounts spent by the two couples, it is perfectly acceptable for the man of the couple which spent less to say, "Let me figure out what we owe on this." Where there is very little difference it might be considered niggardly to be meticulous about the division of cost.

• •

In a night club, when a large party enters with the host and hostess, shouldn't the maître d' seat the guests to avoid confusion? T.E.R., YUMA, ARIZONA

No. The maître d' does not know the guests and wouldn't know where to place them so that all will be congenial. The hostess seats her guests, or, if there is a host alone, he performs this function.

• •

We like to dine at a smörgåsbord restaurant. When we take guests should I, as hostess, lead them to the table,

or should I let the men, including my husband, go to the table and choose the women's food? Or doesn't it matter who goes first to the table? L.E.J., ADRIAN, MICHIGAN

A smörgåsbord meal is very informal, but you could lead the way to the table. If the restaurant is very crowded and there is no waiter to clear the way for you, your husband would go first, followed by any of your women guests. He could offer to serve his companion or merely hand her a plate and suggest that she make her own selections. People usually prefer to do this at the bounteous board.

• •

Recently, when four of us were dining out—two married couples—one of the husbands left the table for a few minutes. The remaining husband, left with his wife and the wife of the other, lit the cigarette first of his friend's wife, then of his own. His wife felt that as her escort he should have lit her cigarette first. Which is correct? MRS. R.L.V., COLUMBUS, OHIO

As one woman was left alone, the husband and wife remaining are, in effect, her host and hostess for the moment. Therefore it was correct for the remaining husband to light the guest's cigarette first, then his wife's.

• •

Recently I was a guest at a club luncheon in a restaurant. Accidentally, I overturned my tomato juice. What was the right thing to do? The waiter didn't see the accident immediately. MRS. R.B.C., SOUTH BEND, INDIANA

A waiter seeing such an accident would immediately change the cloth, or, if that was impossible at a long table, would spread a clean napkin over the spilled food. As the waiter did not do this because he was busy

elsewhere at such a large luncheon, you could have
spread a napkin over the spot yourself, without undue
discussion of the incident. Everyone occasionally has
things like this happen.

• •

**Three or four of us men executives meet once or twice
a week for lunch in a near-by restaurant. Our practice
is for the first one there to reserve a table. But if one is
late, must the others wait before seating themselves and
beginning the meal?** J.A.L., NEW YORK, NEW YORK

The first one to arrive tells the headwaiter or hostess
how many he is expecting in his party. When the majority have arrived, they seat themselves, leaving word
that they have gone on in. For a whole party to wait
for the late-comer may mean that they cannot get a
table reservation at all. For them to seat themselves and
then try to wait until the missing guest arrives would be
to hold up the restaurant unfairly. If the late-comer is a
client or superior, however, the others do wait outside,
even though this may mean a delay in getting a table
when they want it. When there is a long line, the headwaiter or hostess usually assigns a number to a party.
If the party is late assembling, you merely say that you
do not want the table at the time that it is offered but
will let the hostess or headwaiter know when your party
is all together.

• •

**What do you do with the wrapper on a lump of sugar
when you are dining out in a restaurant? Do you put
it on the tablecloth, in the saucer of your cup, or in
the ash tray?** E.F., TOLEDO, OHIO

This is one of those things for which there is no real
rule. You just use common sense. I would say put it
on the tablecloth, for if you put it in the ash tray it may
start a fire, and if you put it in your saucer it may
cause the cup to tip over when you put it back in the

saucer after taking a drink. If it is on the tablecloth the waiter will clear it off along with crumbs.

• •

My friend always insists on wiping off the table silver with his napkin when we go out to restaurants, cheap or expensive. I claim it is just a bad habit with him. He insists it is a sanitary precaution. Should he do this? N.J., PASADENA, CALIFORNIA

He should not do this, even in cheap restaurants. If the silver seems dirty he should quickly ask the waiter to replace it with clean silver. If there is any reluctance on the part of the waiter or of the manager, a complaint should be sent to the Department of Health. No one who must or who chooses to eat in a restaurant in this country need be exposed to any unsanitary conditions. He need only insist on his rights. From a practical standpoint, of course, a dry napkin, however clean, is not going to remove any dirt from the utensils. Soap and hot water are called for.

• •

Will you please tell me what you consider the correct way of disposing of the small tea bag on a string served in a cup of tea in most restaurants these days. It seems kind of messy to remove it and place it in the saucer beside the cup, but, with no special dish provided to hold it, just what should be done with it? MRS. T.L.B., SALEM, MASSACHUSETTS

The only thing to do is to lift it by the tag and perhaps let it drain a little before placing it in the saucer. If you have a butter plate and wish to place it there, that is also permissible. The very best solution of course, for the restaurant, would be to serve the tea in individual pots so that the tea bags could stay out of sight.

• •

What's the proper way to get the attention of a waiter or waitress in a restaurant? P.K., MERIDEN, CONNECTI-CUT

A good waiter or waitress is attentive at all times to the possible needs of the patron. All that should be necessary in a properly staffed restaurant is for the diner to lift his hand—or one finger—in a summoning gesture. If this fails to get attention, the diner calls softly, "Waiter!" or "Waitress!" (not "Sir!" or "Miss!"). Glass rapping, a European expedient, should be resorted to only in desperation. You may also ask another waiter or waitress to fetch yours.

• •

When there is no host or hostess—for example, when friends are eating together in a restaurant—when does one pick up his napkin, and is it still good manners to hold one's left hand in the lap? MR. R.J.L., DENVER, COLORADO

When there is no host or hostess, the diner picks up his napkin as soon as he is seated, but if there are ladies present they take the initiative. When you leave the table temporarily, put the napkin casually to the left of the place setting. A dinner napkin should not be shaken out or tucked in (except for children), but it is laid lengthwise across the knees. It should be used to dab the lips whenever necessary—especially before one drinks any beverage. Such drinks, by the way, should be taken only when the mouth is empty.

It is optional whether the left hand, when one is eating, is held in the lap, American style, or resting in a relaxed fashion to the left of the place setting, European style. I prefer the latter as more natural, because it gives better balance to the body. But there should be no lounging at the table.

• •

A date and I went to a neighborhood restaurant to eat dinner Saturday night. The only available seats were in

a booth for four in which a lone man was already seated. I asked my date to ask this man to share the booth with us. My date said that was not correct and refused to do so. Was he right? A.L.C., DALLAS, TEXAS

It depends on the policy of the restaurant. In a self-service restaurant you take any available seat. In a restaurant with service, especially in one with a headwaiter or hostess, you wait to be assigned to seats. Most restaurants try to seat lone diners at tables for two or one, but where this is impossible they usually do not ask that such accommodations as a booth be shared with strangers. Under crowded conditions, restaurants sometimes ask a man to share a table with another man but not with a woman and vice versa. I feel that your date was right and that essentially his objection was to having your privacy disturbed by a stranger. How could conversation be possible under such circumstances? You might have had an embarrassing situation had the stranger decided to join your conversation. This is the sort of thing that good restaurants try to avoid.

When a man is ordering for the lady he is escorting, what should he say to the waiter? G.M., ATLANTA, GEORGIA

He says, "The lady will have . . ." In a place where their names are known to the employees, for example in a hotel where they are staying, or in a club, he could say, "My wife will have . . ." or "Mrs. Smith will have . . ." The thing you should avoid is saying *"She* will have . . ."

When you are waiting at a restaurant table for someone to join you, is it proper to nibble on something if you are hungry? MRS. G.L., BOSTON, MASSACHUSETTS

Many restaurants have such things as celery, olives, radishes, perhaps cocktail crackers or rolls on the table. You may certainly nibble on these before a guest comes. You may order a cocktail or other before-the-meal beverage if you wish, eating any little appetizer that might come with it, such as salted nuts. You should order nothing more substantial unless it seems obvious that your guest is going to be very late and you might miss an appointment. You should wait a reasonable amount of time, say twenty minutes.

Sometimes when I go to a restaurant I get vegetables served in little side dishes. I like to eat everything off my dinner plate. Is it all right to transfer the vegetables from these side dishes to the dinner plate, and if so, how? H.M., WESTFIELD, NEW JERSEY

You certainly may, and you do it with your fork.

TIPPING IN RESTAURANTS

I am not always certain who to tip and how much to tip in restaurants. Can you help me? P.W., WOONSOCKET, RHODE ISLAND

If one frequents a certain restaurant, it is not necessary for him to tip the headwaiter on each occasion, unless he has had special consideration—worked out the menu in advance with the headwaiter, had his table changed, or ordered some spectacular dish such as crêpes suzette, the completion of which has been presided over by this factotum. The tip is given on the way out. When the headwaiter is also an owner of the place he receives no tip but is thanked on the way out if he shows out his guests.

Such a tip is quietly slipped into the waiting palm in an unobvious manner, but if the room headwaiter is not at his post he is not sought out by the patron. The tendered tip in an expensive place is usually two to five dollars. In a less elaborate establishment it is certainly never silver—always at least a dollar.

The wine steward, if his services have been enlisted, receives 15 per cent of the wine bill in round figures.

In restaurants that employ headwaiters for sections —men who do no more than take the order and pass it on to table waiters for execution—no tip is expected by the section headwaiter, unless, of course, special service has been requested in which he has taken some active part. In that case his tip is not less than a dollar bill and may be two dollars if the party comprises more than two people.

A waiter receives 15 per cent to 20 per cent or possibly more (depending on the place) in round figures (don't leave pennies on the plate unless they add up to an even amount). If the bill is very small, at a counter for example, the server should receive a minimum of ten cents per person. In night clubs, fifty cents per person, minimum.

A cigarette girl usually arranges her change to indicate what she'd like to get, but ten or fifteen cents surcharge on a pack of cigarettes is enough and no one need feel like Shylock for picking up the additional change from a dollar bill.

The bus boy is not tipped. In a nightclub or expensive restaurant the attendants in the men's and women's lounges usually put decoy coins on a plate to indicate what they expect in the way of a tip, as does the hat-check girl, usually a quarter. Unless some service has been asked, the tip need not be, for instance, a quarter, but can well be ten or fifteen cents.

Doormen who perform a service—secure a taxi, summon or bring your parked car—usually receive a quarter.

• •

Why aren't bus boys in hotels and restaurants tipped?
J.L., HOUSTON, TEXAS

Because the waiter for whom he clears the tables shares his tips with him. In resort hotels, however, student bus boys *are* tipped.

• •

In a restaurant, is it okay to leave an extra large tip for especially good service and vice versa for very poor service? Or should one leave the usual standard tip regardless of the quality of the service, whether it is

very poor or extremely good? C.S., MONTCLAIR, NEW
JERSEY

Anyone who works at a job should have pride in what
he does and the way he does it. Most waiters and
waitresses do an excellent job and try to please their
customers. Occasionally, however, one gets surly and
inefficient service. I believe in reward and punishment.
If you believe the service has been deliberately bad—
in effect, no service at all—and if you have the courage
to do so, leave no tip. If the service is good, always
commend either with a kind word or with a little extra
on the tip if you can afford it. While we should think
of a tip as additional payment for service, certainly it
is not required where the services were nil.

• •

**When I was in Chicago I saw one restaurant there
that had the checkroom attendant on its payroll, and it
had a row of boxes labeled with the names of various
charities. There was a sign explaining that tipping was
not permitted, but that patrons could if they wished
donate to these various charities. I thought this was a
very nice idea. However, in most restaurants you are
expected to tip. What's the rule?** L.A., SOUTH NORWALK,
CONNECTICUT

I, too, think that Chicago restaurant had a very good
idea. I know it's very hard sometimes for a man to
have to retrieve his hat at the price of the expected
tip. If he moves around much this can be very expensive. However, here is the rule. At any checkroom in
a hotel specially set up to serve a special affair such as
a dance or ball, the attendant receives a quarter per
person unless the gratuities have been taken care of by
those sponsoring the affair. At a mere cloakroom outside a hotel restaurant the usual tip is also a quarter.

• •

**My husband and I are going to a big testimonial dinner
at a hotel. We've bought our own tickets but will be**

at a table with others we don't know. What does my husband do about tips—if anything? MRS. J.D.B., TOLEDO, OHIO

At public dinners there is sometimes a small card on each table which reads, "Gratuities have been taken care of by the Dinner Committee"—a very good idea. If there is no such card at the table, the waiters, immediately after the service of dessert and coffee and before the speaking begins, come to the host or hostess of each table and place a silver salver before him or her, often with a murmured explanation that something is expected for the table's waiters. Unless all at the table are personally invited guests, the host or hostess makes no attempt to tip for the whole table but after placing a dollar (per service for which he or she feels responsible) on the tray, directs the waiter to the gentlemen at the table, each of whom should leave (at a $10.00 per plate dinner) a dollar and a half for himself and the same for the lady he escorts. Women should never be approached for tips if there are gentlemen at the table.

THEATERS

What do you do with ticket stubs? Is it necessary to hold on to them until the end of the show? MRS. S.D., LONG ISLAND CITY, NEW YORK

Yes, you hold on to them even after you are seated. Someone else may dispute your right to the seats. Or, if you go out during intermission, you are sometimes required to show them before getting into the theater again. If you are entertaining at the theater for business reasons, it is important to keep the stub as a record for tax purposes.

• •

If you are entertaining another couple at the theater, how are they seated? R.E.N., NEWARK, NEW JERSEY

The host (or hostess, in a party of women) produces the tickets at the door and stands back to let the guests file in. Guests then wait until the host or hostess precedes them with the usher to their seats. The hostess in a mixed group places a man first in a line of seats so a woman guest need not sit next to a stranger. She also places a man, usually the host, on the aisle—or in the seat nearest the aisle. When two couples are being seated, the two women sit together in such an arrangement.

CARS AND PUBLIC CONVEYANCES

When a couple takes a trip together in a car, should the wife of the driver sit with him or should the two women sit together in the back seat and the two men together in the front? What if a chauffeur is driving? Who sits with him? Where does the wife of the owner sit? MRS. S.M.G., NEW YORK, NEW YORK

In the first instance, the wife of the driver usually sits with him, but it is mainly a matter of choice and convenience. If the two men have much to discuss and would like to ride together from time to time that is all right, too. If both women wish to sit together they may. If one person finds that sitting in the back causes car sickness he should say so and may then be given a front seat. In a large car three may sit in front if that is convenient for the driver. In this case this might mean that the two women would sit in the front with the wife of the driver in the center seat. In a chauffeur-driven car the owner's seat is to the right, and guests entering a limousine courteously take seats to the left, for it is presumably from the right-hand rear seat that the owner can best direct the chauffeur. However, this is not a hard and fast rule, and the owner may certainly give the seat to a guest. When all seats in a car are to be used the car owner usually indicates who is to sit with the chauffeur. If there is a young man passenger in the car it is usually he who is asked to sit there. Or if a servant is traveling the servant sits in the front seat. If all the other passengers are ladies the owner himself sits with the chauffeur.

• •

What is the correct tipping procedure for taxis in city areas? MR. T.B., ALLENTOWN, PENNSYLVANIA

For taxi fares which come to less than a dollar, you tip at least fifteen cents. If the fare is between a dollar and two dollars, give at least twenty cents. And for a fare of over two dollars, you should leave at least fifteen percent of the total.

• •

Who gets out of a taxi first, a man or a woman? H.A.N., CHICAGO, ILLINOIS

Men are so indoctrinated with the idea that a lady always goes first that they become confused about who should alight first from a vehicle. A man always goes first in this case, turns and assists the lady down from or out of the vehicle by offering her his *hand,* not his arm. In assisting her *up into* vehicles he places his hand under the crook of her elbow for support, allowing her to go first.

• •

When you call a taxi for a woman whom you are unable to accompany to her destination, how do you arrange to pay her fare? It seems awkward to offer her the money, and it isn't always possible to judge what the fare will be. How would you handle this? R.C., SAN FRANCISCO, CALIFORNIA

No, don't thrust the cab fare at the woman. Ask the driver what the approximate fare will be and pay him in advance, including the tip. If the appointment was a business rather than a social one, you have no such responsibility, and if the woman asks you to summon a cab she should pay her own fare. For a man to put a woman into a cab she has not requested with the assumption that she has enough money with her to pay for it is to place her, perhaps, in an embarrassing position.

PUBLIC SPEAKING

Should a woman public speaker wear a hat and gloves?
MRS. T.Y., MIAMI, FLORIDA

A hat is certainly optional today. Gloves should not be worn to the podium. Handling papers with gloves on is difficult and the sight makes other people uncomfortable. A woman speaker should take to the podium only those things she actually needs—her notes, glasses, and perhaps a handkerchief—leaving her handbag if possible with someone for safe keeping.

When the speaker is a man, possibly a politician, and you as his wife are seated at the head table, do you applaud with the others at the termination of your husband's speech, or does this seem immodest? M.F., SAN FRANCISCO, CALIFORNIA

On the contrary, it seems quite natural.

TIPPING FOR SPECIAL SERVICES

HAIRDRESSERS AND BARBER SHOPS

I live in a small town and go to a beauty shop operated by the woman who owns it. She has one extra operator, but she herself usually takes care of me. Now the question is, do I tip her? And when I go into the nearest city, what's the usual there in beauty parlors? Do you tip all of the people who serve you in some way? This gets very expensive, if so. E.J., NEW MILFORD, CONNECTICUT

The operator of a shop with little or no help does not usually expect a tip, because he is self-employed. The operator of a big city shop where there are many employees and who himself has customers is often tipped on the same scale as are his employees. If he is the kind of operator who has a supervisory job mainly and who takes only an occasional customer, he is usually not tipped, for he is classed as an artist of professional standing, but if in doubt ask at the desk, "Does one tip Mr. Paul?" In most beauty shops the tip varies, depending on the location of the shop and the cost of the services. In very expensive shops each operator who serves you, plus the maid who takes your coat, is tipped. The manicurist receives fifty cents or even more, depending on what the charges are for the manicure. If a separate operator does the shampooing she is tipped a quarter. An operator who cuts and sets your hair gets a dollar or more, depending on the cost of the service rendered. The maid who takes your coat will get at least a quarter, or more if she performs some special little service for you such as getting you coffee or sewing on a button.

• •

When I take my son to the barber shop the price for his haircut is $3.00. What tip should I leave if his hair is cut by the man who owns the shop and what if it is cut by one of his employees? When my own hair is cut in a beauty shop what tip should I leave? My husband goes to a barber shop that charges him $5.00 for a haircut. What would be an appropriate tip? MRS. T.A.K., MINNEAPOLIS, MINNESOTA

The tip for your son's haircut should be 45 cents in either case. For a man's haircut of $5.00 a dollar tip is expected. If the only service a woman has in a beauty shop is a haircut at $5.00, her tip should be 20 percent or $1.00. If the haircut is included in the other services of a beauty parlor, tip as suggested above.

TAXIS

In most cities taxi drivers are courteous to their patrons and thank them for whatever tip they may care to give them. However, on a recent trip to New York I found that no matter what I tipped a New York taxi driver he was more likely not to thank me than to thank me. It so happens that even though I am a woman I am inclined to overtip. Maybe they expect a small tip from me because I'm a woman. Do you think women do undertip generally? By the way, what is the standard taxi tip in metropolitan areas? What about country areas where metered cabs aren't used? R.N.O., SAN FRANCISCO, CALIFORNIA

In general, women are thought to undertip, but I find that women who have been in business tend to tip on the same scale as do men. It seems to me, too, that more and more New York taxi drivers are taking their tips without thanks. The patron doesn't discover this until after he's given the tip, of course, so he has no redress. On unmetered cabs in country areas, 10-15 per cent is given, with the higher amount usual where luggage is handled.

HOSPITALS

I expect my first baby very soon and have made my hospital arrangements. I expect to have a private room and floor nursing. Do I tip the nurses and, if so, how much? MRS. P.DEB., LARCHMONT, NEW YORK

No, you never tip nurses, for they are professional people. You may, however, give your own nurse a gift when she leaves you—books, candy, pantyhose, handkerchiefs, lingerie (but only for a woman patient to give), costume jewelry, a plant, or wine are all possibilities. A pleasant custom is that of sending flowers or a plant to one's nurse, either when you leave the hospital or when her duty terminates.

DELIVERIES

Is it proper to tip the carry-out boys at the large supermarkets? I know some give tips and others do not.

Most of these boys are high school students. L.T.,
BRIDGEPORT, CONNECTICUT

Yes, tip a quarter unless the market has put this service charge on your bill or absorbs the cost of the
service itself.

• •

**I would like to know how much to tip a boy who de-
livers flowers and how much to tip a boy who delivers
a package.** A.G.S., CLEVELAND, OHIO

Most people do not tip in either of these cases except
at Christmas and a quarter is usual. Of course in large
apartment houses deliveries are made through the
superintendent and such messengers do not see the
householder. The important thing to remember about
tipping, if it becomes a serious financial burden (which
it can), is that one does not have to tip. And certainly no one should be expected to tip beyond his
means, no matter what is customary. If either of these
deliveries, however, should be made to a hotel room or
suite, then a quarter is given.

• •

**Why don't you mention letter carriers in what you
write about tipping? Our letter carriers are underpaid
and receive little overtime pay during the year. All carriers look forward to their Christmas gratuities and to
the "Big Pay Day" on January 2nd, when they are paid
for their long hours just previous to Christmas. It is
practically the only time carriers are permitted overtime
pay as the department is anxious to keep down expen-
ditures and forbids overtime the rest of the year. I can
inform you that the great majority of the public who
do remember the letter carrier do so with cash. And
that is the way he prefers it.** W.B.L., PATERSON, NEW
JERSEY

It has long been assumed by many people that civil
service workers have such a dignified status that a tip

might offend them. However, economic pressure has brought about a change here, too. The average gratuity to the letter carrier where money is given seems now to be five dollars in rural and suburban communities where deliveries are often difficult in winter. In cities where the postman is rarely seen by tenants there is less sense of personal service. However, at Christmas in some cities the carriers frequently deliver in person through the buildings and receive an average of $5.00 each per apartment. Tips are usually left in mailboxes, otherwise. Most large apartment houses collect from the tenants to cover a gift to the mailmen at Christmas. Householders gauge their gifts on the volume of mail received. Some give small personal gifts, but money is the most practical. It should be given by check or cash enclosed in a greeting card or envelope with a few words of holiday greeting and appreciation.

My husband and I work together as sales representatives from our home. We employ an answering service. Are we expected to tip at Christmas, and if so, how?
MRS. E.S., NEW HAVEN, CONNECTICUT

Answering service employees do expect tips. If you are on a 24-hour basis, the expected tip is $5 per girl with a possible contribution to the kitty for relief operators. If you are on limited service, perhaps just during certain hours, find out the number of operators servicing your account. Tip each one a minimum of $5 with perhaps additional to anyone who seems to have given you extra attention, perhaps adding something for the kitty. Send the check to the company itself with an indication as to how it is to be divided. Or, you may send individual checks to the girls, possibly with one greeting card for all, or individual greeting cards.

I have a 3-room cooperative apartment in a hotel. Cleaning service and maid service are both included in the overhead. The maid dusts and does minor cleaning. I tip her every month, but what do I do at Christmas for her, the linen room maid, housekeeper, and the

morning, afternoon and evening desk clerks? MRS. R.J., MINNEAPOLIS, MINNESOTA

For the maid $10, for the linen room maid $5, for the housekeeper $10 to $15 (this depends on how much help she is to you, and how polite) are suitable. Between $5 and $10 each should go to the day and afternoon desk clerks. The night clerk would get $5 or possibly less. You may want to give more or less in each of these cases, depending on the kind of service you have received. Don't omit the doorman if there is one. If you are in and out a great deal and find him helpful with parcels, taxis, etc., the right amount would be about $10.

CORRESPONDENCE

STATIONERY

On a man's stationery is the named printed "Mr. John Doe" or simply "John Doe"? For instance, on the envelopes, should it ever be printed or written "Return to Mr. John Doe" or should it be "Return to John Doe"?
J.A.D., BURLINGTON, VERMONT

A man's stationery is printed or engraved "John Doe," and that is how his return address reads, too, unless he has a special title such as Doctor or Colonel.

• •

I want to have some social stationery engraved for my husband, who is a doctor. Should it read "James Thomas, M.D.," with his address, or should it read "Dr. James Thomas," or should I also just use his initials, and, if so what should they be like and where placed? What is a good size for a man's social stationery? S.N.G., NEW YORK, NEW YORK

At the top of his stationery you may use your husband's name and title with or without the address. It should read "Doctor James Thomas." In the case of a very long name the title may be abbreviated to "Dr." If you use initials they may be dye-stamped in color or be in simple block form at the top of his stationery or upper left. Or if you prefer you may use his address alone, complete with zip code, upper center, with or without his telephone number. Size 7¼ by 10¼ is good for a man's stationery and is suitable for both type-

170

writer and longhand. It should be in cream, buff, gray or white with engraving or printing in black, blue, dark green, brown or perhaps maroon.

• •

I want to order some nice personal stationery for my husband. What is the best color and is it correct to have his name at the top? D.E.P., FLINT, MICHIGAN

A man's social paper should look masculine—in size, in color, and in quality. He sticks to cream, buff, white, or gray with engraving or printing in black, blue, dark green, brown or perhaps maroon. He may use his initials, dye-stamped in color in simple block form at the top of his stationery or upper left, or his name, Geoffrey Lansing (no Mr., of course), with or without the address. Or he uses the address, upper center, alone, with or without his telephone number. Where return address is desired on the flap, the engraver usually uses the same dye he used on the paper itself to save cost. If the paper is printed, just the address alone may be used on the flap, if you desire. If the name is also used, it is used without "Mr."

• •

When I was a girl I was taught that a lady never used any stationery other than white, unless perhaps it was blue or gray. Now I find stationery, and inks! in all colors of the rainbow. What do you think about this? MRS. W.R., MONTEREY, CALIFORNIA

There are all kinds of note papers for women these days, some of them much too fancy for my taste. For some correspondence, however, the old rule of pale blue, gray or white should hold (see replying to wedding invitations, page 116, letters of condolence, page 134). For conservative correspondence, only blue or black ink should be used. For social correspondence where special papers are used, they may be used with contrasting inks, now so widely available. The use of green, brown, or violet ink is now quite acceptable for informal social correspondence. Green ink and even brown ink are used even in business if it is co-related with the letterhead. Red ink, which used to be limited to Christmas or for use in ledgers, now is used on social paper to match red engraving or printing or just because the user likes it. The taboo on red ink has disappeared.

LETTER WRITING AND SIGNING YOUR NAME

Would you help me in the matter of letter salutations? In school we were taught to use "Dear Sir" on business letters, but is this the correct form when writing to a company or business where usually a secretary handles the mail? MRS. H.B., BAY CITY, MICHIGAN

When you are writing to someone in a firm, a man whom you don't know, his name and address is at the upper left of the page in this manner:

Mr. John Brown,
The Ajax Corporation,
47 Main Street,
Ridgefield Conn. 06877

Dear Sir:

If you have regularly been writing to Mr. Brown, your salutation may be "Dear Mr. Brown."

When you are writing to a corporation and do not know the name of anyone to address there, the form is:

The Ajax Corporation,
47 Main Street,
Ridgefield, Conn. 06877

Gentlemen:

(Unless you know it is an all-women's organization, in which case it would be "Mesdames.")

The usual form of closing is, in a case like this, "Sincerely," or "Sincerely yours." It is important to put on a business letter your own return address, both on the letter itself and on the envelope. You should also be careful to include the date—not merely "Tuesday," as you would use it in a social letter—but the month and the day and the year, so that the company may file your letter correctly.

• •

When you are writing to a woman in business and you don't know whether she is "Mrs." or "Miss," what do you do? J.A, WILLOW RUN, MICHIGAN

You address her as "Miss" or optionally "Ms." When you receive a letter signed "Anne Smith" with no "Miss" in front of it, you assume that she is "Miss." If she is "Mrs." she properly places beneath her name in parentheses the information—"(Mrs. John Smith)" or, more likely these days if she is a business woman, divorced or a widow "(Mrs. Anne Smith)" for the guidance of those wishing to write her.

When I don't know a woman's proper title, I find the use of Ms. very helpful. I note that some business offices, publishers, and even some departments of the government now use this form of salutation for women whose surnames are preceded by a given name. I note there is a difference, too, and that Ms. in some cases is followed by a period (from some government offices) and when it comes from England it is written M/s so there seems to be a lot of confusion. J.G., PHILADELPHIA, PENNSYLVANIA

And many women object to it—and violently although they may have to accept it in time. In the meantime if you know a woman's title is Mrs., use it unless you happen to know she prefers Ms. It is always safe to address a woman as Miss if you don't know her title and this has always been the social rule. That Ms. by the way is pronounced "mizzz." The use of the period seems general. Be selective in using it.

• •

When writing a business letter, do you sign thus: "Mrs. John Jones, Richmond, Utah," or "Mary Jones" and under it in parentheses "Mrs. John Jones" and no address except the heading of your letter? A.L.B., RICHMOND, UTAH

In writing a business letter, the usual procedure is to write your address and the date, including the year, clearly in the upper righthand corner (of course if you are writing on imprinted or engraved stationery which includes your address, it is not necessary to write it as well but the date including the year are both necessary). Just before the salutation you write, upper left, the name of the person you are addressing, the name of the company, and its address. If you have no name in the company to whom to direct your letter you write "Gentlemen" unless you know it is an all-women organization. Here the salutation is "Mesdames." A married woman signs such a letter "Mary Jones" and under her signature "(Mrs. John Jones)" (but see preceding comment). An unmarried woman signs herself "Mary Green" and writes "(Miss)" in front if she wishes, although it is assumed that she is "Miss" unless she has indicated to the contrary. She should use the "(Miss)" if her first name is one used by both men and women —for example, "Cecil." She may also type or print beneath her signature, especially if it is not legible, "(Miss Mary Green)."

• •

My son, fifteen, is in boarding school. When I write him, do I address him as "Master," "Mister," or as plain "Robert Brown"? J.A.B., NEW YORK, NEW YORK

As plain "Robert Brown." He is "Master" until the age of twelve, and today "Mister" beginning at age eighteen.

Previously, socially, a man did not use the title, "Mister," before the age of twenty-one, but with draft age eighteen, it is now accepted that a boy reaches manhood at that age and is certainly entitled to a "Mister."

• •

When sending a card or letter to a doctor (male or female) how is the envelope addressed? MRS. M.L.K., PITTSBURGH, PENNSYLVANIA

If you are paying a bill you may address him either as "Dr. George Johnson" or as "George Johnson, M.D." If you are writing to him socially you must address him as "Dr. George Johnson." Your check for medical services should read "George Johnson, M.D." This is a tax precaution as Dr. George Johnson isn't necessarily an M.D.

When you get a bill from a group of doctors who are in a private corporation (PC), to whom do you make out your check, the first name on the list or the doctor who treated you? L.B., BUFFALO, NEW YORK

The best procedure is to make out your check to the doctor who treated you to simplify tax matters.

I am writing to a friend in England whose friends use "Esquire" spelled out after his name in writing. Should I do the same when sending a formal engraved card to him? D.C.B., BUFFALO, NEW YORK

Yes, for all formal purposes. For ordinary letters "Esq." is quite correct. "Esquire" was originally used as a lesser English title. It indicated a knight's eldest son and the younger male members of a noble house whose hereditary title was borne only by the oldest male heir. Now professional men and all those working in the so-called genteel callings—arts, letters, music—and members of the House of Commons and the landed gentry are addressed in writing with "Esq." following their names. Often, too, older gentlemen of standing are called "Squire" in conversation. It might be interesting to note here that should one be sending engraved invitations to England they are always addressed to the wife alone. Where there is no inner envelope one writes on the top of the invitation "Mr. and Mrs. Brown." If there is an inner envelope, as in a wedding invitation, the phrase "Mr. and Mrs. Brown" appears on the inner envelope alone. Greeting cards, however, are addressed "Mr. and Mrs. Carter Brown."

I am a legal secretary. When my boss writes to other lawyers, he addresses them as Robert Gray, Esq. (Mr. Robert Gray, to his social address). With many lawyers now receiving the J.D. (Doctor of Juris Prudence), should we address those men we know to be using the J.D. as Dr. Robert Gray, as Robert Gray, J.D. (and Dr. Robert Gray socially)? I assume that Robert Gray, J.D., Esq. would be incorrect and that the Esquire would be reserved for those lawyers whose status concerning the J.D. is not clear. T.O'K., DALLAS, TEXAS

If you know a lawyer has received the J.D. and uses it, he is addressed professionally as Robert Gray, J.D. (the Esq. is omitted). The salutation would then be Dear Dr. Gray, (if you are sure that he prefers this form of address). Presently most J.D.'s prefer to be addressed as Mr. professionally and socially.

Is a woman lawyer ever addressed as Esquire as are her male contemporaries? Would she then be Miss Marian White, Esq. (to indicate that she is a lawyer)? Or just Marian White, Esq. or what? L.G., CINCINATTI, OHIO

A few women lawyers insist that the male title, Esquire, is their right as well as that of male lawyers although it really doesn't make any sense to call a woman "Mr." The proper way to address a woman lawyer is as Miss Mrs. or possibly Ms. Marian White. If she uses the J.D. (Doctor of Jurisprudence), she would be in business correspondence Marian White, J.D. and in the salutation of the letter, Dear Miss White; or if it is her preference, Dear Dr. White. Many holders of the J.D. do not call themselves "Doctor" at present although they are entitled to do so socially and professionally.

• •

What is the proper form of address for a married woman, for a widow, for a divorcée? A.F.L., NEW HAVEN, CONNECTICUT

A married woman is "Mrs. John Smith" socially. In business, however, it is now virtually a necessity for her to be "Mrs. Ann Smith" to conform with computer practice. A widow is always "Mrs. John Smith" socially no matter how long she remains a widow unless she *prefers* to use her given name. A divorcée either returns to her maiden name or combines her maiden name with her married name, becoming Mrs. Jones Smith, or increasingly, Mrs. Ann Smith socially and in business.

• •

You have said, I know, you prefer the use of the maiden name of a married woman as a middle name for the sake of clarity; that is, "Jane Doe Smith." What happens when "Jane Doe Smith" becomes a widow and in a few years remarries, this time to "John Adams"? Would her name then be "Jane Doe Adams" or "Jane Smith Adams"? I am asking this question from a legal standpoint, realizing that socially she could use either form. M.S.V., PITTSBURGH, PENNSYLVANIA

Actually there is no choice here. Once she is married to another man, she ceases to use, legally and socially, the name of her former husband. Therefore, she is correctly "Jane Doe Adams," which indicates that she was born "Doe." Socially she is "Mrs. John Adams." Legally she signs herself "Jane Marie Adams," "Jane Doe Adams," "Jane Adams," depending either on the name, if any, used in the paper she is signing or on some indicated legal requirement.

• •

Is it ever correct for a married woman to sign her name "Sincerely, Mrs. R. C. Jones"? S.C.L., LONG ISLAND CITY, NEW YORK

I cannot say often enough that a woman always signs herself with her given name plus her maiden name or married name. If she is also "Mrs. Robert Jones," she writes this in parentheses beneath her signature, if the person to whom she is writing doesn't know this. A single woman may put "Miss" in parentheses before her name to anyone who doesn't know that she is "Miss," and especially if her name is also one used by both men and women, for example, "Marion." "Marion Jones" is her signature, handwritten. "Mrs. Robert Jones" is her title—never written as a signature. This is one of the most common mistakes women make.

• •

I am separated from my husband. When writing my name should I use my husband's full name or should I use my first name, then, of course, his last name? L.S., FORT WAYNE, INDIANA

Although separated you are still married to your husband. Therefore you are "Mrs. John Smith," but understandably you may prefer to be "Mrs. Clara Smith," rather than the still correct "Mrs. John Smith." You make the choice.

I always sign my business correspondence "M.J. Brown." Friends now tell me that this signature doesn't indicate whether I am a man or a woman and even if I put parenthetically (Miss M.J. Brown) beneath my signature, it still is improper. Is this so? M.J.B., CHICAGO, ILLINOIS

Yes it is. For a woman to sign her initials, M.J. Brown, does seem masculine, even with the parenthetical addition. You should sign Mary J. Brown, or Mary Jane Brown. If you prefer, you can drop the middle name or initial entirely. Incidentally, a return address for a woman should always bear her title, in your case it should be Miss Mary J. (or Jane) Brown.

My father-in-law died recently. My husband is a "Junior." My mother-in-law is still alive. Does my husband drop the "Junior" and because of this give me my mother-in-law's name, or should he retain the "Junior" until she dies? D.E.B., ALBANY, NEW YORK

Your husband drops the "Junior." Your mother-in-law continues to use her husband's name unless and until she remarries. But if she lives near you and there is any possibility of confusion, she may add to it "Sr." After the death of his father a man keeps "Jr." only if he was the son of a very prominent man whose name continues in the news long after his death and who therefore might be confused with his son.

• •

I am a successful businesswoman with my own business. For many years my husband and I ran it together, and I used his name. Last year I became a widow, and now I am getting married again. Everybody knows me in business under my former husband's name. Should I try to change my name in business to my new social one? H.E.W., ELIZABETH, NEW JERSEY

This is a question which many married businesswomen have had to solve by keeping the name of a former husband because in business it has become somewhat of a trade-mark. It is an awkward decision to make, but the alternative, if you are very well established and have been so for many years, is to reeducate all of your business acquaintances throughout the country to call you by a new name, something which may be difficult to accomplish. Your dilemma points up the wisdom of Lucy Stoneism to a certain degree. It has always seemed wise to me for a woman who establishes herself in business or a profession to use her maiden name. I believe this gives protection, too, to her husband, should she engage in any activities that might run counter to his own professional or business interests.

• •

With a joint checking account, is it correct for the wife to sign checks "Mrs. John Jones"? K.A.R., RICHMOND, UTAH

The correct way to sign checks drawn on a joint account depends on what is on the signature card at the bank. This usually reads "John and/or Mary Jones." The wife may use a middle name or initial for more complete identification if her first name and her husband's name are common. I prefer to see women have their own checking accounts. Joint checking accounts often cause trouble.

• •

After discovering the convenience of the typewriter, I began typing all my personal letters. This makes them easier to read because my handwriting is poor, and proper punctuation is often left out of handwritten correspondence. While typewritten letters do not have the "personal touch," I believe they benefit the receiver in that there is no time lost in deciphering illegible words. However, some of my friends object to typewritten letters. Would you be kind enough to give me your opinion on the subject? B.J.G., LINDEN, NEW JERSEY

This strikes a note of sympathy with me, as my own handwriting is highly illegible, and I know that many of my friends would prefer not to hear from me, rather than get a letter in longhand which leaves them baffled. The use of the typewriter in social correspondence is completely acceptable now, with three exceptions— letters of condolence, the bride's thank-you letters, and letters of felicitation in the case of a wedding or an engagement which should be hand-written. But otherwise social letters may be typewritten, may even be dictated on social stationery. Thank-you notes are usually handwritten but if the thank-you is part of a long, chatty letter, it may certainly be typed. People with severe physical difficulties in writing—arthritics, for example—may certainly be excused for typing everything.

• •

Please settle an argument between my husband and myself. I say he can write his name "the Second," since his father's brother had the same name. He says he can't. Who is right? W.B.B., HARRISBURG, PENNSYLVANIA

You are right, but there is no point in it, if his uncle is no longer living or there is no possibility of confusion. It may be written II or 2nd.

GENERAL INVITATIONS AND REPLYS

Can you issue a formal invitation on a calling card or just informal ones? How is this done? L.H., MIAMI, FLORIDA

You may use your calling card (which should be engraved, of course) to issue *informal* invitations. The card is sent in a small envelope that meets postal requirements or a regular correspondence size envelope. Sometimes a joint card is also used for the issuing of invitations, as is the joint informal. On the visiting card carrying a message, you may or may not—as you wish —draw a line through the engraved name if the message is signed informally with a given name. For example:

> *Birthday party for Lillian*
> *Saturday, August 9, 5–7*
> ~~Mrs. Henry Eugene Cox~~
> *Do hope you can come.*
> *Love, Julia*

R.S.V.P.

> 471 Bunting Lane
> Cold Spring Harbor
> New York 00000

A joint card is used this way,

Cocktails Sunday
Mr. and Mrs. Joseph Asa Benet
Sept. 6th, 4–6

Bayside Avenue
East Islip, New York 11730

• •

Is it considered more correct to write informal invitations or to telephone or give them in person? Y.H., CHARLESTON, SOUTH CAROLINA

Such invitations may be telephoned, given in person, or written.

• •

Today when you are writing invitations, the word "informal" does not seem definitive enough. To some people it seems to mean bare feet and shorts, to others perhaps an open-necked sports shirt with no jacket. When I write "informal" I mean jackets and ties for the men, preferably dark suits, but not dinner jackets. When I wear a long dress, I like to see my women guests do so. How can I make this clear? MRS. B.O'R., BOSTON, MASSACHUSETTS

You are right. "Informal" seems to mean different things to different people in different communities. If you are writing out your invitations, you might say exactly what you mean; for example, "Most of the girls will wear long dresses and the men jackets and ties." If you are using fill-in informals with a return telephone number, explain the same thing on the phone. Wise guests these days ask their hostess what they are expected to wear if they are not familiar with the customs of the household.

• •

In using a fold-over informal, is it proper to use all of the available writing space or should you limit it to the space opposite the engraved or initialed front—and should you ever write on the back part? B.W., EL PASO, TEXAS

The informal is designed for brief notes and looks better when it is reserved for that. However, it is not actually incorrect to lay the informal flat and to begin writing at the top continuing on over to the back section. It would be unattractive to see writing on the front section where your name or initials may appear, if they are put on in such a way as to form a design that dominates that first page. If they are at the top and small then you may, if you wish, begin your note on that first page. The new card informals with a monogram or initials upper left or center or with a name and address engraved in the upper section are meant to have writing on the face. For example:

> 46 East Fifty-first Street
> New York, N.Y., Zip Code
> Mrs. Humphrey Arden Hanshow

> *Tea, Saturday, April 12th*
> *4–6*

• •

Sometimes my husband and I receive invitations on visiting cards with an R.S.V.P. in the lower left-hand corner. Sometimes they come without an R.S.V.P. when it is for a cocktail party or a tea. In either case what do we do? May we use our own visiting card for a reply? Is it all right to telephone our acceptance or regrets? MRS. K.P., WILMINGTON, DELAWARE

Where there is no R.S.V.P. on a visiting card invitation, the hostess expects you to come if you can. It is not incorrect to let her know that you'll definitely be there. It is pleasant if you don't get there to let her know in some way afterwards that you appreciated the invitation. You might even send your card later saying, "Hear the tea was a great success. I wish I could have been there—and thank you. Marie." For such little messages on visiting cards salutation and closing are never used and on informals are not necessary, although the inside of an informal is often treated as if it were note paper. Yes, you may telephone your acceptance or regrets. If you use your calling card or an engraved informal in accepting an informal invitation requiring a reply, you do it this way (in black ink):

We accept with pleasure for
the 6th at eight
~~Mr. and Mrs. Lawrence Armitage~~
Lucy

Love to come Friday
~~Miss Laura Sue Ramsey~~
at five
Laura

If the couple is not on a first-name basis, a line is not drawn through the names on their joint visiting cards. As it is the wife who replies to invitations with the example given, she writes in longhand "Lucy," not "Lucy and Lawrence."

• •

Is it correct to send out invitations written in pencil or typed out over the hostess's name? MRS. W.F.M., DALLAS, TEXAS

No, it is not. When invitations are sent they should be hand-written, engraved, or, under certain circumstances, printed. Ink should be used.

• •

We are buying a house ten miles from the city we now live in. Would it be proper to send printed cards announcing our new address and phone number to friends we see only occasionally? If we do it, should our child's name be included? MRS. S.J.S., WACO, TEXAS

Yes, this is perfectly proper, and you may include the name of your child if you wish. Some people use printed post cards for this purpose, listing all the essential information.

• •

I would like to invite a very old friend who knows most of my friends here to my small apartment so she can meet with them before she goes off into another community to live and work. As I have a job, it is convenient for me to entertain only on week ends. Because of this, although I want to be informal, I would like to know how many people are coming. Also I want to know whether I should write informal notes or use cards on which I would write "Reception in honor of Miss _____." C.S., GREEN BAY, WISCONSIN

As most of your friends know your visitor, the nicest thing would be to write small notes saying that you are giving an "open house" for her on Sunday, the _____ of _____, from, say 4 to 8. This way you could say in the note that you would like to know if they actually plan to come; for example, "Will you let me know if you're coming?" It is not usual to use the R.S.V.P. on a card issued for a reception.

Last year I sent my Christmas cards very early because I was enclosing in each one an invitation to a special pre-Christmas party. One of my friends didn't reply because she didn't open her card in time. If I do something of the kind in the future, would it be all right to put on the envelope something like "Open Before Christmas"? MRS. W.S., FORT LAUDERDALE, FLORIDA

A good idea. Remember Christmas invitations can go out very early, as much as one month or five weeks in advance, so if you do put them in your Christmas card, run the legend you suggest and perhaps add "Invitation Enclosed." In addition, you might call your friends and ask them to save the date, saying that the invitation is on the way.

THANK-YOU NOTES

Just what is a bread-and-butter note? M.P., NEW YORK, NEW YORK

A bread-and-butter letter is a letter of thanks written for entertainment overnight or longer. Technically, a bread-and-butter letter may consist of a mere "Thank you for the lovely week end," written on the face of your visiting card with a line through your title (Mrs., Mr., or Miss and your last name, too, if you are on a first-name basis) but it is better to make it a little more human even when it must be quite brief. It is usually handwritten, though if your handwriting is highly illegible it may be typed. Here is a possible example:

Monday

Dear Mildred,
Your party and the entire week end, as always, were great fun. I enjoyed meeting the Le Beaus and found them just as stimulating as you promised. In fact, just talking to M. Le Beau stirred me to dig out my French grammar again.

Love,

Josephine

• •

I think one of the most common complaints I hear from my friends is that nobody, especially the younger generation, bothers to thank anyone any more for gifts. They just take them for granted. This goes for brides (and some of them even send thank-you *cards*) and for grandchildren away at college who don't even bother to express thanks for Christmas checks or other gifts. What do you suggest? A.T., EL PASO, TEXAS

Lack of appreciation is indeed a modern fault. People, including children, who don't acknowledge gifts do not deserve to receive any in the future. Sometimes one needs to be quite flat about it. "Johnny, I sent you a check for your birthday and you didn't bother to thank me. I feel appreciation is a very important thing in life. Unless you can assure me that you will thank me in the future for gifts that I send you, I plan not to send you any more." This may seem harsh, but it can teach a very important lesson.

When my husband and I go to an elaborate dinner at somebody's house should I write a thank-you note to my hostess? Just when are thank-you notes obligatory?
MRS. B.L., RICHMOND, VIRGINIA

A verbal thank-you is enough unless you have been entertained overnight as well. In this case a thank-you note is always obligatory. When a party has been given especially for you, it is very polite to write a thank-you note to your hostess—and actually it is never impolite to do so even when it is not strictly necessary. A thank-you note should always be written when you have received a gift through the mail and do not have the opportunity to thank the sender either by phone or in person. And even when you have made personal thanks it is never impolite to write a note as well. Thank-you notes must always be written for wedding presents, even when the bride has had an opportunity to thank the donor in person. The bride's notes need not be long and most people understand if there is a time lag of several weeks between the receipt of the gift and the dispatching of the thank-you note. An example of such a note follows:

> Tuesday, May 4
> (Address, if address is
> unknown to your correspondent.)

Dear Aunt Mary,
Bob and I were thrilled with your generous wedding check. We put it with others we have received to help us furnish our apartment. We hope to be able to ask you over to see it soon.

> With much love,
> Helen.

• •

Several young people have not acknowledged wedding presents I gave them, although they certainly have had plenty of time to do so. How do you learn tactfully if the presents were received? MRS. C.T., NEW ORLEANS, LOUISIANA

If possible, call the store and see whether they have received a return receipt upon delivery of the gift. Give the bride, at the most, three months to respond. After that, if you haven't heard, you may certainly drop her a line or call her saying something like this, "I wonder if you received the gift that I sent you. It was a——. I know how the mails are and how difficult deliveries often are, so I thought that I would check." Remember, some brides don't realize that if possible they should thank donors for all gifts they receive before the wedding, or as soon after as possible, mentioning exactly what the gift was and writing at least a few words of appreciation. Commercial "Thank you" cards should not be used. Fold-over informals are best for this purpose and if they are engraved they should have the bride's name alone, for example, Mrs. John Cavendish, or her monogram. The notes must be signed by the bride alone, never "Mary and Bill." For this reason joint informals should not be used.

· ·

Have we gotten clear away from the idea that greeting cards are merely to supplement when a personal greeting is not possible? I refer especially to the sending of printed thank-you cards to guests who have been present at a shower or birthday party and have already been thanked in person at that time. J.A., ALBUQUERQUE, NEW MEXICO

A verbal thank-you is enough, but a note is never amiss. Thank-you cards should never be sent unless they include a written message. Most conservative people do not use them, even this way, but prefer regular stationery or informals, with no "thank-you" imprinted upon them.

• •

My son is being confirmed, and we are having a large reception in his honor. I know he will receive many gifts and I wonder if it would be proper for us to have a printed thank-you note made up, as his handwriting is very illegible. B.T., BROOKLYN, NEW YORK

Where your son has had an opportunity at the reception to thank the donors adequately in person, he need not write a note in addition. Where he has not had a chance to thank people this way, he must write a note, although it can be quite brief. Do not use printed "thank-you" cards. Don't let him use "thank-you" fold-overs for his notes or informals. Informals are for feminine use.

• •

I am to be guest of honor at a stork shower. My hostess is a close friend. Is it enough to call her on the phone the next day to thank her for the shower, or should I write her a note? What about the girls who will give gifts? W.P.L, PASSAIC, NEW JERSEY

Verbal thanks are enough, but if you can manage little notes, this is always especially courteous. As your hostess is a close friend whom you presumably see all the time, it is enough to thank her by phone the next morning—as well as, of course, the day of the shower.

• •

I have a nine-year-old daughter and an eleven-year-old son. When they are casually entertained at the homes of their friends, overnight, is it really essential for them to write thank-you notes to the mothers involved? MRS. J.A.A., BOSTON, MASSACHUSETTS

The word "casually" is your cue here. If they frequently visit back and forth and there is no special entertainment arranged for them, then a proper verbal thanks to the mother of the children they are visiting is enough. But again, a careful mother does train her children to write thank-you notes, and certainly one, occasionally, at least, under these circumstances, is never amiss. A child who is specially entertained at someone's home overnight or longer always writes the mother after his return home.

• •

My husband and I received a gift from the company for which he works. The card was signed by the president and the vice-president, whom I have never met. The gift was sent to us both at home. Should I acknowledge it in a personal note, or should my husband just thank these officers personally by calling at their offices? MRS. B.L.J., BIRMINGHAM, MICHIGAN

As the gift was sent to you both at home, you yourself should write a personal note of thanks, addressing it to the president of the firm and saying in the body of the letter that your husband and you both wish to thank him and Mr. X (the vice-president) for their kind thought, etc. You sign it yourself, with your married name in parentheses beneath your social signature if your name is not on your stationery. Of course, it would always be correct, in addition, for your husband to thank these executives personally if calling by at their offices would not too greatly disrupt his own routine. If it is a very large organization and he feels that he cannot take the executives' time for these thanks, he can leave word with the secretary for them.

SPECIAL LETTERS

I live in the suburbs and every once in a while some order I give by mail goes wrong. Just how do you cope with a situation like this—do you telephone the store

or write an indignant letter? What I want to get is action. H.G., BRONXVILLE, NEW YORK

Just remember that individuals in stores are people, too. They are probably besieged by indignant shoppers. The one who will get service will be the one who writes politely and fully—or who calls on the telephone and is considerate and patient with her complaint. Here is a letter, fully explanatory, and giving full benefit of the doubt. It should get results.

786 Decatur Road
Thomasville, Georgia 31792
April 3, 1968

Nu-Fairbanks Seed Company
400 Bond Street
Richmond, Virginia 23223

Gentlemen:

Your company has always given such excellent service that I regret having a complaint to make now. On June 22 you mailed me a package of grass seed I had ordered and which arrived with the carton open and most of the seed gone. I took the matter up with the post office here, and they informed me that the package had not been properly prepared for mailing, nor had it been insured. As the mistake seems to have been made by your shipping department, I am sure you will make good on the order by having the carton more carefully packed before sending it out to me again. Thank you.

Sincerely,
Jane Doe (handwritten)
(Mrs. John Doe) [may be typed]

• •

Like all housewives, I have occasion to write some business letters. Can you give me a simple form that I can follow and that will be more or less foolproof? MRS. G.N., SARASOTA, FLORIDA

Yes, here is the form:

> 1212 Main Street
> Weehawken, N.J. 07087
> May 4, 1968
> (Put the year)

R. H. Mabee Co.
1200 Boston Post Road
Westport, Conn. 06880

Gentlemen:

Will you please send me two lounging chairs as adver-
tised in last Sunday's *Times* @ $35.75 each. I enclose
my check.

> Sincerely, (or Sincerely yours,)
> Adele Lewis (handwritten)
> (Mrs. Frank J. Lewis) [may be typed]

CHRISTMAS CARDS

**My husband is in the service and stationed abroad. I
am wondering if it would be considered proper to sign
our Christmas cards as always or to omit his name, using only mine and our son's?** MRS. F.S., JR., MACON,
GEORGIA

Include him, as always.

• •

**Do you approve of Christmas cards or greeting cards
of any kind being sent third-class mail—that is, with
the flap tucked inside the envelope and the envelope
unsealed?** MR. D.W., SYRACUSE, NEW YORK

Actually, any communication with a friend which requires an envelope deserves the dignity of a first-class
stamp. But because of the cost of postage today, many
people are sending their greetings third-class mail, but
they should be forewarned that if the address is wrong

or the person has moved, this mail will not be returned or forwarded. It goes to the dead letter office. I'd prefer the use of postcards for Christmas greetings to third class mail.

• •

Is it correct to send Christmas cards with the name imprinted, rather than personally signed? A.M.C., BEACON, NEW YORK

Most people with large Christmas card mailing lists make things easy for themselves by picking one personal card and having it imprinted or engraved if they do not care to sign each one. Others who have the time and the real interest pick individual cards to suit each friend and of course sign each one of these personally. I, myself, like a personal signature, at least to a close friend, even when the card is engraved or imprinted. I like a little message too when I haven't heard from this particular friend for some time. Notes sent with Christmas cards are better on a small separate piece of paper than written on the card itself as these cards are often displayed and sometimes the communications are highly personal. To be avoided in Christmas cards is news of divorce, deaths, accidents and the like that may bring shock or sadness to the recipient.

• •

What's correct if you get a Christmas card from someone to whom you haven't sent one and it comes too late for you to send one of yours so it will arrive in time for the holiday? D.O'C., HOUSTON, TEXAS

If you have a very personal card that perhaps includes a photograph of your children, send it anyway with a little note on it that indicates, delicately, that your friend was not on your original list. Say, perhaps, "It was so nice to get your card. Our late wishes are just as merry." Of course, it is not necessary to acknowledge a greeting card, but often you want to when you receive one from a friend at a distance whom you can't thank personally on casual encounter. A brief note, a pretty post card perhaps at another time of the year— or a suitable return greeting card will thank him for remembering you.

• •

When a husband and wife are signing Christmas cards, whose name comes first? A.S., STRATFORD, CONNECTICUT

The one signing usually places his or her name second, out of courtesy. Therefore, it would read, "John and Mary Smith" or "Mary and John Smith." However, if the names on the card are imprinted or engraved, the husband's name, preferably (British style), comes first, and the names are used after the message. Informal names are always used on informal cards. "Mr. and Mrs." is used only on formal cards and there is an increasing tendency away from them.

CORRECT FORMS OF ADDRESS

Occasionally I would like to write to my congressman or representative. Can you tell me how to address them properly? H.C.C., SPRINGFIELD, MASSACHUSETTS

You are to be congratulated on your public-spirited feeling. Following is a list of personages many people may at one time or another wish to write to. Congressmen and representatives are on the list:

THE PRESIDENT OF THE UNITED STATES
WRITING TO *For domestically mailed letter, address:*

> The President
> The White House
> Washington, D.C. 20510
> Add U.S.A. on letters from abroad

If his wife is included: The President and Mrs. Adams

Letter opening: Mr. President: (*business*)
                   Dear Mr. President: (*social*)
Closing: Most respectfully yours, (*business*)
          Sincerely yours, (*social*)

UNITED STATES SENATORS AND STATE SENATORS
WRITING TO The Honorable Angelo Cognato
            United States Senate
            Washington, D.C. 20510

If wife is included, the form is:

The Honorable and Mrs. Angelo Cognato
Home address
Letter opening: Sir: (*business*)
                   Dear Senator Cognato: (*social*)
Closing Very truly yours, *or* Sincerely yours,

NOTE A woman is The Honorable Genevieve P. Schuler
(always with given name). If husband is included,
the social form is: Mr. and Mrs. John Schuler, home
address. Official invitations read: The Honorable Genevieve P. Schuler and Mr. Schuler, home address.

REPRESENTATIVES AND ASSEMBLYMEN
WRITING TO The Honorable Lincoln Chadwick
            House of Representatives
            Washington, D.C. 20510

If wife is included, the form is:

The Honorable and Mrs. Lincoln Chadwick
Home address
Letter opening: Sir: (*business*)
                   Dear Mr. Chadwick: (*social*)
Closing: Very truly yours, *or* Sincerely yours,

NOTE A woman is The Honorable Lucy Butterfield. If
husband is included, the social form is: Mr. and Mrs.
Amos Butterfield, home address. Official invitations
read: The Honorable Lucy Butterfield and Mr. Butterfield.

PROTESTANT CLERGYMEN WITH DOCTOR'S DEGREE
WRITING TO The Reverend Joseph E. Long, D.D.

If wife is included, the form is:
    The Rev. Dr. Joseph E. Long and Mrs. Long
Letter opening: Reverend Sir: (*business*)
                Dear Dr. Long: (*social*)
Closing: Respectfully yours, (*business*)
        Sincerely yours, (*social*)

CLERGYMEN WITHOUT DOCTOR'S DEGREE
WRITING TO The Reverend Frank K. Hanson

If wife is included, the form is:
    The Rev. and Mrs. Frank K. Hanson
Letter opening: Reverend Sir: (*business*)
              Dear Mr. Hanson: (*social*)
Closing: Respectfully yours, (*business*)
        Sincerely yours, (*social*)

ROMAN CATHOLIC PRIEST
WRITING TO The Reverend Father James L. Cullen
    Letter opening: Reverend Father *or* Dear Father
        Cullen:
    Closing: I am, Reverend Father, etc.

ROMAN CATHOLIC BROTHERS
WRITING TO Brother William Shine
    Letter opening: Dear Brother William *or* Dear
        Brother:
    Closing: I am, respectfully yours,

ROMAN CATHOLIC SISTERS
WRITING TO Sister Mary Annunciata
    Letter opening: Dear Sister:
    Closing: I am, respectfully yours,

RABBI WITH SCHOLASTIC DEGREE
WRITING TO Rabbi Nathan Sachs, D.D., LL.D.
              Temple Emmanuel
              Bridgeport, Connecticut, Zip Code

If wife is included, the form is:
   Rabbi (*or* Doctor) and Mrs. Nathan Sachs
     (Some prefer Rabbi to *Doctor*)
   Home address
Letter opening: Sir: (*business*)
             Dear Rabbi (*or* Doctor) Sachs:
               (*social*)
Closing: Very truly yours, (*business*)
     Sincerely yours, (*social*)

RABBI WITHOUT SCHOLASTIC DEGREE
WRITING TO Rabbi Harold Schwartz
         Beth David Synagogue
         New York, N.Y. Zip Code

If wife is included, the form is: Rabbi and Mrs. Harold
                              Schwartz
                            Home address
Letter opening: Sir: (*business*)
             My dear Rabbi Schwartz: (*social*)
Closing: Very truly yours, (*business*)
     Sincerely yours, (*social*)

MILITARY FORMS OF ADDRESS

In the modern Army, rank is used in all grades for both men and women in the service.

Doctors in the service have a starting rank of Lieutenant, and common Army usage dictates that they be addressed by this rank, but junior officers are not infrequently called Doctor. Once, however, they reach Captain or above, they are generally addressed socially by the Army title so long as they remain in the Army. Officially they are always addressed by rank.

Chaplains in the Army and Navy are always called, officially and socially, Chaplain, no matter what the military rank. There is no ruling, however, expressed in regulations, which would prevent men from referring to Catholic priests as Father.

Non-commissioned officers are addressed officially by title, i.e., Sergeant, for all grades of Sergeants—First

Class, Master, Sergeant, etc.—but there is no regulation prohibiting the use of Mister socially.

A Warrant Officer in any branch of the service is called Mister officially and socially.

In the Navy, Commanders and above are addressed socially by their Navy titles. All below that rank are Mister. Properly a Lieutenant Commander is Mister, but recent custom accords him the courtesy title of Commander socially, with his actual status indicated to all by his two and a half stripes.

Any officer in command of a ship, whatever its classification, is Captain for the period of his command, no matter what his usual title may be.

Cadets of the U.S. Military Academy are Mister socially and in conversational references, but Cadet officially.

National Guard and Reserve officers not on active duty do not use their titles socially or in business affairs unless their activities have some bearing on military matters. Whenever the rank is used, the proper designation must follow the name, i.e., ORC or NG.

Socially and in ordinary military use Lieutenant Colonels, Major Generals, Brigadier Generals, and Lieutenant Generals are known as Colonels and Generals, respectively.

Vice-Admirals and Rear Admirals are Admiral.

All officers of the military services retain their rank after retirement.

TEEN-AGERS AND PRE-TEENS

DATES

I am fourteen but my parents won't permit me to go on a date because they say I'm too young. The boy I like keeps asking me to go out with him, and I have explained I'd like to but I can't. What do you suggest I do? B.J.W., CHICAGO, ILLINOIS

Talk it over with your parents and see if they can come to some understanding with you in the matter of limited dates with limited hours and specific places to which you are allowed to go.

• •

When I take out my girl who is considerably shorter than I and it begins to rain, should I let her carry the umbrella and I walk out in the rain, or should I attempt, in spite of the disparity of our heights, to hold it over her? G.C.G., BATTLE CREEK, MICHIGAN

You hold it over her unless you are so burdened with packages that this seems impossible, in which case she walks under the unbrella and you walk outside of it.

• •

I have always been very fussy about my dates and refuse to go out with boys who are unattractive looking. I figure that if I am seen with one of them, more attractive boys will pass me by, figuring I can't do any better. My sister says the idea, though, is to keep in cir-

culation, and any date is better than no date. Who is right? E.H., EASTON, CONNECTICUT

Some of the most attractive men I have ever known have been quite homely. One of the things a girl gets to know, in time, is that a handsome man is not necessarily the most attractive escort. If you have been sitting home a lot lately, I would agree with your sister that almost any date is better than none. If you do circulate, you are likely to meet someone in time who will really appeal to you. On the other hand, never accept an invitation from a boy you really dislike, just for the sake of the entertainment he can offer. He is sure to sense your feelings during the course of the evening. Under such circumstances it is always more fun to stay home with a good book.

• •

Some of the fellows in our neighborhood have a habit of calling up girls they don't know, trying to make blind dates. Sometimes they call me and some of my girl friends, saying they know who we are through fellows in high school. My mother says I should have nothing to do with them, but it seems all right to me. I said I'd ask you. J.W.I., NEWARK, NEW JERSEY

Your mother is right. Blind dates are very dangerous unless they are arranged by someone you actually know and can trust. Even then it is safer to take another couple along on a blind date. This way you have some protection in the event of some disagreeable occurrence. Boys who do their blind dating in packs on telephones are usually pretty poor pickings themselves, or they wouldn't have to get dates this way.

• •

I am a girl thirteen and have started going steady with a boy who is very quiet. Whenever he calls me I have nothing to say to start a conversation. What could I say

to him to start a conversation? D.M., PASADENA, CALIFORNIA

First, you're much too young to go steady, but the best way to get a boy to talk is to ask him a question about himself. Most people, especially teen-agers, are only too ready and willing to talk about themselves, whereas it is often difficult for them to talk about impersonal things, especially when a conversation is just beginning. That is why convention has us ask, "How are you?" to which the traditional reply is "Fine, thank you. How are you?" Conversations, like automobiles, have to warm up. Therefore don't be afraid of the tried and true subjects as beginners, such as weather, school activities, sports, etc. Eventually, as young boys and girls get to know each other, they can get into fairly deep subjects, I well remember.

• •

I am a girl of fifteen. My mother says nice girls don't call up boys. I think this has changed, don't you? M.D.S., PHOENIX, ARIZONA

Yes, it has changed somewhat. A girl should really have some excuse for calling up a boy unless she wants to seem to be chasing him. Perhaps she needs to call him about homework or to invite him to a dance or, under certain circumstances, to some entertainment at her own home. If she knows the boy very well and sees him all the time, she could call him just to talk as she might any other friend, but she should be very careful not to overdo it.

What do you think about a 15-year-old boy going on a Dutch treat date? P.R., HARRISBURG, PENNSYLVANIA

Dutch treating in a group is quite acceptable, but is less usual for a single date. Preferably, a boy should be able to suggest plans for his date that are within his means. Many a girl would rather go for a walk in the park and have an ice cream soda a boy could manage, than to be asked to share the cost of a date. There are exceptions to this, of course. Dutch treating is getting much more common.

When you have a blind date and can't stand the guy and he calls you up afterward to see if you will go out with him, what do you do? I like to be honest in my relationships. Do you think white lies are really moral? How can I tell this fellow he's a creep?

I believe in the sparing and kindly use of the white lie which has always been a sometimes need in the practice of good manners. To tell this boy flatly that you did not enjoy your date, that you don't want to see him again, seems needlessly cruel. Instead, using the white lie technique, you can say when he calls that you are "busy"—and you *can be* "busy"—washing your hair, helping your mother. Do not explain why you are not available. If he tries to pin you down about a future date, be kind, pleasant but vague. Say something like: "Well, I really don't know what I'll be doing that far ahead. I think I do have some things to do then." Unless the boy is completely hardshelled, he will get the idea that you don't want to see him again. But if you handle your end properly, you won't bruise his ego. Just remember that you do not have to give any explanation as to why you can't accept another date with him. In handling the situation, put yourself in his place. Hurting people's feelings is not the way to social success, hence the occasional necessity for the white lie.

• •

I'm a teen-age boy and I get a lot of calls from a girl I can't stand. Her mother is a friend of my mother's, and my mother says I have to be polite. I say I have a right to go out with the girls I pick and this girl should be made to stop chasing me. What do you say? T.S., JR., NEW YORK, NEW YORK

Perhaps it's the mothers who are to blame, not the girl. Undoubtedly the girl is being told by *her* mother to include you in her various entertainment plans. Perhaps you should accept an occasional invitation, but any girl will get the idea in time that you're not interested in her. It is not necessary that you squire her around on your own initiative, you know. If you don't invite her to go out with you in turn, she'll find another boy who'll enjoy her company for her own sake, not because he's asked by his mother to act as her escort. Of course, mothers should know such machinations are usually most ineffective.

• •

Recently I double dated and afterward the other boy called me up and asked me for a date. My mother says that I shouldn't accept it unless we inform both the other boy and the other girl involved of our intentions of going out together. Do you really think this is necessary? MISS J.E.O., BELOIT, WISCONSIN

As you met through the boy who took you to the dance, I think it would be good manners for the second boy to ask the first if he minded if he invited you as his own date on the occasion you mention. At the same time, if you know the other girl well, you might ask her if she has any objection to your going out with her previous date. If the two had been dating steadily, your action might seem unfriendly. However, as so much dating is so very casual, very probably neither will object if you two have a date together after having met this way. It is nice to ask, however, but you should be prepared to refuse the date if the other girl is obviously hurt or the boy with whom you went out at first seems upset. If the attraction between you two newly-met young people is very strong, then, of course, later on you probably would date anyhow. It is good manners to be sporting about these relationships even at the most casual stage. Just think how you might feel if the whole situation were reversed.

RESTAURANT ETIQUETTE

When I am at a very nice restaurant with my boy friend, how do I order dinner? A.M., HOUSTON, TEXAS

During the noon hour even in luxury restaurants each diner is expected to give his own order to the waiter to speed the service. Therefore, when you sit down you look at the menu presented to you, either by your escort or by the waiter, and choose your main dish, the entree, first so you can decide what first course would go well with it. You then tell the waiter what you would like, usually waiting until after your meal to give your dessert order if any. The procedure is usually different at night in luxury restaurants where there is time for some old-fashioned courtesy. You wait until the menu has been handed to you by your escort or the waiter, then you wait for your escort to make some suggestions on what might be nice to eat—he may be thinking painfully of his pocketbook, though rightly he shouldn't take you to a restaurant where this matters to him. But you, of course, as a considerate person, will not order the most expensive dish unless you are sure that it really doesn't matter. There is much less ceremony about this kind of thing these days, however, so if your waiter asks you what you want without referring to your escort, you may tell him just as you would in an unpretentious restaurant or eating place where the meal is table d'hôte and there is little if any choice. At the end of the meal remember that it is your responsibility to indicate when it is time to go. Except under exceptional circumstances, your date should not make the first suggestion to leave. Note, too, that others may be waiting to use your table.

• •

When I get taken to a nice restaurant by a date I never quite know what's expected of me once we get inside the door. I feel so lost when my date goes to check his hat. I don't know where to stand, and I don't know whether to go with the headwaiter or waitress if they arrive before my date does from the checkroom. Could you give me explicit advice on this subject? J.O.L., JEFFERSON CITY, MISSOURI

Your feeling of helplessness can be a great social asset in this instance. Just allow your date to take full charge.

He probably feels just as unsure as you do, but you mustn't let him know that you know it. If he doesn't escort you out of the line of traffic at the entrance while he checks his hat, you step out of it yourself although you don't follow him. You wait quietly without seeming too interested in your surroundings until he rejoins you, then together you approach the entrance to the dining room. There if the headwaiter or hostess steps forward, your escort states the places he requires then steps back and lets you follow the individual who is to direct you to your table. If no one does step forward to guide you, then your escort steps in front of you and you follow along until he has found a table and pulled out a chair for you. You allow him to seat you.

• •

At the end of a restaurant meal when a boy and girl are dining together which one indicates that it's time to leave? R.J.L., BOISE, IDAHO

The girl. She places her napkin unfolded at the left of her plate, looks questioningly at her escort, and then prepares to rise. If he suggests they linger she may do so if she wishes. However, her decision must be abided by.

DANCES AND PARTIES

We are having a formal dance from nine to twelve p.m. and are inviting escorts. Does my escort see that I have a way of getting there or should I? Should I dance every dance with my escort? How often may I go to the powder room? Would it be impolite to leave him to talk to a girl friend? When we go home should I give him my coat so he can help me with it? Do I kiss him good night? Do I thank him for the evening or, since he is my guest, should he thank me? "ANONYMOUS," CHICAGO, ILLINOIS

Taking your questions in order. Your escort calls for you and gets you home at a time agreed upon with your family. You are not obliged to dance every dance with your escort, but he should not leave you until he sees that you have someone with whom to dance. You go to the powder room as often as necessary—and I mean necessary. You mustn't spend the whole evening in there primping or gossiping. Do not leave your guest to talk to a girl friend, but, if you wish, ask him to accompany you to another group. When it is time to go home you allow him to help you into your coat if he is with you. He doesn't follow you into the girls' dressing room, if there is one, for this purpose. You kiss him good night, briefly, only if you want to. A girl is never obliged to kiss a boy just because he expects it. It is always the boy who thanks the girl for her company, but a girl should always say that she has had a very good time—even when she hasn't.

• •

A friend of mine is giving a Sweet Sixteen Party for her daughter. Is it quite all right to invite several friends or aunts of the girl to attend—sort of chaperones, so to speak? The party will be held at a well-known inn. MRS. M.K., HARRISBURG, PENNSYLVANIA

At sixteen, teen-agers usually like to have a minimum of chaperonage, and while the girl's mother and father of course will be there and standing next to their daughter as the guests come in, I think they should discuss with their daughter whether or not any of her mother's friends or the girl's aunts would be really welcome. The parents, after all guests are present, might even dine together by themselves in the restaurant, keeping very much in the background on this important occasion.

• •

Do you feel that a party of all girls or all boys in their early teens can be given in the home of one of them in the evening without the parents or some other older person actually being in the house during the whole period? A.H.S., BOSTON, MASSACHUSETTS

Yes. A chaperone is needed only in mixed groups, under the circumstances. But again, children need the support of their parents in such social situations, and parents should not fail to appear at some time during the evening to greet the guests and lend the feeling of family solidarity.

• •

When a boy and a girl go to a restaurant and the girl wants to go to the powder room, what does she say? What does the boy say if he has to go to the men's room? Does the person remaining at the table order, or wait until the other returns?

In both cases the boy or the girl merely says, "Will you excuse me a few minutes?", rises and goes off without any further explanation. They don't usually leave at the same time. One more often stays to hold the table. If the girl is left alone, she waits for the boy to come back to place the order.

For years I have wondered what a girl is supposed to say to a fellow after they have danced together and he takes her back to the table. The fellow usually says, "Thank you." Then what does the girl say? I hear that some girls don't say a thing. I usually say, "You're welcome." MRS. B.MC K., DETROIT, MICHIGAN

I think it is nice for girls to show their pleasure under such circumstances—or at least to simulate it. Instead of the trite phrase "You're welcome"—which is correct enough, mind you—I think it is nice for a girl to say in different ways, "I enjoyed it too," and to sound as if she means it. Even a girl who isn't such a very good dancer can make the boy feel so appreciated that he comes back and asks her again in preference to a girl who seems to be doing him a great favor by dancing with him at all.

• •

I go to an all-girl school, and whenever we have a formal or semi-formal dance it is customary for the girl to invite a boy to escort them and take care of all the expenses, with the exception of the tickets. What would you consider proper notice to give a boy when asking him to the dance? I think the possibility of his having to earn the money himself should be taken into consideration. Also, can you tell me a pleasant and tactful way of telling a boy what kind of flowers you want? So often they bring a shade that doesn't go with the girl's gown. B.A.J., PITTSBURGH, PENNSYLVANIA

As these dances don't take place very often during the year, you should be able to let the boy know a month or more in advance where you think there might be some problems financially. For ordinary invitations, as you know, two weeks is considered sufficient time. Most boys know that they are expected to send or bring a corsage to the girl they take to a dance, but sometimes they just can't afford it. Therefore, I would hate to have you suggest what kind of flowers you would like to wear. Heavy corsages should be avoided. A single gardenia is preferable to a ribbon-swamped purple orchid. In cities and in some schools and communities the girls no longer wear corsages, but any girl, of course, loves to receive cut flowers.

• •

I have had several friends over to my house for a day or evening. Every time I do so I feel like a boring hostess and that my friends want something to do. Do you know of a way to cure me of this feeling? A.M.P., FORT WORTH, TEXAS

You don't say how old you are, but I assume that you are a teen-ager. Feelings of inadequacy overcome much more mature hostesses from time to time, especially when a party doesn't seem to "jell." I myself love good conversation, but sometimes one does find guests who will not talk readily. For this there is no cure except activity of some kind—dancing, music playing, a record session, cards, or any of the parlor games that are popular in your set. For a young hostess it is always well to have such entertainment quickly available, if not actually planned, for such occasions. Never, however, insist as a hostess that your guests play a game in which they seem on the whole disinterested. Often people have lots of fun doing nothing in particular, just relaxing in each other's company, without strictly planned entertainment or scintillating conversation. You don't have to be "doing something" every minute to have a good time.

• •

I have invited a boy to a junior prom. We are both graduating from junior high school. I hope he is going to send me flowers. Should I get him a boutonniere? If so, what kind and color? Should I give him a graduation present—I think he is giving me one. D.K., SAN DIEGO, CALIFORNIA

No, don't give him a present. If he hasn't planned to give you one himself, he might be very embarrassed at receiving one from you. Even if he does give you one, it isn't necessary for you to reciprocate. That's one of the nice things about being a girl—when you receive a gift you are not expected to give one in return to a boy. You usually wait on this until you are engaged. If your escort brings you flowers it is all right to give him a boutonniere from them, but don't order one separately for him. It is best, always, to let the boys take the initiative in this giving business. They like us to be the receivers—I guess because it makes them feel so manly.

• •

Would you help us with this problem? A is having a Sweet Sixteen Party at a night club. B says guests should bring gifts to be opened there. C says it is not a proper place or setting for a gift-opening. What do you say? MRS. M.G., JAMAICA, LONG ISLAND

As gifts are usually brought to birthday parties, I do not see that it makes any difference in this case that the setting is to be a night club, but gifts should not be left unguarded.

• •

My boy friend's family entertained me at their home in another part of the state. Would it be all right to send his mother some flowers in thanks? M.D., PITTSBURGH, PENNSYLVANIA

Yes, quite all right and very nice too.

• •

My daughter is giving a dinner party for six before the Junior Assembly. The other boys have called their dates and asked what kind of dresses they're going to wear so they can send corsages. However, my daughter's date has not called her. She's afraid she'll be the only girl at the dance without flowers. Would it be all right for us to get her some flowers and keep them in the refrigerator just in case? W.E., NEW YORK, NEW YORK

That would be a good idea, but keep the flowers very modest—the sort of thing the boy would probably send himself. Perhaps he feels that the safest thing to send, if one doesn't know the color of the girl's dress, is white, and perhaps that's why he didn't ask. In a situation like this, tactful parents or a foresighted girl can save an awkward situation. Perhaps the boy couldn't afford the flowers, even though you are paying for the dance tickets. Perhaps he forgot. But if he appears without flowers he may tell your daughter quietly the real truth —either that he forgot them or, without embarrassment, that he is just squeaking through on his allowance this month and that the flowers will have to wait until next time. At this point your daughter, with perfectly good

humor, might say, "As a matter of fact, I have some—
so everything's all right."

• •

**Do you have any sort of rules for parents regarding
teen party behavior?** MRS. W.R.T., HOUSTON, TEXAS

Yes, here are some excellent ones, circulated by the
Parents Association of the Loomis School, Windsor,
Connecticut.

1. Insist that your boy or girl go to no party to which
   he or she is not invited and that none be allowed to
   your parties who is not invited.

2. Have no parties at your home unless you are there.
   Every party of teen-agers should be adequately
   chaperoned.

3. Impress upon your son or daughter the full extent
   of the responsibility involved when he or she is
   driving someone in a car.

4. Alcoholic beverages should not be served to boys
   or girls of high school age.

5. Parties should end at a reasonable hour. Insist that
   your boy or girl telephone you if he or she is to
   be out later than agreed or if there are other changes
   in their plans.

6. Boys should ask the parents of their dates what
   time the girls are expected home and should comply
   with the parents' wishes. They should also advise
   the parents where they are going.

• •

**I am twelve years old and am about to have my first
big party with boys and girls. At other parties I go to
they play kissing games. I know they will expect to
play them at my party, but I suppose my mother will
object. Do you think kissing games are all right?** J.M.L.,
TALLAHASSEE, FLORIDA

They are very usual at your age and even later and have been played, one way or the other, by generations of children. I'm very sure your mother knows all about it and played them herself at your age. So long as they stay within the rules of good taste I see nothing wrong with them. Your mother, however, is the final arbiter in the matter, so, if she seriously objects, do substitute something else.

• •

My daughter reported to me that at a record hop she attended, several of the boys and some of the girls were smoking "pot." She refused to join in, but I told her she should have come home immediately. She thinks I'm square and that it is enough she doesn't smoke herself. J.N., PHOENIX, ARIZONA

It isn't enough. There have been instances where people at such a party who were not smoking were arrested even though they had no marijuana in their own possession. Some communities are very strict in the matter, others somewhat lenient. The safest thing is to leave any party where the law is being broken in any way.

• •

I have just received my driver's license but have a jalopy. My girl, who also has her license, has a new car. Her parents are uneasy about her going out in my car. If we go on dates in her car, at least occasionally, who should drive? Should I pay for the gas?

I would hate to see your girl furnish the transportation all the time, but there might be occasions on which she would be more comfortable going in her own car, for example to a dance. And I think you'd be more comfortable under the circumstances buying the gas and driving. Be sure that you are a good driver, however, and that her parents understand that you are.

• •

Among our children's friends are some who have issued invitations for "Bring Your Own Bottle" parties, in their own homes. Wouldn't it be better not to have a party than to ask guests to supply their own liquor? Is this acceptable today? MRS. P.M.M., CHAPPAQUA, NEW YORK

Such parties are very common indeed among the young to whom the cost of liquor can be of major consequence. Guests bringing their own bottles mark them with their own names and take them home afterwards if there is any appreciable amount left in the bottle.

DRESS

I have been having an argument with my mother for a long time about wearing earrings. She said I was too young to wear those button-type earrings, and I say I am not because all the other girls my age wear them. She told me to write you and find out if you think a fourteen-year-old girl is too young to wear earrings. A.S., WACO, TEXAS

You have almost answered this yourself. You say all the other girls your age wear them. Generally, what the others in the group do, so long as these things are not really harmful, can usually be a safe guide to parents. I can't see anything particularly harmful in button earrings at your age, but if they really disturb your mother, why don't you wait a while? I know what she means. She doesn't want you to try to look like a grown-up young lady when you are still only fourteen. She doesn't want you to look in any way "cheap" by using a lot of make-up, tottering around in very high heels, wearing your dresses cut too low. My own mother used to call this "gilding the lily." There's something wonderfully young and fresh about the age of fourteen in a girl, and it is very nice if she just looks fourteen.

• •

My fifteen-year-old daughter wants to get a very low-necked gown for the junior prom. She says a lot of the other girls are wearing them and that I'm just old-fashioned. Should I stick to my guns? S.K.Q., ST. PE-TERSBURG, FLORIDA

Within reason. Some really charming and youthful dresses for that age group have fairly low necks. It's the dark, slinky, siren type of dress that makes a girl that age look as if her mother weren't keeping an eye on her. Your daughter shouldn't be allowed to dress like a woman of the world—although it is hard to convince youth that youth itself is a precious and all too fleeting thing.

• •

I am twelve years old and four feet eight inches tall. My parents say that I cannot wear lipstick because I am small and too young, but I would like very much to wear lipstick. They think I should wait a few years. What do you think? M.F., FAIR LAWN, NEW JERSEY

I hate to see girls of your age wearing lipstick, but I know that in some communities girls as young as you wear pale lipstick to parties at least. If this is the case in your community, maybe you can get your parents to compromise and let you wear it only under certain circumstances.

• •

I am nine and a half. I would like to wear junior panty-hose to parties but my mother says I must wear socks, especially as I am small for my age. Who is right? M.K.J., OAK PARK, ILLINOIS

Some girls your age do wear junior-sized pantyhose to parties but I much prefer tights in pastel colors or white, or socks. As teen-agers love to wear socks of various kinds, I don't see anything too little-girlish about your wearing socks to parties at your age.

I am a girl of fifteen. I have been invited to a football game by a boy and to dinner in a nice restaurant afterwards. May I wear a slacks suit under a storm coat? Would it be all right to go on to the restaurant in this outfit? A.F.S., INDIANAPOLIS, INDIANA

Add a scarf or a wool hat to keep your head warm. A girl who is cold at a football game is no fun. You may go right on to the restaurant in your football clothes.

I am seventeen and buying my first tuxedo to take on a Carribean cruise. I expect to have very limited use of it at other times. Should I buy tropical weight in white or colored jacket, or get one in all-black? J.H., BOSTON, MASSACHUSETTS

The most practical investment will be in a tropical weight, (worn all year round now) black tuxedo. With the trousers you can wear an odd sports jacket in, for example, linen or madras. A black dinner jacket is always in good taste even in the tropics and the ship will be air-conditioned.

My sister and I like to go barefoot as much as possible. My parents go along with this, but my mother insists that we wear shoes to the table even when we are in blue jeans. We think she is unreasonable—at least when we don't have guests. How can we convince her? C.B.R., NEW ORLEANS, LOUISIANA

Don't try to. Your mother is responsible for teaching you manners. While it is probably a good idea to go barefoot at least part of the time (but not, I hope, on city streets), it is unattractive to see bare feet—and dirty ones, too—at the dinner table. You will note that many stores and restaurants have signs "No bare feet." There is a reason for this. Many people find bare feet, under inappropriate circumstances, repulsive.

Is it proper to wear a grannie dress to a morning wedding at eleven o'clock?

It would be the choice of many teen-age girls and some of the youthful mothers may well follow suit. Grannie dresses go just about anywhere at any time of the day.

I am eleven and I want to have my ears pierced. My mother is terribly against the idea. I just want to wear tiny gold rings in my ears now. She not only doesn't like the idea, but says I'm too young. What do you think? R.L., NEW YORK, NEW YORK

Even tiny babies have pierced ears and wear earrings among certain ethnic groups. But many young girls, your age and much younger, have their ears pierced in order to wear the earrings you describe. If you really feel you want to do it at your age and your mother finally agrees, have the jeweler mark the place on your earlobes where the holes should go. Then have a doctor pierce your ears under absolutely sterile circumstances. Don't take a chance on having a bad infection.

INTRODUCTIONS AND GREETINGS

My mother has a different name than my own because she's been married twice. When I bring my friends home, should I just say, "John, this is my mother," or should I say, "John, this is my mother, Mrs. Barclay"? B.S.J., TACOMA, WASHINGTON

The latter is correct. Otherwise, the guest might be embarrassed by calling your mother by your name and then finding out later that he has misaddressed her.

• •

I live in an apartment hotel where many older ladies live. Should I, a high school senior, stand if they happen by to greet me or for an informal chat while I am dining? Also when girls my own age are arriving and leaving at a party, shall I then rise? Please tell me also if a teen-age girl (sixteen) should curtsy. K.C., BATTLE CREEK, MICHIGAN

Yes, at your age it is courteous for you to rise for women very definitely older than yourself—women in the category, say, of your mother's friends. You would not have to rise for young marrieds. At a party, unless you are a hostess or a member of the family, it would not be necessary for you to rise when other women guests are coming or going. At your age you should definitely not curtsy—in fact I'm against the curtsy for all except little girls who move perhaps in the diplomatic set or who just love to curtsy.

• •

So few parents seem to be teaching their sons to stand up when lady guests enter a room that I am wondering if I am old-fashioned in teaching my son to do so. Also, do the men rise when friends greet us while we are eating in a booth? A.C.W., OAKLAND, CALIFORNIA

You are right, of course. Parents should teach their sons this essential of etiquette just as early as they are able to absorb the information. Boys should also stand when male guests enter the room, even their own contemporaries, and come forward to greet them with a friendly handshake. They should rise, too, for their fathers returning home after a day's work. No, the men do not arise when they are seated in a booth, although they may half rise and make apologies for not fully rising. However, no lady ever lingers unless she can seat herself quickly so as to prevent the men's discomfort.

• •

I am fourteen. How do I introduce boys and girls at a party? Do you mention the last name? A.D., INDIANAPOLIS, INDIANA

You say, mentioning the girl first, "Sue, this is Joe Adams, Joe, Sue Clarke." In introducing two boys, say, "Joe—Bill Burke, Bill, Joe Adams." Always try to add something to an introduction that will help the two start a conversation. For example, "I think you were both at the Scout Jamboree in New Hampshire last year."

GIFTS

I am in high school and have been going with a boy about a year. Would it be all right to give him a nice shirt and tie for his birthday? "PATTY," DULUTH, MINNESOTA

Well, the shirt I would consider too personal, but the tie is permissible these days. Other possible gifts would be a sweater or socks you have knitted yourself, gloves, scarf, or handkerchiefs.

• •

I have been dating a boy steadily for seven months. I have been over to his house for dinner, and I also have been in the family's company quite frequently. Is it proper for me to give something to his parents at Christmas? And perhaps to his brother and his brother's girl, at whose house I have been a guest several times? And my parents want to know whether they should give my boy friend a gift. D.S., BRONX, NEW YORK

It would be quite normal for you and the young man to exchange Christmas presents. I do not advise, however, that you give to the others you mentioned or that your family give a gift to the young man.

• •

I know you advise that gifts should not be accepted unless one is engaged; that is, expensive gifts. While vacationing I dated a fellow who was introduced through a personal friend. He visited my family and took me out quite often. At the end of my vacation he brought me a "going away" gift, a costume jewelry bracelet, which I know must have cost at least twenty-five dollars. I accepted it rather than hurt his feelings. Was I in error?
T.D., HARRISBURG, PENNSYLVANIA

No, costume jewelry does not come within this ban. An unengaged man should not give to a girl such things as real diamonds, pearls, or mink coats. He must avoid anything so personal as underthings. A recent news picture showed an important American diplomat fastening on his daughter's wrist a large rhinestone bracelet which, it was explained, was a "gift from one of her boy friends." So, you see, gifts of costume jewelry are quite all right, even though the cost is sometimes as high as that you mention. After all he could also have sent you a large spray of orchids that could have cost the same amount of money or entertained you at an equally expensive dinner.

• •

I have a class ring I got from a boy in grammar school. Now we are both in high school, and, although we date occasionally, it really doesn't mean anything to me any more. Should I give it back to him or just not wear it and say nothing? V.S., DETROIT, MICHIGAN

Give it back to him, and say something about how much fun it was wearing it but that you feel you don't want to wear anything like that now. He'll understand.

LITTLE COURTESIES

In bad weather, when girls have to wear storm boots to parties, should the boys help them off and on with them? M.I.S., PORTLAND, MAINE

Yes, especially if these are removed out-of-doors, on the porch, or in a lobby. If the girls have a separate dressing room where they are asked to remove their outer things, they manage their storm boots by themselves. And a girl who has removed her storm boots in the dressing room doesn't appear with them helplessly in her hand, at departure time, to get her escort's assistance. If he is something less than crazy about her he may consider her just a nuisance at a moment when he has many things to think of himself—making his adieux, collecting his own belongings, getting the car, etc.

• •

My brother was visiting us and was ready to leave when I asked my eighteen-year-old daughter to get her uncle's coat. She replied that a girl does not get a man's coat, that he should go and get it himself. Is it proper for a girl to hand the male guests their coats, whether they are friends or relatives? MRS. M.A.C., WEST ORANGE, NEW JERSEY

As your assistant hostess she may properly get a male visitor's coat. If you were alone and had male visitors you would be likely to at least make the gesture of opening the closet door and getting out the coat, although you would not necessarily help a man into it. Even when she is much older, if there is no acting host in the household to perform such a function for male guests, she will be the one to make this slight gesture of farewell. Like you, too, she also rises to welcome her guests, male or female, and again rises to see them off.

• •

My family isn't poor, but we come from a neighborhood you couldn't exactly call fancy. My mother was careful to teach us good manners, but I guess they aren't the same manners other people expect sometimes from a fellow. Recently I began going around with a girl who lives in a big apartment house the other side of town. She says I embarrass her sometimes—like the time I got out of the cab and helped her out in front of her house. She said I should have let the doorman do it. How can I learn? J.B.M., SPRINGFIELD, MASSACHUSETTS

Your girl, young like yourself, is just learning, too, or she wouldn't be so sensitive. It would never occur to me to be offended if my escort chose to escort me out of a cab while the doorman stood by. Usually, where there is a doorman, it is more convenient for him to perform this service while the gentleman pays the taxi driver. Also, this is the doorman's function, and he may be jealous of it. Certainly, when he is busy with many other passengers, you would help your girl out of the cab rather than keep her and the cab waiting. As for learning, read etiquette material and ask your girl. Women love to teach manners and are flattered by being asked what's right.

• •

I am fourteen and have a friend who hasn't been taught things concerning cleanliness at home. I feel, as her most intimate friend, I should try to help her along these lines. But when I approach her it seems I am too blunt and she is hurt. How should I bring up this tender subject? P.C.I., LITTLE ROCK, ARKANSAS

Don't—in so many words. Put yourself in your friend's place. You wouldn't like to be told that you needed a manicure, that your hair could do with more frequent shampooing, that your shoulder straps are soiled. In telling your friend these things, no matter how kind your intentions, you make her feel inferior and resistant to your advice. Instead, why not suggest that you do some of these things together? Ask her to give you a shampoo and help you with your hair, and you do the same for her. Give yourselves manicures together and perhaps ask her to help straighten up your bureau drawers. Make her feel that she does know these things, and you will find that she will take pains to acquire any knowledge that you can so tactfully give her without seeming to preach. Learning these things at your age can be a lot of fun—and boy-catching, too. Your friend is sure to find that out and want desperately to be as attractive as possible.

• •

My teen-age son often comes home from various public places with ash trays he has taken as souvenirs. He tells me all the other boys and girls his age do likewise. I tell him that no matter what they do it is still stealing, and I won't permit him to keep these things in his room. He thinks me unreasonable. Do you agree? MRS. T.S.C., BUTTE, MONTANA

I think *he* is unreasonable. The purloining of other people's property is stealing. However, some restaurants and night clubs do expect a certain amount of this "lifting" of such things as ash trays, and they consider it good advertising for these things to be taken out of clubs and into people's homes. If a boy or girl wishes to have one of these things with the name of the public place upon it and asks permission to take it, that is another thing. Just be sure how your son came by these articles. Anything not honorably come by should be taken back—or if necessary, sent back with a note of apology.

• •

I am a boy in boarding school. I love to get letters, of course, especially from girls. When I meet them on vacations, is it all right to ask them to write to me, or do I have to write to them first? J.O'N., ROWAYTON, CONNECTICUT

You should ask them if you may write to them, and then you write the first letter and hope they'll answer you. Girls, by the way, should not write to boys in boarding school without being asked to do so, unless there's some very good reason, such as the tendering of an invitation.

• •

I know that it is not necessary for men or boys to remove their hats in public buildings such as stores or office buildings. I do wonder, however, if a school building would be considered in the same sense as a store? MRS. E.B., MORRISTOWN, NEW JERSEY

Since a school is a place for learning, it should be a place where boys are taught good manners. For this reason, they should remove their hats upon entering, even though a school may be considered a public building.

SPECIAL PROBLEMS

My son has had an allowance since he was six, and I think he's handled it very well. Now he is fifteen, and he would like me to increase his allowance so that he can buy all his own clothes, and perhaps even have a checking account. Do you think this is wise? MRS. F.O.M., WICHITA, KANSAS

It depends very much on the boy, but your boy sounds as if he could stand the increased responsibility. It would be valuable to teach him now how to handle a checking account. He might open a special account in your local bank—and, at his age, it is permissible. He must learn the responsibility of handling his money well, of never overdrawing, of keeping careful account of what he spends and of what he deposits. Certainly, fifteen is not too early to learn this. If you can, go back with him over your own accounts and determine what you have been spending a year for his clothes, and then add something to it for the future year when he will be growing and needing, perhaps, more clothes for social things. You can then arrive at the amount he needs for school, for spending money, and for clothes. If he is the kind of boy you describe, I think that he could well manage this whole sum given to him once, or, divided, twice a month. It should be put into his checking account, and he should pay his bills himself. An arrangement like this obviates the many arguments the mothers and fathers of teen-agers have as to whether or not a boy or girl may have a certain article of clothing he desires. The answer is, "If you can afford it out of your allowance and nothing else suffers seriously, by all means, use your judgment and get it if that seems important."

• •

My daughter is sixteen years old and is a junior in high school. She would like to go to a private school. I have not had a college education, and I shall have to meet the head of the school for an interview. Do you suppose I will hinder my daughter's chances of being accepted at the school? I know if I had the social background, she would have no difficulty in being accepted. I have a friend who has several degrees and who is now doing research work at one of the foremost universities. He has gone to private schools all his life. Wouldn't it be better for him to go with my daughter when she visits the school? I myself am a widow. M.A.S., ORANGE, NEW JERSEY

Your friend's educational background has nothing to do with the desirability of your daughter as a student in the school to which you want to send her. In all good private schools, children come from all sorts of backgrounds in this country and from abroad. You do not have to have a college education to be a well-informed and attractive person. I am sure your daughter is proud of her mother and wants you to go with her. Surely the school would prefer it that way. The top schools, of course, have rigorous scholastic requirements and more or less pick and choose among children they think will represent the school well. They are interested in character and genuine social attractiveness, rather than in family background and the social position of the family. An attractive boy and girl, with adequate marks, who has something within himself to offer, has the best chance.

• •

A few weeks ago I was invited to my boy friend's home. While there I was invited to stay over night and did so. My parents say this is wrong. What do you think? Would it make any difference if we were engaged? M.M.M., INDEPENDENCE, MISSOURI

I assume that you were properly chaperoned by the boy's parents and that you, of course, phoned home to ask your parents' permission to stay there and the boy's mother spoke to your mother. All of these points of etiquette in order, there should be no problem for your parents concerning this invitation that you accepted. You could accept it in this way, even though you were not engaged. You may also invite the boy to your house with your parents' permission.

• •

This year I am going to an all-girls' school. I have never attended one before and I am having quite a time convincing my friends that I want to go. They think I will miss out on a lot of activities and boy and girl relationships. I tell them that I will have plenty of time for that later. How can I convince them that I really want to go without hurting anybody's feelings and that it is not as bad as they think? N.N., SEATTLE, WASHINGTON

It seems to me that *you're* the one who is worried, rather than your friends. I myself went to boarding school, but in Europe, where even the holidays did not mean that I would return to my former friends. For many children good boarding schools mean increased concentration on work and often better marks, and social life, when it comes, is enormously appreciated. Often, actually, boys and girls away at school enrich their friendships, not only in their new environment but with those left behind, through correspondence. And such a child coming back on school holidays has the advantage of a certain prestige over those who continue to go to school locally. And when they do come home they seem to be almost fresh, new personalities in their groups because of their absence. This may mean that a girl or boy who didn't have too much success with the opposite sex before going away to school comes back with a glamor that makes previously indifferent friends eager for his or her attention.

How is a class ring worn—toward the wearer or away from the wearer? Is there any change after graduation?
B.S., MEDICINE HAT, MONTANA

Generally, the design on the ring is worn toward the wearer. I find that in some schools after graduation the design is worn away from the wearer. This is true also in West Point, where class rings originated in this country. It is true also at the Naval Academy and the Air Force Academy.

BABIES AND CHILDREN

CHRISTENINGS

We are going to have a home christening for our baby. Should formal invitations be sent out? We plan to have it at five o'clock and follow it with a buffet supper. Should both the minister and his wife be invited or just the minister? Isn't there some traditional punch that is served? I.W.R., LONG BEACH, CALIFORNIA

Formal invitations are not sent for a christening. Close friends and relatives are invited by telephone, by word of mouth, and by note. The clergyman's wife is included in the invitation. The traditional drink at christenings was a caudle cup (a mixture of wine or ale with eggs, sugar, and spices), but this has, in the main, been replaced by champagne, plain or in a delicate punch. Often at afternoon christenings a dry sherry is served. It should be kept in mind that this is a celebration in honor of the baby, following a formal religious ceremony. It has a character quite different from a cocktail party and should be kept on such a plane that even the most conservative baby could not object to the behavior and bearing of his elders.

• •

At what age is a baby christened, and is it permissible for male children to wear christening dresses? U.S.Y., DETROIT, MICHIGAN

It depends upon the denomination. The matter should be discussed with your clergyman. You should know

227

that some Protestant denominations permit home christenings but that Catholics do not, except in cases of dire emergency. Some Protestant denominations do not permit christening or baptism until the child has reached an age of understanding. The Baptists, for example, have a dedication of babies, but actual baptism usually does not take place until about the child's tenth year, and of his own free will. Yes, a boy may wear a christening dress too.

• •

Is it proper to have a grandparent for a godparent in the Presbyterian church? Do the parents ask the prospective godparents whether they wish to serve before the baby's arrival or shortly thereafter? MRS. J.R.L., LOUISVILLE, KENTUCKY

Although relatives do often serve as godparents, I do not recommend the choice of grandparents as godparents. Godparents should be the approximate age of the child's actual parents or younger, because the association with the child should run at least through his formative years. The godparents have the implied responsibility of parenthood should the actual parents die before the child reaches maturity, even though legal guardian arrangements are usually noted in wills.

Among Presbyterians, baptism (the proper term for this denomination) is one of the two sacraments. However, godparents are not usually appointed but may be if the parents so desire.

CHOOSING A NAME

A fine Irish name for a boy is "Florence." It has long been in our family, and I would like my daughter-in-law to give it to her first son in order to maintain the family tradition. She says that "Florence" is a girl's name in this country and that she would be handicapping a son by using it, tradition or no tradition. What do you think? F.A.O'N., ROANOKE, VIRGINIA

I feel that practicality should come ahead of tradition. "Florence" is not a fighting name for a boy in Ireland, but it well could be here. Giving a boy a name that could be mistaken for a girl's name is to put him at a psychological disadvantage. There are so many handicaps to overcome on the way up to adulthood, why add one more in a name?

• •

I want to name my baby for my mother-in-law, if it's a girl. Should she be called "Junior"? A.J.R., MIAMI, FLORIDA

No. A girl is never called "Junior," which is a masculine suffix.

• •

If my coming baby is a son we should like to name him for his grandfather. However, my husband had a brother who was named for his father and was therefore "Junior." This brother is mentally ill and will never recover. He is institutionalized. Would it be proper for us under the circumstances to call the new baby "Junior"? A.G.L., INDIANAPOLIS, INDIANA

You could not possibly call the baby "Junior" for two reasons. One is that even though his uncle is in a mental institution he still retains his identity, and you may not take it from him. Secondly, "Junior" means "the son of," and your baby will not be the son of his grandfather, obviously. If he is a boy you may call him, however, "Second," naming him for his grandfather.

• •

If my coming baby is a boy I want to name him for my husband who is not a "Junior." Some people tell me "Junior" is old-fashioned and not used any more and the numeral "II" is correct. I'd appreciate your advice. R.F.H., CEDAR RAPIDS, IOWA

The term "Junior" actually means "son of." Therefore the child of a father who receives the same name as his father is "Junior." However, if the child is to be named for his grandfather (whose name differs from his father's), he cannot be "Junior" but he is "II" or "2nd." The same is true if he is named for an uncle or a cousin who bears exactly the same name in full, or, if he is named for a very illustrious ancestor, in which case he may be known as "II" or "2nd," "III" or "3rd," depending on how many others still living are named exactly for that ancestor. So therefore the term "Junior" is not in any way old-fashioned, although there is a trend away from it, fortunately, but it must be used correctly. I prefer to see a child, even when named for his father, have some portion of his name belonging to him alone, either in the first name or the middle name, so that he does not have to be called "Junior" or "little John" the rest of his life—or at least while his father is alive. This is something he may grow to resent.

BIRTH ANNOUNCEMENTS

My husband and I have been married seven years and are adopting our first baby. It will be one of the happiest moments when he arrives. Could my husband pass out cigars to his co-workers and friends? Our other problem is that we live in a small community, and the arrival will be announced in the local paper. How can it be stated properly and yet made to sound as if he were born to us? MRS. F.H.H., CHESHIRE, CONNECTI-CUT

Of course your husband may pass the cigars, but you should be perfectly frank about the baby's being adopted. You may announce his adoption by sending individual notes to friends and relatives, but you may also have a card engraved. Here is one suggested way of doing it:

Dr. and Mrs. Arthur George Adamson
take pleasure in announcing that
Bruce McKay Adamson
(age one month)
has been adopted as their son.

Eighteen Fox Lane
Red Hook, New York 12571

Please do something like this and do not pretend to anyone that you have borne this child yourself, for in the years to come he will certainly happen upon the deception. The actual birthdate of an adopted child is not given in birth announcements unless of course there is no real reason to conceal it—for example, if an uncle adopts a niece or nephew after a family tragedy. But baby's actual birthdate is the one he celebrates.

• •

I am to have a baby in the near future. Of course I want to send out birth announcements, and I am just not sure to whom to send them. Also, there was a surprise baby shower for me. Is it necessary for me to send announcements to all the families that were present? G.K.C., AUGUSTA, GEORGIA

Stationery stores have very charming little birth announcements which are quite proper to send out. I would send one, if you are sending them, to the various girls who came to the shower for you. A more formal —and more expensive—way of announcing the new baby is to have tiny calling cards with the baby's name attached to your own calling card with white, pink, or blue ribbon. Any good stationer will show you how this is done.

BABY SITTERS

How old do you think a baby-sitter should be? Some of my friends employ girls of eleven and twelve to sit

with their babies in the evening. I don't think this is right, do you? B.B.T., POUGHKEEPSIE, NEW YORK

A child of twelve or perhaps thirteen during the daytime might be satisfactory as a baby-sitter if she is truly responsible and if the mother is within hailing distance. She might be employed to go along with the mother shopping to help with a small child, too. But for evening sitting an older person should take care of a child, especially a tiny baby. A boy or girl in the late teens, known to be stable, conscientious, and really fond of children, would be suitable. For overnight or longer periods, children should be left with an older woman if possible. Sometimes a man and his wife are an even better choice if the house is in an isolated district. A mother should always consider that an emergency might occur with which an immature person might not be able to cope.

• •

Do you think that teen-age girls should be allowed to have their boy friends in while they are baby-sitting? L.J.D., PELHAM, NEW YORK

No, I do not. Baby-sitting is a serious business, and the person taking on this responsibility should not have anything else on her mind. Wise parents do not permit their teen-age daughters to entertain their boy friends when there are no adults in the house. A very responsible girl might be permitted occasionally to have another girl visit her while she is sitting, but she should not be allowed to have a party or, as I have said, to have in boy friends.

CLOTHES

Can you suggest some suitable baby presents aside from the usual sacques, bonnets, blankets, etc.? R.R.W., CHARLESTON, WEST VIRGINIA

One of my own favorites is that silver dumbbell which makes a fine comfort when the baby's teeth come in. Every baby is enchanted, too, by the wide variety of nursery mobiles now being offered. Hung above the crib, they fascinate him for hours on end. For the infant who is literally going to get "everything," there is nothing better than a savings bond or a contribution to his savings account.

• •

How soon before a baby is expected should a baby shower be given? Who should give a shower? MRS. L.M., NORWALK, CONNECTICUT

Baby showers are usually given about one month before the baby is expected. A shower may be given by a friend of the mother-to-be, never by a relative. Shower gifts may be in neutral colors—white, pale green, or yellow, or in the traditional pink and blue now worn interchangeably by boys and girls.

PARTIES

I am having a graduation party for my son at our home. I am inviting forty people or more, mostly relatives. The relatives have small children—some eighteen of them—and usually take them along when they are invited out. Certainly on this occasion I would like the grown-ups to enjoy themselves without worrying about the children. How can I word my invitations, telling them not to bring the children, and yet not offend? Y.M.A., CHICAGO, ILLINOIS

Tell them just as you have told me. Say that there will be so many coming that if the children come too there will hardly be room for the grown-ups, and ask them if on this occasion they will make arrangements to leave their children at home. If this seems really difficult, perhaps one relative can arrange to take all eighteen, with several sitters, paid for out of a common fund, so that the grown-up party may proceed happily.

• •

In a few months, I expect to become a grandparent. I have been asked to give a baby shower for my daughter. I have declined, simply because I don't think it is proper to give a shower before the birth—so many unfortunate things could happen. MRS. E.R., ORANGE, NEW JERSEY

I agree with you only in part. Showers are usually given before the baby's birth, because we do look on the coming event with optimism—which is good and normal. However, you are right in another respect. Arrangements for the shower—any shower, as a matter of fact (with some ethnic exceptions)—should not come from within the family. The shower proposal should come from friends of the mother-to-be, otherwise it looks as if the family itself is soliciting presents for the newcomer. I know you will be able to put this tactfully to those you think should be the sponsors.

SPECIAL PROBLEMS

My first baby was born dead. Friends gave me many gifts in anticipation of his birth, and now I don't know whether I should return the gifts or what I should do. G.S.N., PRINCETON, NEW JERSEY

The use of the word "first" in your letter to me indicates what most women know in their hearts—that they will try again after such a tragic circumstance. Do not return the gifts, as this would sadden your friends. Keep them in the hope of having another baby soon.

• •

When I take my baby shopping, I leave his carriage in the sun outside of the supermarket. Often when I come out I find some strange women leaning over him, dis-

arranging his blanket, breathing in his face, and, in general, trying to entertain him. I don't like strange people to touch my baby, but I don't know how to say so without being rude. Can you suggest something? MRS. B.T., MIAMI BEACH, FLORIDA

I can think of almost nothing you can't say so long as you say it politely and with a pleasant look on your face when an admonition must be made. I would say to such a person, "I'm trying to get the baby to go to sleep, and I hope you don't mind but I'd rather you wouldn't disturb him in any way." Then if she's someone who really can't understand even this and continues to hover over the baby, say, "It's really not very sanitary to put your face so close to a small baby. I never allow it." If you can remember when you have to say something like this that the person who has been attracted to the baby has a tremendous need for maternal expression, you will say what you have to say in the most kindly, yet firm manner. She doesn't really mean to make a nuisance of herself. And, of course, if you can leave the baby with someone while you shop it is a far better idea than leaving it unattended.

• •

I have a little girl who shuffles as she walks. I have tried everything to get her to pick up her feet but it does no good. What can you suggest? MRS. J.A.F., SPRINGFIELD, MISSOURI

First, check with your doctor to be sure there is no medical reason for this condition. If there is none, check your daughter's shoes. Be sure that her shoes fit properly. If she is wearing loafers, be sure they are not so wide they slip off her feet as she walks. Properly fitting shoes should correct this. You should also tell her that "Ladies never shuffle as they walk but pick up their feet gently and walk straight ahead, toes straight." A shuffling walk is irritating to hear and most unattractive to observe, tell her. Explain that movie stars must all learn to walk beautifully.

I have a son who has a nervous habit of clearing his throat every few minutes. What can I do? MRS. L.O.N., WICHITA FALLS, TEXAS

There may possibly be a medical reason for this. If you've checked with your doctor and there is none, then at a moment when he seems fairly relaxed, explain to him what he is doing. He is probably quite unconscious of it.

• •

My daughter has a little friend at school who comes from a decidedly underprivileged home. The child comes here often and seems to appreciate it. From time to time she invites my daughter to her home, but as her mother has many other children and they have so little money, I feel this is an imposition, and I don't allow my daughter to accept. However, I am worried about this because obviously the little girl wants to show her appreciation. What should we do? MRS. D.D., DENVER, COLORADO

Let your daughter go. Perhaps in this household full of children, the mother has more to give than many more privileged people—financially—imagine. You can help your daughter to maturity by letting her understand that parental love is not dependent upon a bank account, that security is not definitely determined by how one lives, in a material sense.

• •

Can you give me a list of the important "don'ts" that might serve as a guide for my two boys, aged eight and ten? E.S., CHEYENNE, WYOMING

Well, they don't:—
1. Scratch, pick the teeth, spit, comb the hair, or tend the nails in public.
2. Chew with their mouths open or with obvious noise or lip-smacking.
3. Leave a spoon in a cup, or eat with a knife, or tuck

in their napkins, or suck their fingers instead of wiping them on a napkin.

4. Sit down to a meal unwashed and uncombed or improperly dressed.

5. Fail to greet others in the household when they arise or return home.

6. Tilt chairs or lounge on the dinner table or put their elbows on it, except between courses (and then preferably one elbow at a time, if any).

7. Go up and down stairs like elephants and bang doors after them.

8. Pass in front of others without excusing themselves.

9. Use a flat "Yes" or "No" in answer to questions. Instead, "Yes, Mother," or "Yes, Mr. Roberts (or Sir)."

10. Swear in a way that is considered offensive (though most children need a list of acceptable "swear words"—perhaps one list for use in the parents' presence, another list for away from home where there is likely to be more rigidity in the matter).

11. Put more than a manageable mouthful in their mouths at one time. Talk with their mouths *full* (conversation is permissible with *some* food in the mouth).

12. Burp, sneeze, or cough without attempting to turn away from others, and then only behind the cupped hand or a clean handkerchief.

13. Behave noisily and conspicuously in public places.

14. Enter a room whose door is closed without knocking and waiting for permission to enter.

15. Interrupt a conversation except for an important reason and then only after asking permission to speak.

• •

I am constantly appalled at the atrocious manners exhibited by today's children. They seem to have no regard whatever for the comfort or sensitivies of others. Is this the result of the so-called "permissive" method of upbringing? I don't think much of it. MRS. E.T.R., LANCASTER, PENNSYLVANIA

I feel that basically children's manners are really absorbed from their parents. This does not mean that I think children should be permitted to be rude or unmannerly as a result of outside influences without having it called to their attention. There are certain accepted manners which children should be continually encouraged to cultivate. They should learn that mother and father do certain things to be socially agreeable and that these courtesies will be expected of them, too, as soon as they are able to cope with them. I have never seen a child with well-mannered parents who grew into an adult completely devoid of social grace. But I have seen such a child, in rebellion at constant goading about his manners, go through a savage period in which the only conformity with social customs was enforced with damaging tension to both child and parents. Such a nagged child gets to believe he *is* a boor and that nothing can remedy the fact, so he might as well be as primitive as possible just to show them. Most children eventually rise to the social graces in their own good time. In the meantime, they should hear us deliver the courteous phrases for them, without irritation. And they need to be told quietly, before and after social events, what will be expected of them as a matter of course.

• •

Do you think very young children, just able to print little notes, should be made to write thank-you's to adults who have given them presents at Christmas and for birthdays, or do you think verbal thanks is enough? Would it be better for the mother to write such notes?
MRS. D.B., BALTIMORE, MARYLAND

It is really never too early to have children do their own thank-you's if they can. Notes on plain lined paper saying merely, "Thank you. Love, Bobby" will be treasured by someone like grandma. Having mothers take over the chore really teaches the children nothing in the way of appreciation. If they don't learn early, then they may never learn at all. Teach them to enjoy such social needs.

I have been correcting my children when they say "sweat" instead of "perspire." They tell me I am way behind the times, that "sweat" is now accepted and that "perspire" is now nice-nellie. MRS. K.F., PITTSBURGH, PENNSYLVANIA

"Perspire" is still in the running and many people do prefer to use it. But, I feel there is nothing wrong with "sweat." There is more forthright language, fewer euphemisms now.

My baby was born on February 29th. Does this mean that we celebrate his birthday only every four years? MRS. O.M., MILWAUKEE, WISCONSIN

Actually, the legal and official date of birth is February 29th which does come only once in four years. This does not mean, however, that the child gains a year only once in every four. Legally a year passes each February 28th and this is the date on which he should celebrate his birthday with a "real" one coming up just once in four years.

When my grandfather takes me out, he makes me eat my pizza, a hot dog or ice cream cone where we buy it. He says nice people don't walk along the street eating things, that it is okay to do this only at a fair or something. Isn't it okay to eat things on the street now? E.F., ST. PAUL, MINNESOTA

If your grandfather buys these things for you at stands, sometimes the stand owners want you to move on as the space is limited. If you are very young indeed and are walking along the street with an ice cream cone in your hand, you could very easily knock it against somebody. Some places, such as stores, won't let you walk in eating food. Eating food as you walk along the street still is considered very informal, but you do see many people doing it. The important thing is to be considerate of other people, not to litter and not to annoy others in any way with your eating. Sometimes it is indeed best to eat the food where you get it, for there is always the matter of sticky fingers, smeared faces and of course the disposal of leftovers, napkins, etc. Tell your grandfather that a lot of very nice people eat on the street today, but they do use judgment about it.

My husband and I, who are Christian, are invited to the *a bris* of a friend's second son. We didn't know them when the first son was born. As you know, *a bris* is the ritual circumcision of a male Jewish child. Are we expected to take a gift, and if so, what is suitable? MRS. W.L., PORTLAND, OREGON

It is usual to give a gift to the first male child in the family on such an occasion, but optional for the others. As you didn't know these people before, I suggest you take a gift now. This could be anything that you would take to a christening, for example a silver spoon, napkin ring or silver baby cup. Bonds are always popular. If you decide on the latter, it should be made out jointly with his mother in the baby's full name, Robert Louis Kamin, *or* Mrs. Sarah Kamin (this is the government requirement regarding a married woman. The husband's given name is not used with the title, Mrs., in this case).

BUSINESS ETIQUETTE

INTRODUCTIONS

I am a secretary who works for two men. We all work in one office. Is it correct for my bosses to introduce me to an outside visitor? Recently we had a visitor from England who spent an afternoon with my bosses. He sat not more than three or four feet away from me. I felt embarrassed at not being introduced, particularly when they left the room and I was alone with him. What do you think? J.M., DETROIT, MICHIGAN

Yes, you should have been introduced to him. In a case like this, which concerns business, a subordinate woman worker is introduced to a male superior. (*His* name is mentioned first: "Mr. Prentiss, my secretary, Miss Garcia.") Socially, of course, a man is always introduced to a woman.

• •

I am an office manager. When a new secretary comes in, do I introduce her to the other girls on the staff or vice versa? How do I introduce her to the non-executive men, to the executives? B.K., SAN FRANCISCO, CALIFORNIA

In introducing the new secretary to the other girls in the office, you may say, "Miss Brown (or "Anne"), this is Miss Smith, who will work with us here in this department now. Mary (or "Miss Smith"), this is Anne Brown (or "Miss" or "Mrs. Brown")." In introducing her to her male co-workers, not her superiors, you in-

241

troduce the men to her, saying, "Miss Smith (or "Mary"), this is Mr. Jones (or "Bob Jones"), who operates the Comptometer." In introducing her to executive males, you say, "Mr. Wittlesey, this is (or "I'd like to present") Miss Smith, our new secretary." Optionally you may say "Miss Mary Smith." Many offices are now very informal with most employees calling each other by their first names. In many cases employers call employees by their first names, and sometimes vice versa. Follow the practice of the particular office in which you find yourself.

CARDS

When a business firm has cards engraved for Christmas, is it proper to send them to a business associate's home, addressed to husband and wife, or should they be sent to the associate's office, addressed to him alone? MR. W.C., CHICAGO, ILLINOIS

When they are sent to him at home, they should be jointly addressed. When they are sent to his office, they should be addressed to him alone.

• •

If a man or woman has a degree which he is entitled to use in his profession, how is it used on his business card and how socially? How does he sign his name in business and how socially? P.C., STATEN ISLAND, NEW YORK

Clergymen, doctors of medicine (or allied sciences such as psychology and dentistry), judges, senators, mayors, military or naval officers, governors, professors who make teaching their profession and are holders of university professorships, all use their titles on their social and professional cards. Regarding the doctorates; the letters indicating the title follow the name on the business card, for example: LL.D., M.D., D.D.S., and so forth and are not preceded by Mr., Dr., or Miss. Holders of purely honorary degrees usually omit them on both social and professional cards. And, although they may be called doctor, socially, they do not use their degrees in social signatures. For example, Dr. Robert Brown signs himself "Robert Brown" socially, never "Robert Brown, M.D.," never "Dr. Robert Brown." The title on a social letter may be printed or engraved on his stationery and is always used on the return address. A medical doctor signs himself in business correspondence, "John Jones, M.D." Some Ph.Ds (those at Yale, Harvard, and Vanderbilt Universities, for example) usually choose not to call themselves "Doctor" although they frequently use the Ph.D in professional correspondence. Increasingly, Ph.Ds use the title socially and professionally, however, and this includes social engraved announcements and invitations.

How does a man's business card differ from his social card? There are many occasions on which I am never sure whether I should send my business card. For example, if I have a customer who's celebrating a wedding anniversary and I want to send flowers, do I send my business card or my social card? Of course, I send the flowers for business reasons. W.F., RICHMOND, VIRGINIA

You know, of course, the main difference between a man's social card and his business card is that his social card always carries "Mr." before his name, his business card does not. His business card is larger than his social card, and for an executive it is always engraved or printed in black conservative type faces or script. Business cards used for advertising purposes may be printed or engraved in colors, but those of the top executives of the company shouldn't be. In sending flowers under the circumstances you give, you send your social card, as you are making a social gesture on a social occasion. But if the man doesn't know you and your connection with the firm you wouldn't intrude upon him at such a time. On the other hand, if he were opening a new store you could certainly send flowers accompanied by your business card.

• •

I am a woman about to be promoted to an executive position in our firm. Should my card read "Louise Severy," or "Miss Louise Severy"? L.N.Y., NEW YORK, NEW YORK

It should read "Miss Louise Severy." A woman who is "Mrs." in business should also use this title on her card, so people may know how to address her. Some women may prefer to use Ms. but some title is needed.

• •

I am a doctor and have both personal and business checks. I plan to have them imprinted by the bank. Should my business checks carry my title differently than my social ones? DR. E.M., BRUNSWICK, NEW JERSEY

Yes. The imprint on your business check should read:
            "Edward Moore, M.D."
with the address. On your personal checks the name appears as

            "Dr. Edward Moore"
with either your business address or home address, depending on how you manage your personal bookkeeping.

GIFTS

I worked with two girls for eight years, and we became very good friends and exchanged Christmas gifts. Then, three years ago I changed jobs (but we still exchanged gifts), and this year I would like to stop buying gifts for them as I haven't seen them for three years and I want to cut down my Christmas list. I would like to write them a nice letter and tell them so but I can't seem to find the words to do it without hurting their feelings. How do you think this should be handled? V.D., MONTREAL, CANADA

Do it in a simple, direct, and friendly way. Write them well before Christmas and say that, while you have always valued your mutual giving at this season of the year, you find that this year you must cut your Christmas giving to your immediate circle but that you hope that as friends you will always exchange cards and at least once a year give each other news. Undoubtedly they too will be vastly relieved that you have taken the initiative in what is so often an embarrassing situation.

• •

My boss gets a lot of presents at various times from firms that supply us. The salesmen's cards are usually enclosed, and I wonder how we should handle the thanks on this. Should we just thank the salesman when he comes around, do I write for the boss, or does the boss dictate a letter? MISS M.E.W., OAKLAND, CALIFORNIA

I think it depends very much on the status of the salesmen in relation to your boss. Certainly your boss should not take his time to write a personal note to every salesman who sends him a calendar or some other gift advertising services offered. However, you may, verbally, when you see the salesman, thank him if you wish, but in such cases his gift is really a business getter and merely requires passing acknowledgment at your convenience. There are some salesmen who are definitely in the executive class themselves and who give gifts of some importance to major customers. In a case like this your boss should dictate a brief note of thanks, if he himself has personal contact with the salesman. If he never sees him, you yourself could write such a letter of acknowledgment which might begin, "Mr. Brown has asked me to thank you, etc." Where business gifts are exchanged between people who are on a social basis as well, the acknowledgments are always on the social level —often handwritten on personal stationery. However, many executives dictate such letters on special executive stationery, and this is quite acceptable too.

TELEPHONE COURTESY

I am a personal secretary for a major executive of my firm. When my phone rings should I say, "Miss Brown speaking" or should I say, "Mr. Carstair's office, Miss Brown speaking" or just "Mr. Carstair's office"? M.J.B., FLEMINGTON, NEW JERSEY

You say "Mr. Carstair's office," and add, if you wish, "Miss Brown speaking." Don't say, "This is Bob Carstair's office, Anne Brown speaking." This implies that you are on a first name basis with your boss (and you may well be) and that you expect the caller to call you "Anne." Such assumptions may make the caller quite uncomfortable.

• •

A new clerk is in the office—not a secretary, just a clerk. Usually answering the phone calls from the outside, she says "Miss Monroe speaking." At times she will put the name of the company first but always manages to put her name in also. As her name wouldn't be of any advantage to the customers, I am curious to know if this is the right or wrong procedure. She is not on the selling end. A.M.F., BANGOR, MAINE

Such a clerk should answer "The Jones Company," not "Miss Monroe speaking." As she has no official capacity, presumably the outside world is not interested in her name, and in this instance I can see no reason why she should announce it. On the other hand, if the phone call came in to her desk from the switchboard she would assume that someone wanted to talk to her in particular and would answer, "Miss Monroe speaking" —the proper business procedure.

• •

In calling up a doctor—or someone else whom you are going to consult for a service—is it correct to ask, "How are you?" first, or should you say, "Doctor, this is Mrs. So-and-so, I have a headache, etc."? A.S.L., SOMERVILLE, MASSACHUSETTS

Just announce your name and say immediately what you want. It is best to ask for an appointment or to ask the doctor to come to see you—if he makes house calls—without going into a lengthy discussion of your symptoms over the telephone. Illness is most interesting to those immediately concerned, but a doctor must protect himself emotionally from his patients' troubles in order to best serve them. It's more important to him and to you that he act to relieve your trouble than that he commiserate with you at length. At that, most doctors are reasonably sympathetic. If they didn't have innate sympathy for the troubles of others it is unlikely that they would have become doctors in the first place.

• •

How should an executive (a man) answer his business phone? I was taught it is very impolite for a man to use his own title when referring to himself, except to servants or other employees. Can you set me straight?
MR. H.A.M., WINSTON-SALEM, NORTH CAROLINA

In this country, an executive answering his own phone says merely "Black," or "John Black." He refers to himself as "Mr. Black" to servants and to employees who do not call him by his first name. To his clients or customers, he identifies himself on the phone as "John Black" if they know him well and as "John Black of the Ace Company" if their contact is more casual. If he is calling upon a woman on a business matter, he says, "This is Mr. Black," adding his company's name, if needed.

FAMILIAR PROBLEMS

Does business etiquette differ from social etiquette in regard to a gentleman's treatment of a lady? O.L., MOSCOW, IDAHO

Yes, in many cases it does. A subordinate woman employee, for example, usually rises if a top male executive approaches her desk to give her some instruction. She does not do this for her immediate superior, as it would mean she would be jumping up and down all the time. She rises for a superior woman executive too, under the same circumstances—that is, if her desk is visited by a superior with whom she is not in constant contact. She rises too for an important client or customer of the firm to whom she is introduced, whether male or female. Neither men nor women in business today expect social etiquette under business circumstances, merely general politeness and consideration.

Is it correct for an employer to address his secretary and other women employees by their first names? M.C.J., DETROIT, MICHIGAN

Many informal offices do this. It frequently encourages the employees to call the employers by their first names. In certain businesses, for example advertising, this seems to work well enough, whereas in others it would seem highly unsuitable, for example in law. There is also the danger of outsiders immediately calling all employees by their first names which can break down formality completely, although it is frequently comfortable and conducive of business and professional efficiency. People who seemingly have no last names and no titles, do not always inspire confidence at an executive level.

• •

When taking dictation must the book be placed on the lap of the stenographer, or is it quite proper to use the space on the boss's desk? L.B.B., SEATTLE, WASHINGTON

It's certainly much more convenient to put it on the desk and probably produces neater notes.

• •

As I am going to continue working after my marriage I thought it would be simpler for me to still use my maiden name. What do you think? H.S., ST. LOUIS, MISSOURI

I think it makes things much simpler if a girl who continues to work after her marriage uses her maiden name in business.

• •

Recently I saw a salesman come into a store with his hat on and with a cigar in his mouth. He removed neither the hat nor the cigar while talking to the manager of the store. I thought this very rude. MRS. O.W.H., ROANOKE, VIRGINIA

It was not only rude but poor salesmanship. Anyone, man or woman, should remove anything he is smoking when he speaks to anyone, whether or not he is trying to make a sale. A salesman should remove his hat in any indoor situation, even when he is trying to make a sale to a man. Anyone in a buying position is quite consciously influenced by deference on the part of the person who is trying to sell him something.

• •

There is a girl sitting near me in the office who indulges in loud gum-chewing and snapping all day long. What is your opinion of this? What can I do to stop it? L.D.F., WINTHROP, MASSACHUSETTS

Gum-chewing, I feel, is often a good release for tension, but it should certainly be done most privately. Undoubtedly your co-worker is not conscious of the fact that she makes so much noise. If you speak to her yourself she may be offended. The best thing is to take this problem to the office manager, as such things come within her, or his, province.

• •

In my work I travel quite a lot. Is it ever correct for me to permit a strange man to buy me a drink, either alcoholic or nonalcoholic, on these trips? MISS W.P., CHICAGO, ILLINOIS

No, never permit strangers, especially men, to buy drinks for you. And do not accept any invitations from such strangers for entertainment at the end of the journey, unless you arrange for friends or business acquaintances to join you. This rule applies even to older women traveling for business or social purposes.

• •

Recently when I went into a business office and told the receptionist my name, I heard her go to the office of her employer and say, "*A* Miss Woodward is calling." This seems very rude to me. W.B., PEORIA, ILLINOIS

Yes, it was. If you had not given her a card, she should have asked whom you represented. She should then properly have said, "A lady to see you" and handed him your card, or if you had no card, "Miss Woodward calling." If her employer didn't know you he might then ask her to find out, tactfully, why you were calling, or he might have sent out his secretary for the same purpose or to invite you in.

• •

Do you think it is good taste for a receptionist to smoke at her desk? MISS A.C.G., SPRINGFIELD, ILLINOIS

No, I do not. A receptionist should be the most courteous face of the company. She should look pleasant, act pleasant, and be all attention when anyone approaches her desk—even a salesman. She can't be any of these things to smoke or eat at her desk. She may, of course, smoke away from her desk in her periods of rest.

• •

Would you please give me some information on Christmas gifts to an employer? I am a private secretary to an executive in a large corporation and have received nice gifts from the boss and his wife at Christmas time and on several other occasions. I have often thought of getting him something for his desk, or perhaps something for their teen-age daughter but don't wish to embarrass him. Would a nice plant sent to his home directly from the florist be in good order? J.C., NEW HYDE PARK, NEW YORK

• •

No. Do not give them gifts yourself, although you may send a Christmas card, of course. At the executive level, gifts are sometimes exchanged between the boss and his employees, although not necessarily so. Actually such gifts from an employer are gifts from the corporation or the company, not gifts from him personally. They are part of his business expense. Should you have much social contact with the family, that is, if you are entertained by them as a friend rather than as an employee, you then, of course, may give Christmas gifts if you want on a personal basis—not on a business one.

• •

I am a woman executive and one of my main duties is entertaining customers for the firm. When these customers are men is it permissible for me to pick up the luncheon check as a representative of my organization? MRS. R.K., CHICAGO, ILLINOIS

Yes, you may, saying something such as, "This is business—you're the firm's guest." It is highly convenient for a woman executive to have her own credit card and to use it rather than cash at times like these. Most sophisticated businessmen understand the procedure and don't insist on "grabbing" the check when a woman executive is prepared to play hostess for business reasons. The less discussion of the matter the better.

• •

The wives of some of our executives here make a habit of dropping in at their husbands' office in the midst of our busiest days. They use the company's phones, ask their husbands' private secretaries to make hairdressing appointments for them. Sometimes they even park their children with us for an hour or so if they can get away with that. Mostly, I think the husbands feel about this the way we girls do, but they don't dare say so. But it might help if you said something about it. MISS L.B., NEW YORK, NEW YORK

Women who have worked themselves rarely are guilty of this kind of discourtesy. They understand all too well that their husbands work for a corporation and that social encroachments on the corporation's time are actually dishonest. Of course, there are exceptions when an executive's wife might have her husband's secretary do something for her—but the request should always come from the husband. A secretary resents very much being ordered around by her employer's wife. And, as I have said, this takes time away not necessarily from her employer's work, but from the corporation for whom he works. I would say that a wife's visits to a husband's office should be limited in the extreme. And a man even with the most charming children should think twice before having them descend upon the office except on very special occasions, perhaps during the Christmas holidays when he might like to show them off. But he needs to be in a very secure position in order to do even this.

I am a business woman, soon to make my first trip abroad professionally. I have used my maiden name in my career and feel that using my married name on my passport might create some confusion, as I am traveling with a group which does not know me under that name. Is it possible to apply for a passport in my maiden name? MISS W.H.Y., PLAINFIELD, NEW JERSEY

When the State Department grants such requests, the subsequent passport reads "Sheila Smith Moore A/K/A (also known as) Sheila Smith." You will find, however, that it is under your married name that you will be listed by hotels abroad. It is safer to have mail so addressed and to tell the concierge and telephone operators that you may get calls and mail in *both* names.

As a married woman how do I register to vote? MRS.
D.B., MILLERSVILLE, PENNSYLVANIA

You sign it with your legal name, not your social title;
that is, "Anne May Smith," or "Anne Clarke (your
maiden name) Smith," not "Mrs. John Smith." In most
states, I am told, a person may use any name he chooses
on legal or other documents so long as there is no in-
tent to defraud. If a married woman prefers to sign herself "Anne Clarke Smith" rather than "Anne May (her
baptismal name) Smith," there is usually no objection,
and I feel that this is a more distinguishing name than
one which uses the first two given names—if there are
two—with the married name.

• •

**Is it correct, in a firm, for the name plates on the
partners' inner doors to be shown as "Mr. Jones" or
"Mr. Brown," rather than using the full name or initials, such as "John Jones" or "J. Jones and George
Brown"?** L.R., DETROIT, MICHIGAN

Use "Mr. Jones." And in the case of a woman, you use
"Miss Jones" or "Mrs." or possibly, "Ms. Brown."
If the name is to be put on the door which faces the
public hallway, the name of course is then spelled out
in full, i.e., "John Jones."

**My boss was recently divorced. Frequently, invitations
come in from business organizations to the office addressed to Mr. and Mrs. He wants to do the right thing,
but how does he let these organizations know that he
is now divorced? May he ask to take a date? These
are business functions. What if he gets such an invitation at home from someone who doesn't know about
the divorce? Should he phone the hostess, state the situation, and ask if he may bring someone?** M.D., NEW
YORK, NEW YORK

In the first instance, you may call for him or write a
note saying something like this: "Mr. Willoughby is no

longer married and will be escorting Miss Doris Manning to the dinner. You may wish to correct your records."

In regard to phoning the hostess when he has received a private invitation, this is something he should do himself. He should explain without elaboration that he has been divorced. Unless the hostess asks him to do so, he should not suggest that he bring a date. Most hostesses are delighted to have an extra man. If the hostess does suggest that he bring someone, she should ask for the guest's name and if possible phone or write her to extend the invitation.

Are checks made out to clergymen written with or without their titles? D.E., HOUSTON, TEXAS

It is optional. The name alone without the title is sometimes used, but more commonly the title is included. A Monsignor, for example, would have his check made out to The Rt. Rev. John J. Cleary. The familiar title "Father" or "Pastor" is not used. Instead, for a clergyman, The Rev. Charles R. Billings is correct.

What is the proper way to put a name on a nameplate for my desk. I am a medical secretary in a small medical center and people are always asking me my name. I would like it to read just "Mrs. Roberts" as I dislike being called by my first name by strangers. Is this suitable? MRS. J.R., PERTH AMBOY, NEW JERSEY

Yes, and advisable.

Although I am getting married, I plan to keep my maiden name in business. What should I do about notifying Social Security. Should I tell them of my social name change (I plan to use my husband's name socially) but that I will be paid under my maiden name?

It is not necessary to change your name for Social Security purposes. Social Security goes by number. I have had a long professional career and have never used my married name on my Social Security records. Social Security tells me this is probably very wise as doing so might have caused some confusion. Many women never change the name under which they are recorded at Social Security headquarters. This is probably advisable for working women, especially those who have had more than one marriage.

Should a building custodian, a plumber, a meter reader, etc. be expected to remove his hat upon entering a house or an apartment in the course of his job when ladies are present?

No.

When you are wearing sunglasses and are being introduced to somebody outdoors, should you remove the sunglasses? What if you stop to speak to a friend on the street and you are wearing sunglasses—should you remove them?

I think it depends much on the sunglasses. If they are very dark and really conceal your eyes, people are frequently most uncomfortable trying to talk to you as the eye-to-eye contact is very important. Also people may not recognize you if you approach them with sunglasses on. In many cases it is better to remove them. Sales people in sunglasses, for example, approaching customers frequently get a chilly reaction as people seem not to want to trust those whose eyes they cannot see.

DIVORCE, SEPARATION, AND WIDOWHOOD

YOUR CORRECT NAME

Some questions have arisen between myself and some of my friends, more recently widowed, as to present-day designation of widows. Since we belong to the generation that was taught to resume their personal names in place of those of their husbands, we find some questions left unanswered by current etiquette dicta. I gather from what you have written that in addressing this letter to you I should refer to you as "Miss Amy Vanderbilt." But my friends and I are in doubt as to the *correct designation* of the widow of several husbands or of the divorced wife of several husbands. I would appreciate your comments. MRS. E.S.C., MONTEREY, CALIFORNIA

Most conservatively, a widow of one or more husbands retains the full name of her last husband until she remarries. Increasingly, however, widows—especially the young ones—are becoming Mrs. Sarah Smith, usually because they are returning to a career or entering one for the first time and this nomenclature is virtually necessary in business today because of computers. A widow following only a social life may certainly insist on the traditional Mrs. John Smith if she prefers this. A divorced woman either resumes her maiden name or combines her own surname with her former husband's surname, becoming "Mrs. Jones Smith." Sometimes if she has children by a previous marriage she returns to that husband's surname combining it with her own—"Mrs. Jones Brown"—so she and the children will bear the same name, but increas-

ingly divorcées who do not return to their maiden
names precede their given names with Mrs. A professional woman such as myself usually finds it much
simpler to use her maiden name throughout her professional career despite marriage.

• •

**I was divorced from my husband several years ago and
now he is dead. I would like to know how my calling
cards should read.** MRS. S.C., PROVIDENCE, RHODE IS-
LAND

When you were divorced you no longer could use your
husband's first name in connection with his last. If you
followed the conservative procedure of appending your
maiden name to his name, you became Mrs. Smith
Green. His recent death has nothing to do with a name
that you are to use on your calling cards since you are
not legally his widow, but instead, his divorced wife.
Therefore, you use the name Mrs. Smith Green on
your card. If, however, you are in business and have
been calling yourself Mrs. Muriel Green, you may decide, as do many divorcées now, to use the same name
socially for simplification.

• •

**I am a recent divorcée, and I'm not sure whether it is
proper for me to wear my wedding ring. I have two
children. What do you advise?** V.B., FARGO, NORTH
DAKOTA

A divorcée usually removes her wedding ring, even
when she has children, and wears her engagement ring
on other than the third finger of her left hand. Or she
has it redesigned into some other article of jewelry, if
indeed she wears it at all.

• •

**Within the next few months my divorce will be final.
I have a choice, I know, of returning to my maiden**

name or of using a combination of my maiden name and my married name. However, I have children. Would it be preferable for me to use "Mrs.," retaining my married name and preceding it with my former maiden name for the children's sake? E.F.F., MADISON, WIS-CONSIN

It is usually simpler that way when there are children. However, there are instances wherein a woman has married and divorced twice and has children by the first marriage but not by the second. In this case she sometimes chooses to return to her first married name to simplify matters. She uses it plus her former maiden name. In some rare instances, but also correctly, if for some reason she does not wish to use the name of her former husband or husbands, she returns to her maiden name and for the sake of the children precedes it by "Mrs." rather than "Miss." If her maiden name does not combine well with that of her former husband, for example, "Mrs. Green Brown," she can choose some other name in her family for her *nom de divorce*. Increasingly, however, as so many women are in the business world, divorcées follow the simpler procedure of just calling themselves "Mrs. Mary Brown" in social and in business life. A mother who has long been in professional life may, if she is divorced, assume for all purposes, legal, social, and professional, her professional name and for simplicity's sake be "Miss" at all times, even when she has children. This is not advisable, however, unless she is so prominent that she is generally identified by everybody with her maiden name.

I was in the throes of divorce when my husband died. I have two children who bear his name. I am thus legally a widow, but during my separation period I called myself Mrs. Mary Jones. I understand I am now entitled to be Mrs. John Jones, but I do not want to use my late husband's name. Is there any reason why I could not continue to call myself Mrs. Mary Jones? MRS. T.L., LEXINGTON, KENTUCKY

None. Many widows today are calling themselves the equivalent of Mrs. Mary Jones because of the complexities involving the computer. It is difficult to have two names—Mrs. Mary Jones in business, for example, and Mrs. John Jones socially. I am sure that in the fairly near future most widows will call themselves the equivalent of Mrs. Mary Jones for simplicity's sake.

I am a new widow with an eighteen-year-old son. Would it be proper for me not to wear my wedding ring? Having had a happily married life, I hope I can have a home again. Also, should I be introduced as "Mrs. Bronson" or as "Catherine Bronson"? C.B.S., HOT SPRINGS, COLORADO

Whether or not you continue to wear your wedding ring is a matter of your choice. Also a matter of choice is your title, the conservative "Mrs. John Bronson" or the now acceptable "Mrs. Catherine Bronson."

With very few exceptions, any woman who really puts her mind to marrying can do so. It is only fantasy that a woman must be beautiful, young, talented, physically desirable—to be claimed in the marriage market. A glance around you will show this very clearly. Women —tall, short, old, young, fat, thin, pretty, and ugly— all seem to find husbands. At a time like this I think your friends can be of great help. It is they who spread the word to eligible men whom they invite to their homes, where you will be, that you are available once more. It is easy in conversation to let it be known to any man who interests you that you are a widow. The fact of your previous happy life should make it easy for you to remarry and to make you sought after as a wife.

YOUR SOCIAL LIFE

I am a widow of forty-five and considered quite attractive. I have several young children but no servants. I live in a small community, and I wonder if it is all

right for me to entertain male guests week ends, or will people gossip? R.S.L., CEDAR RAPIDS, IOWA

People will gossip whether or not you have male guests under these circumstances. A woman of forty-five is her own chaperone usually today, and the presence of the children, when your guest is there overnight, should be an additional safeguard. Every woman, however, should value her reputation and conduct herself in such a way that she does not make a public display of her very private life.

• •

My young husband died recently under tragic circumstances. I was left with three young children and the need to readjust as quickly as possible to the situation so as to go back to the job I held before marriage. My days are filled with work for the children, but my evenings are understandably lonely. My friends have been very kind, but I wonder what the new convention is about my going out again with men. Am I supposed not to do so for a year as some of my conventional older friends insist? MRS. M.M.S., LOS ANGELES, CALIFORNIA

Although, as you say, it has been only a few weeks since your husband's death, I feel your own need for social contacts is of more importance than outworn notions of decorum. Today we know that the bereaved must be helped to take their places again in their communities under normal circumstances as quickly as possible. However, in your sensitive state, mourning as of course you are privately, you do not want to subject yourself to the criticism of older people who perhaps do not quite understand how our thinking has changed. If I were you I would accept an occasional invitation from a man to go to the movies or to the theater, to dinner or to the house of friends. I would not go dancing in a public place just yet. It might be better to go out quietly with various escorts rather than to permit the attention of just one. I think that restrained social activity should not be expected of you after about three months from the date of your bereavement. You may then give parties yourself and act as would any young woman of your age under regular social conditions.

• •

My husband is very friendly with his former wife, the mother of his two sons. He visits her to see the children at least once a week and stays to dinner. Do you think I should be invited at this time? He seems to think not. MRS. W.K.L., BOISE, IDAHO

Yes, he is right. He needs to see the children without your presence. Your being there would only remind them of the loss they've had to adjust to and could create considerable tension no matter how fond they may be of you. Under ordinary circumstances it is wisest for their mother not to be present at that time either, and for their father to have dinner with his children alone. But these things have to be worked out according to individual circumstances so that whatever is done is least painful emotionally.

• •

A couple in our neighborhood has been divorced, but both are living in the area. We have no quarrel with either one of them and would like to extend invitations to them for parties we give throughout the year. Are we supposed to make a choice or may we invite them both, so long as we don't invite them together? MRS. K.P., SYRACUSE, NEW YORK

Sometimes when a divorce has been what is called "scandalous," it is difficult for people who have been friends of the couple not to make a social choice when both remain in the community. Sometimes those who were first the friends of the husband continue to see him, and those who were, before the marriage, friends of the wife, continue to see her. Others who knew both equally well sometimes find it necessary to make a choice, but this is only necessary usually when there is bad feeling between the divorced couple. The important thing for friends to remember is not to carry tales from one to the other, if they are entertaining both socially—and, of course, separately. And the divorced people should not ask their friends to give them news of the other or involve their friends in their own personal problems of adjustment. After all, the divorced must make their new ways, socially, and must learn to put the bitter past behind them—especially if they are to be sought-after guests.

• •

Recently I was divorced. My immediate friends, of course, know about it, but I have a wide correspondence. Should I write to my friends explaining what happened or just mention it as the opportunity arises in my regular letters to them? W.F.A., NEW ORLEANS, LOUISIANA

If close relatives are among those with whom you correspond it is wise to write to them briefly, so that they do not hear the news through others. I feel that people are usually rather embarrassed to have to hear or read the intimate details of such things. Certainly it is not necessary for you to write in any detail. As all divorce is really sad you might write first of other things and then say, "You will be sorry to hear, I know, that Harry and I were divorced a few weeks ago." If there is anything to add about children, for example, you will say, "The children will live with me here and seem to be accepting the situation as well as possible." More than this you certainly need not say in a letter, nor has anyone the right to demand a fuller explanation. You will find in time that you will want to say less and less about the causes of your divorce. And it is well for friends to realize that the true causes of your divorce are rarely told and often not really well-known even by the parties involved. A wise man once replied, when asked why he had divorced such a seemingly perfect wife, "Look at the shoes on my feet.

Are they not handsome and of fine quality? And yet, which of you can tell me where they pinch me?"

• •

I have been keeping company with a man for ten years. My invalid brother, with whom I lived, died a few weeks ago. How long should I wait before getting married? C.G.A., MEDFORD, MASSACHUSETTS

It depends very much on the community in which you live and the circumstances. I assume that you must have taken care of your brother, relinquishing marriage yourself. I feel that it is only fair for you to marry as soon as you wish, but if you want to be really proper you could wait three months from the time of his death, which is more or less the modern idea for mourning. Why not discuss this with your friends—people who mean much to you—and see how they feel about it? I am sure that many would urge you to marry now as you have certainly done your duty and it would seem unfair to keep your fiancé waiting longer. I would urge, however, a quiet ceremony rather than a formal wedding.

• •

I am a widow of four months and have started going out with a nice man. He wants to get married but my family thinks I should wait a year to show respect for my deceased husband. I am forty. Would it be disrespectful for me to marry now? MRS. E.R.J., TOPEKA, KANSAS

Many widows and widowers marry this soon after their bereavement. Some, especially the widowers, remarry even earlier especially if they have young children or are very aged. I suggest you discuss the idea with your friends and your clergyman and see how they feel about it and the new man. Should you let his courtship and friendship go on a little longer, it is possible you may feel differently. You must be very lonely now and perhaps a little too anxious to re-establish a married life. Be sure that it isn't this that makes you think you are in love and ready to marry again so soon.

I have been recently divorced. I have two young children and a job that doesn't pay very well, and very small alimony. I am beginning to date again but find that paying the sitter really keeps me strapped. There is no privacy in our small apartment. Some friends, in somewhat the same situation, say that it is now acceptable for the woman's date to pay for the sitter as part of the cost of the evening. Is it?

It is recommended, I understand, by Parents Without Partners when there is a financial problem such as yours. What you must consider, however, is that many of the men who will date you are either divorced themselves and paying alimony, or just coming up in jobs that don't pay too well either. The cost of entertaining a woman is expensive enough without having to add what should, in my opinion, be her own personal expenses to the tab. I would much prefer your finding other women with whom you could exchange baby sitting services so that you would not have to accept baby sitting money from a man. This, it seems to me, puts you very much under obligation. Try to be a free agent. If you can leave your children with friends from time to time, then you should be able to entertain men guests at home at least part of the time. A man who finds himself comfortable in the attractive home of a woman, may very well find her attractive enough to become her husband. Also, if you are able to entertain at home you are free to invite men to dinner or to a party without waiting to be asked yourself.

DRESS

BUSINESS

Do you think it's all right for a junior executive to wear slacks and a sports jacket to his office, especially when the senior executives do so? H.R., DENVER, COLORADO

Yes. In certain organizations such as banks, for example, where the senior executives conservatively wear business suits, the younger executives frequently wear sports jackets and slacks and even in some cases sports shirts in the summertime. Follow the custom of the office in which you are, or when in doubt discuss the matter with the Personnel Manager. I prefer to see employees err on the side of conservatism, however. They seem more serious about their jobs than when they wear clothes that are utterly unsuitable even where guidelines are not or cannot be enforced.

What type of clothing do you consider most suitable for a secretary to wear to work? G.H., LA JOLLA, CALIFORNIA

It depends on the community in which she works. If she is in a large city, she preferably wears street clothes, pantsuits rather than slacks unless the latter are worn with a jacket, tailored suits, simple knits or wool for winter or cotton, linen or other suitable materials for summer. In hot weather pantyhose may be dispensed with in most offices if legs are well groomed. Heels should not be high. Make-up should be becoming but conservative and hair worn in such a fashion that it

265

does not interfere with work. I do not like to see office workers' long hair hanging down or for that matter any extreme of fashion. If boots are worn in winter, bedroom slippers should never be substituted for them indoors instead of suitable shoes (I have seen this).

Maybe you can help me. I am a single man just making my way in my profession. Shall I buy expensive shoes at $45.00 and up—if I can afford only a few pairs—or shall I buy inexpensive but neat looking shoes and use my budget money for better suits, hats, and top coats? Other men I know say that it pays to buy an expensive suit and shoes, if only a couple, rather than several suits and several pairs of shoes that are not expensive. What is your view on the situation? K.H., CHICAGO, ILLINOIS

My grandfather used to say that he judged a man by his shoes. Certainly shabby shoes, or ones that lose their shape and crack easily, can spoil the entire impression of a man's wardrobe. I agree with your friend that you should buy the most expensive shoes that you can in relation to your over-all budget. Inexpensive shoes lose their shape and wear out so quickly that in the end they are really no saving. Two good pairs of shoes, brown and black, with an inexpensive pair of summer shoes, should take you through the year and maybe much longer. If you watch the sales you should buy those $45 shoes for $30 or $25, you know.

PARTIES AND OTHER SOCIAL OCCASIONS*

What is the proper attire for a cocktail party from five to eight for the hostess and for the guests? MRS. A.H., BELOIT, WISCONSIN

The hostess wears a short or long cocktail dress or hostess pajamas suitable to the time of the year. The wom-

---

*The subject of Dress is also discussed in the Wedding, Funerals, and Your Manners Away from Home Sections.

en guests wear fairly dressy clothes such as silk suits, black or jewel-colored cocktail dresses, cottons, linens or wools (depending on the season) with or without hats. The men wear dark suits in the winter, linen or any of the tropical weaves in the summer or, in the country, sports jackets and odd trousers. Depending on the household, less formal attire might be equally welcome, for example, in the summer, sports shirts and shorts for the men. When in doubt, ask the hostess.

• •

At a cocktail party is it correct for ladies to remove their hats? A.R.H., NEW HAVEN, CONNECTICUT

If they wish. And of course they may even come without hats if that's their preference.

• •

Recently several couples who were staying at the same hotel during a convention were invited to dinner in the hotel dining room. With one exception, we women wore dressy, street-length dresses and no hats. One of us wore a severe suit and a hat. The dinner was at eight o'clock in the main dining room. The rest of us felt that the suited one did not display good taste. We'd appreciate your opinion. H.G.S., TRENTON, NEW JERSEY

As you were all attending a convention, perhaps she was unable to change in time, as you were. You were, of course, more appropriately dressed as, in this instance, the hotel dining room is treated as your own home under party circumstances. If it was necessary for your friend to dress in her business clothes she should have made a brief, unembarrassed apology.

• •

When women dress formally, shouldn't men follow suit?
F.L.A., PEORIA, ILLINOIS

Our growing informality has placed women, sometimes, in an awkward position in regard to their clothes.
Many times I have been in a smart restaurant and seen
a woman dressed in dinner clothes followed by an escort
in a sports jacket and sometimes with his hands in his
pockets (probably out of sheer embarrassment). When
a man can't or won't dress for an occasion it is bad
taste for the woman whom he escorts to be dressed to
the hilt, and while I feel a certain informality in entertaining tends to relax us all, it shouldn't relax us so
much that we become completely graceless.

• •

**In going down a receiving line, should ladies remove
their gloves?** G.B., CHICAGO, ILLINOIS

No, not unless they are being introduced to the President of the United States or to royalty which has made
such a request (that ladies remove their right gloves) to
those attending them. A lady would also remove her
right glove for a very high church dignitary on a par
with the President in position. I would like to note here
that aside from the above it is a rather masculine
gesture for a woman to strip off her glove to shake hands
with anyone in the United States. Even when she is
shaking hands with a woman who is ungloved she does
not remove her gloves here.

**I enjoy wearing long dresses and long skirts which are
often sold as "at home" dresses, "patio" dresses and
the like. Are they limited to home wear? Should they
be worn only at night? Could I wear one to an afternoon wedding?** S.T., STATEN ISLAND, NEW YORK

"At home" dresses now go out just about everywhere.
You see them on cruises, crosstown at a neighbor's
dinner party, at a cocktail party, and even at the theater.
Young people very frequently wear them just about
everywhere—sometimes even to work (which I don't
like). I have seen them on young guests at morning
weddings. When in doubt, ask your hostess what she
would like you to wear.

ACCESSORIES

I am confused as to when to wear a hat and gloves. Many of us here in the Midwest are averse to wearing either, except for comfort. Some of us have one pair of gloves and one hat for each season. But I know there are times when we should wear either or both. Could you give me a few basic rules for life here in the Midwest? Also, does one have to wear white gloves all summer? It seems there are local customs that are accepted etiquette on these things, but where does one go to understand them? Usually I have followed the trial-and-error way and have had embarrassing times. MRS. J.A.F., MONROE CITY, MISSOURI

The wearing of a hat anywhere these days is usually optional. It is not true that if you go without a hat you should discard your gloves. Many women, however, no longer wear gloves in the summertime, either in the city or in the country, except perhaps to weddings and formal parties. Even then rarely are gloves worn indoors but are put away with outer wear even at balls. One should never eat or smoke wearing gloves.

I have been asked to speak at a woman's club. Ordinarily I never wear a hat and haven't been in a woman's club for years. I know that women speakers used to wear hats, but is this true today?

No. Women speakers rarely do. In fact, you see a hat on a woman speaker only if she is in the older age group and then it may be only a token ribbon or a veil.

• •

When a man is wearing a suit with a vest, is it proper for him, when taking off his suit coat, to also remove his vest, or should he leave the vest on? MRS. C.L., ATLANTA, GEORGIA

Since, in most cases, vests are not made of the same fabric all around, a vest should be removed when the jacket is removed. Of course, jackets should not be taken off unless permission is given.

• •

Is it ever correct for a man to go without garters?
MRS. R.V., CHARLESTON, SOUTH CAROLINA

Men who wear over-the-calf executive length socks with elasticized tops don't need to wear garters, nor are garters needed on sweat socks or colored-wool short socks for sports wear. Evening and other dress socks, not elasticized, require garters if a man wants to avoid looking sloppy.

• •

My wife says that it is incorrect to wear black shoes in the country. What do you think? J.A., NEW YORK, NEW YORK

Well, it depends. The choir boy would wear black shoes even in the country church, and black shoes are for formal attire anywhere—for example, cutaways or director's jackets or the very popular Edwardian "Prince Edward" often worn at country events such as weddings which are of course accompanied by black shoes. Black loafers may certainly be worn in the country with the right kind of clothes, especially in the evening.

• •

Is it really good taste to wear the cross as jewelry, as I see so many girls doing? M.O.K., TOLEDO, OHIO

The cross worn as costume jewelry does not have religious significance. Worn this way, however, it is always a plain cross and never a crucifix.

• •

My girl objects to my wearing a diamond ring it took me a long time to save for. She says it's in bad taste for

men to wear diamonds. Do you agree? C.J.H., KANSAS
CITY, KANSAS

Yes, in this day and age, with the possible exception
of small diamond chips in cuff links, diamonds have
become very feminine and are considered ostentatious
on men. Because men bestow diamonds on women, it
is not considered ostentatious for a woman to wear
them—if she has them. If a man wears a big diamond
he is presumed to have bought it for himself to wear as
a beacon of his success—and, practically, as a form of
easily negotiable wealth. In some parts of the country,
for example Texas, a large diamond ring or a stickpin
can suit the style of the wearer; whereas in New York
a man with the same standing wouldn't wear one. It is
interesting that neither Neiman Marcus in Texas nor Tif-
fany in New York sells diamonds like this for men. You,
however, need not be bound by these standards but may
suit yourself.

• •

**Is it ever proper to wear an oxford shoe with a moder-
ately dressy afternoon dress?** MRS. A.S.N., DENVER,
COLORADO

Well, it isn't fashionable, but many women with foot
trouble, it seems, have no choice, as their doctors insist
that they have this kind of support over the instep.
However, there are dressy oxfords in suede, and many
special manufacturers make shoes with firm support
that look better than the oxford with dressy clothes. A
woman whose feet hurt can't enjoy herself, so their comfort should be a major consideration in her social life.

SPORTS

**In recent years bowling has become a very popular
sport for women as well as men. A group of women
in our community has formed a bowling league, and
now the problem of correct attire at the bowling lanes**

has come up. We would appreciate your opinion. MRS. J.B., EAST MEADOW, NEW YORK

For bowling, with some of the unflattering positions one must assume, I recommend well-tailored slacks, flared skirts or culottes. Straight skirts should be avoided, as they inhibit movement.

• •

My daughter is going to start riding lessons. What can I tell her about the proper choice of a riding habit and what to wear with it? I don't want her to be laughed at, and as I've never ridden myself I don't actually know what's right. W.A.J., KANSAS CITY, MISSOURI

Just tell her that she should avoid fussy femine riding clothes. Actually, women's riding clothes are adapted from men's fine gabardine, whipcord, linen, etc. Jodhpurs when they are worn should be worn by the quite slender and should fit properly. Jackets are always mantailored and in conservative woodsy colors either matching or contrasting with the trousers. She should never wear anything such as lapel jewelry with a riding jacket, although a small boutonniere such as a man might wear is acceptable. If the hair is short or can be done in such a way as to keep out of the rider's eyes a hat is not necessary unless she will be riding alone when it is advisable to wear a hunting cap. A hat, when worn, is usually a soft sport felt hat with an unbound brim, again in soft woodsy colors. The shirt worn with a country riding habit is usually white and may be open at the neck or worn with a suitable tie. Don't invest in expensive habit until you investigate what the others are wearing. Many young people ride in sports shirts and jeans, especially if they begin their training bareback in the country. Boots are a necessary protection, however, and sneakers should be taboo.

• •

What do you consider proper wear for a woman on the golf course? L.E.L., SCARSDALE, NEW YORK

In warm weather knit shirts in man-made fibers or cotton, sleeveless or with short sleeves, are worn with golfing skirts (above the knee or knee-length), Bermuda shorts, or the short golf pants-skirts (skirt panel in front, over shorts). All colors are acceptable, but apart from grassy green or bright yellow, the preference is for pastels or white. Traditional golf shoes with metal cleats are essential, but sturdy leather walking shoes could be worn in an emergency. (No heel-less, toe-less shoes or sandals, please.)

In cold weather, a loose pullover or cardigan may be worn over a shirt with comfortably cut wool skirt or slacks. A windbreaker may be worn on a windy or cold day. Leather golf gloves are available for women in pretty pastel shades or even in bright colors. Half-socks, which come just above the top of the shoes, are most comfortable in warm weather and knee socks, or tights, on colder days. Long hair is usually tied back in a pony tail or controlled with a headband or ribbon. Visored headbands also come in colors now as do regular visored golf caps preferred by some women on windy or sunny days.

• •

I am a married woman in my late thirties. I have a pretty good figure, and I would like to buy a bikini bathing suit. My husband objects, saying that only young girls should wear such revealing suits. I disagree. What is your opinion? MRS. C.S., LONG BEACH, CALIFORNIA

I agree with your husband. If you get one be absolutely sure of your figure. I feel that bikinis are usually only for the very young—and the slim ones at that.

• •

I am on the heavy side and wonder what would be the best kind of bathing suit for me to wear—I mean fabric and cut and color. MRS. J.L.M., LOS ANGELES, CALIFORNIA

So-called dressmaker suits are best for you—a tailored suit with a brief skirt that covers your thighs gracefully. Avoid midriff suits and those in shiny materials. Many of the new suits have built-in—or woven-in—features that improve the figure considerably. Black, navy, brown, dark green, dark gray all make you seem slimmer than the vivid colors. Get an early and thorough tan if you can manage it, and this too will seem to make you slimmer.

RELIGIOUS SERVICES

Will you please say whether it is proper for men to go to church without wearing their coats and to communion in shirt sleeves? My nephew and quite a few men go to church and communion in their short sleeves. I told him he should not go up to the altar without his coat. MRS. J.C., WACO, TEXAS

On the Sabbath, and especially for communion, it is usual for a man to approach the altar in coat and tie. He may come and go to the church in his shirt sleeves if that is the custom of his group and the weather is intolerable, and on weekdays take communion as he is.

• •

I occasionally visit churches other than my own when visiting friends. What is the etiquette regarding proper dress in the different places of worship? MRS. J.P., JACKSONVILLE, FLORIDA

"Sunday best" seems to have almost disappeared. Young clergymen are much more interested in getting people to church than in decreeing what they should wear there. I prefer to see people conservatively dressed in church, but generally speaking hats are unnecessary. Orthodox synagogues do require some headcovering for married women, but a wig will qualify. Roman Catholic and Protestant congregations see most of the women hatless these days. Pantsuits are acceptable even in cathedrals. Slacks and shorts are seen at mass in Catholic churches, although generally there is some attempt usually to dress up on Sunday. In Reform synagogues the matter of married women's headcovering, or lack of it, depends upon the individual rabbi. Many are quite permissive in the matter. If hats are worn to church, they should be of a reasonable size so as not to obscure the view of those behind. In warm weather, sleevelessness is quite general, but there should be decorum in the matter of low backs and cleavage. Bare legs (well groomed) are optional. My own prejudice is against bare feet in church—except perhaps among monks and friars. Gloves are optional, although a woman dressing up to go to church will probably wear gloves which may be removed during the service. The right glove at least is removed for communion when the Host is taken in the hand.

I was taught as a little girl that one must never cross one's legs in church or wear a lot of perfume. Yet I find many people ignoring both of these customs or whatever you call them. MRS. J.F.S., GLEN COVE, NEW YORK

Neither of these is a matter of church regulations. We are so used now to sitting with our legs crossed that the Victorian edict of having a lady's feet strictly on the floor at church and for social occasions is no longer valid. Plenty of perfectly nice people cross their legs in church. However, heavy perfume is certainly not a good idea, for it draws attention to a single worshiper and possibly distracts those around her.

INDEX

277

ABOUT THE AUTHOR

MISS AMY VANDERBILT is the author of AMY VANDERBILT'S ETIQUETTE, the standard work and the most complete etiquette book ever written. It has sold over 2½ million copies and is the only American etiquette book translated into foreign languages: Portuguese, Spanish and Japanese. The latest major revision has 120,000 more words than the previous one, and 200 more pages. Plates are kept standing by the publisher, Doubleday, to permit changes and additions frequently. She has also written AMY VANDERBILT'S COMPLETE COOK-BOOK, over a million in sales, and *AMY VANDERBILT'S EVERYDAY ETIQUETTE,* a Bantam paperback with nearly 1,200,000 in print. The total sales of the three books are nearly 5½ million copies. She is also a daily columnist for the Los Angeles Times Syndicate internationally. Her column is run in English, Spanish, Portuguese, French and Chinese. She is a contributing editor to the *Ladies' Home Journal,* where she has a monthly column on etiquette. Her daily column reaches some 75 million readers, and through the *Ladies' Home Journal* she reaches 7 million more. In addition to all her writing, Miss Vanderbilt is a member of the Board of Directors of the Women's Auxiliary for the New York Academy of Sciences. In private life she is the wife of Curtis B. Kellar, General Counsel of Mobil Chemical Co., a division of Mobil Oil Corporation. She is the mother of three sons and the stepmother of five more children, two boys and three girls. Her brownstone house, which has appeared in many decorating magazines, is located in the Gracie Square area of New York. She has a vacation house near Woodstock, Vermont, set on thirty-one acres with a large remodeled barn.

Facts at Your Fingertips!